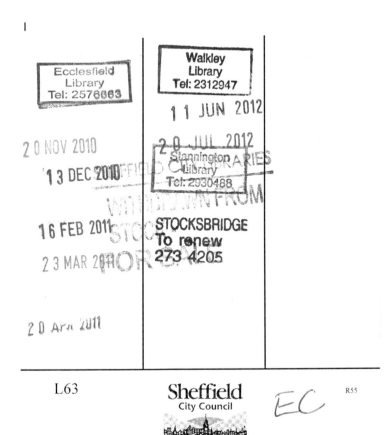
Please return/renew this item
by the last date shown.

Items may also be renewed by
phone and Internet.

LIBRARIES, ARCHIVES & INFORMATION

ALSO BY DILIP SARKAR

Spitfire Voices

Life as a Spitfire Pilot in the Words of the Veterans

DILIP SARKAR

MBE FRHistS

AMBERLEY

For Hannah Louise Sarkar

First published in 2010

Amberley Publishing Plc
Cirencester Road, Chalford,
Stroud, Gloucestershire, GL6 8PE

www.amberleybooks.com

Copyright © text and all photographs
Dilip Sarkar 2010

The right of Dilip Sarkar to be identified as
the Author of this work has been asserted in
accordance with the Copyrights, Designs and
Patents Act 1988.

ISBN 978 1 4456 0042 0

British Library Cataloguing in Publication Data.
A catalogue record for this book is available
from the British Library.

Typeset in 10pt on 12pt Sabon.
Typesetting and Origination by FonthillMedia.
Printed in the UK.

CONTENTS

GLOSSARY

The following abbreviations are commonly used throughout the text:

AAF Auxiliary Air Force
AASF Advance Air Striking Force
a/c aircraft
ADU Aircraft Delivery Unit
AFDU Air Fighting Development Unit
AOC Air Officer Commanding
ASI Air Speed Indicator
ASR Air Sea Rescue
ATA Air Transport Auxiliary
ATC Air Training Corps
BEF British Expeditionary Force
CFI Chief Flying Instructor
CFS Central Flying School
CFS Central Flying School
CGS Central Gunnery School
CO Commanding Officer
CWGC Commonwealth War Graves Commission
E/A Enemy Aircraft
FAA Fleet Air Arm
FTS Flying Training School
ITW Initial Training Wing
JG *Jagdgeschwader*
KG *Kampfgeschwader*
LAC Leading Aircraftsman
LDV Local Defence Volunteer, the Home Guard
LG *Lehrgeschwader*
MOD Ministry of Defence

MTB Motor Torpedo Boat
MU Maintenance Unit
NCO Non Commissioned Officer
n/k not known
OTU Operational Training Unit
PDU Photographic Development Unit
POW Prisoner of War
PRU Photographic Reconnaissance Unit
RAFVR Royal Air Force Volunteer Reserve
RDF Radio Direction Finding, radar
RN Royal Navy
R/T Radio Telephone
RVT *Riechverteidigung*
SAAF South African Air Force
SFTS Service Flying Training School
StG *Sturkampfgeschwader*
UAS University Air Squadron
u/s unserviceable
USAAC United States Army Air Corps
WAAF Women's Auxiliary Air Force

The following German words and explanations may also be useful. In an effort to preserve authenticity, the original German is used throughout the text wherever possible.

Alarmstart Scramble, to take off urgently.
Eichenlaub The Oak Leaves, essentially being a bar to the *Ritterkreuz*.
Experte A fighter 'ace'. Ace status, on both sides, was achieved by destroying five enemy aircraft.
Freie hunt A fighter sweep.
Gruppenstab Group staff.
Geschwader The whole group, usually of three *gruppen*.
Geschwaderkommodore The group leader.
Geschwaderstab The group staff.
Geschwaderstabschwarm The group staff tactical section.
Geschwader-gefechtstand Group tactical operations HQ.
Geschwader-maschine An aircraft belonging to the group.
Gruppe A wing, usually of three squadrons.
Jagdwaffe The fighter force.
Jagdbomber A fighter-bomber, or *Jabo*.
Jagdflieger Fighter pilot.
Jagdgeschwader Fighter group, abbreviated JG.
Kanal The English Channel.

Kanalgeschwader Fighter and bomber groups based on the Channel coast.
Kanalfront The Channel Front.
Kampfgeschwader Bomber group, abbreviated KG.
Kampffleiger Bomber pilot.
Lehrgeschwader Literally, a training group, but actually a precision-bombing unit, abbreviated LG.
Oberkannone The 'Top Gun'.
Ritterkreuz The Knight's Cross of the Iron Cross.
Ritterkrueztrager Holder of the Knight's Cross.
Rotte A pair of fighters, comprising leader and wingman, into which the *Schwarm* broke once battle was joined.
Rottenflieger Wingman.
Riechverteidigung RVT, the organisation charged with the aerial defence of Germany.
Schwarm A section of four fighters.
Stab Staff.
Staffel A squadron.
Staffelkapitän The squadron leader.
Staffel/Gruppen Kommandeur The squadron/wing commander.
Stuka The Ju 87 dive-bomber.
Sturkampfgeschwader Dive-bomber group, abbreviated StG.
Vermisst Missing.

Each *geschwader* generally comprised three *gruppen*, each of three *staffeln*. Each *gruppe* is designated by Roman numerals, i.e. III/JG 26 refers to the third *gruppe* of Fighter Group 26. *Staffeln* are identified by numbers, so 7/JG 26 is the 7th *staffel* and belongs to III/JG 26.

The abbreviation 'Me' is used throughout the text for Messerschmitt, although 'Bf' is also correct. As Battle of Britain pilot Flight Lieutenant Keith Lawrence DFC said, however, 'To us they were simply "109s".'

Rank comparisons may also be useful:

Feldwebel Sergeant
Hauptmann Squadron Leader
Leutnant Pilot Officer
Major Wing Commander
Oberfeldwebel Flight Sergeant
Oberleutnant Flight Lieutenant
Oberst Group Captain
Oberstleutnant Lieutenant Colonel
Unteroffizier Corporal (no aircrew equivalent in Fighter Command)

INTRODUCTION

During the twentieth century, aviation, and military aviation in particular, remained a very young science. The Wright Brothers, of course, had only made the world's first powered flight in 1903. Just a decade later, aeroplanes were being used as war machines. Pilots were seen as extremely glamorous figures – fighter pilots especially so. The general public avidly consumed tales of aerial derring-do during the Great War. Every nation had its favourite: in Germany, Manfred von Richthofen – the fabled 'Red Baron'; in France, Georges Guynumer; in Britain, Albert Ball. Between the two world wars aviation became even more alluring as the boundaries were pushed further still by adventurous aviators. A whole new generation of young men was inspired to follow in the footsteps of their august heroes.

This new generation of would-be fighter pilots was no stranger to war. Born shortly after the First World War ended they had grown up in the shadow of it – barely a family of the major combatants escaped losing a loved one during the 1914–18 conflict – and from 1933 onwards war with Hitler's Germany was an ever-present prospect. None the less there was no shortage of aircrew volunteers. By 1938, the RAF's bi-planes had been replaced by new monoplanes: the Hawker Hurricane and Supermarine Spitfire. To become a fighter pilot was the ambition of most volunteers, and for the majority of them to fly a Spitfire was the ultimate aim. As Battle of Britain pilot Ken Wilkinson said, 'If you were a fighter pilot then you were a cocky so-and-so, but if you were a Spitfire pilot then you were cockier still!'

The Supermarine Spitfire, designed by the genius R. J. Mitchell, was iconic: its clean and beautiful lines charismatic. The Spitfire was a revolutionary design which really looked and, with its gutsy Rolls-Royce Merlin engine, sounded the part. Indeed, over seventy years since its first flight, it still does today, captivating the public's imagination in a way unparalleled by any aircraft before or since. None the less, as Gordon Mitchell, son of 'RJ', said, 'My father was heard to say on a number of occasions that "A Spitfire without a pilot is just a lump of metal",' by which he meant to show the high regard and respect he had for the pilots whose job it was to fly his 'lump of metal'.

1. The Spitfire's designer, Reginald Joseph Mitchell (centre) photographed at Eastleigh airfield, near Southampton, on 5 March 1936 – after the prototype's first flight. With him, from left, are Supermarine's Chief Test Pilot, 'Mutt' Summers, who made the historic flight, Major R. J. M. Payn, S. Scott-Hall, Supermarine's Resident Technical Officer, and Test Pilot Jeffrey Quill.

2. The prototype Spitfire, K5054.

3. The Supermarine factory on the banks of the River Itchen at Woolston, near Southampton. Compare this to the photograph in Chapter 3 after the bombing on 26 September 1940.

For many aviation-minded youngsters in Britain and the Commonwealth who grew up between the wars, their dream to fly a Spitfire became a reality owing to the Second World War. If not for that global conflict, the vast majority of these fit and intelligent young men would not have had the opportunity to fly. Private aviation was the preserve of only the very wealthy, and between the wars essentially all RAF officers were pilots. Owing to the socio-educational prejudice prevalent in British society during the 1920s and 30s, only public schoolboys were commissioned. As war with Nazi Germany became an increasingly unavoidable prospect, however, Britain re-armed and expanded the RAF. A small number of NCOs were selected to become pilots, and grammar schoolboys were permitted to fly as sergeants (but not commissioned) in the RAFVR. By 1939, therefore, it was not just public schoolboys occupying the cockpits of RAF fighters but a much wider cross-section of society: ordinary people, it could be argued, who responded extraordinarily courageously and tenaciously to defend both democracy and their chosen way of life.

During the Battle of Britain in 1940, there were many more Hurricanes than Spitfires. The Spitfire enjoyed superior performance but was more difficult to build, its advanced design requiring the workforce to learn new production techniques. Nevertheless, by the summer of 1941, it had taken over as the RAF's front line fighter. In the years ahead, Mitchell's 'lump of metal', designed as a

4. Spitfires under construction at Woolston.

5. An early Spitfire having its markings applied at Eastleigh.

short-range defensive interceptor, was used successfully in roles never envisaged by the designer. The Spitfire dropped bombs, fired rockets, operated from aircraft carriers, escorted bombers, and photographed targets deep within enemy territory, and was developed through a succession of twenty-four different marques. It was not until 1948, twelve years after Mitchell watched his prototype's maiden flight from Eastleigh airfield in Southampton, that the last of 22,500 Spitfires rolled off the production line. The type actually remained in RAF service until 1954.

For all of those young men who aspired to fly the Spitfire, surely there could have been no greater thrill. The war also offered an unprecedented and unexpected opportunity to travel, providing experiences impossible in peacetime. But there was a high price to pay: all too many of these educated, fit, and intelligent young men took off never to return, for reasons as varied as perishing in flying accidents to falling in battle. Their graves can be found in cemeteries the world over, or their names read on memorials to the missing. Others were wounded and maimed for life, both physically and mentally. Naturally, survivors are proud of the days when they flew Spitfires as much younger men, often recalling their wartime experiences with great clarity and detail.

While I will always consider the sight and sound of a Spitfire the most evocative and inspirational image of all time, it is not the technical aspect of the Spitfire story that moves me. My interest has always been in the human element, the stories of those who flew R. J. Mitchell's 'lump of metal'. One of the pilots in this book, Peter Fox, described himself as 'an also-ran', and it is the 'also-rans', in fact, who fascinate me most. There were thousands of 'also-rans' – men who would never have flown or travelled if not for the war, men whose lives were completely disrupted but who went off and 'did their bit'. A classic example is another pilot in this book, Ron 'Cloudy' Rayner: a jeweller after the war and a true gentleman in every sense. It is almost impossible to imagine him dive-bombing and strafing his way across Sicily and through Italy. Indeed, when I told him that the pilot of an FW 190 he had shot down was killed he characteristically replied 'How sad' – and meant it. 'There is not a day goes by', he added, 'that I don't think about what we did.' This from a man awarded the Distinguished Flying Cross and with a logbook brimming with evidence of heroic exploits. So, if any readers think that being a Spitfire pilot was a glamorous business, they should think again.

The famous survivors, men like Douglas Bader and 'Johnnie' Johnson, published their personal memoirs and were the subject of biographies. After the war, there was an insatiable demand for such literature, which shows little sign of abating. Peter Fox's 'also-rans', however, had no platform from which to recount their experiences, and it is only in comparatively recent times, since the famous pilots have died, that any serious interest has been shown in recording their stories. Another reason for this is because, although there have been advances in recent years, academic historians are still often mistrustful and suspicious of oral histories. Oral history, they say, is unreliable because it can be influenced by the events and perceptions of the years since the events in question, and, of course, the memory fades. All of this is true, but, as the facts are recorded and a matter of public record, meaning that oral accounts can be verified and cross-referenced, does this matter? Eyewitness accounts are in my view essential to providing colour and atmosphere to history. Over the years, therefore, I sought to record memories and provide a stage from which they could be shared. The casualties are another issue: they have no voice, apart from publication of their letters and diary entries, so official records and memories of others must speak for them. In that context oral history is crucial, because as wartime survivors are now fading fast so too are those who made the ultimate sacrifice passing from living memory. In how many cases, I wonder, is no likeness known, no photograph archived?

In this book I have reproduced the oral accounts of various survivors, who speak of their own experiences and memories of friends who died. The Spitfire experience related is wide-ranging, which is as it should be, thus providing an accurate impression of flying to battle in Spitfires during the Second World War. The stories of certain casualties have also been included. Often the research has involved significant detective work, not least the saga of how Douglas Bader was not brought down over France by the enemy but accidentally by one of his own pilots. This book therefore represents a comprehensive study of life as a Spitfire pilot – essentially in their own words. Just as my book *The Few: The Story of the Battle of Britain in the Words of the Pilots* (Amberley Publishing, 2009) represents an important collection of first-hand accounts concerning the summer of 1940, so too does *Spitfire Voices* contribute to increasing our knowledge and understanding of flying R. J. Mitchell's 'lump of metal' between 1939 and 1945.

Dilip Sarkar MBE FRHistS, Worcester, July 2010

I

PILOT OFFICER LAURIE WHITBREAD

Herbert Laurence Whitbread was born on 21 August 1914 in the picturesque and fortified Shropshire town of Ludlow. Laurie lived with his parents and sister at 4 Linney View, Ludlow, attending the local primary and grammar schools. At the latter he was a popular pupil, excelling at sport. In 1933, he became House Captain of Wright's, a master, George Merchant, later describing Laurie in the House photograph as 'sprawling in his majesty, flanked by his henchmen and surrounded by his minions'. At Ludlow Grammar School, Whitbread's name became synonymous with boxing and rugby, and our hero also represented Shropshire at hockey. His best friend was fellow-pupil Charlie Knight, the son of Revd and Mrs Lacey Hulbert of St Mary's. Charlie's younger sister, Margaret, remembers Laurie as 'a second brother', and humorously recalls him dressing up in her father's cassock to walk around the town! After leaving school, young Laurie became an apprentice at Fisher and Ludlow in Birmingham, manufacturing sheet steel for the automotive industry. Ken Brown, another Ludlovian, worked with Laurie but was not surprised when his friend left the firm in 1939 to become a fighter pilot.

On 12 January 1939, Laurie sat for interview at the Air Ministry and subsequently received a Short Service Commission. Having volunteered for aircrew, by May Pilot Officer Whitbread was undertaking his *ab initio* flying training at Desford, where he recorded the following notes in his diary:

9 March: Flying lots in afternoon – instructor to myself from 1.30 to 4.30. Managed OK. Stalling, gliding, turning, and taxying.
11 March: Looking forward to first solo.
25 April: RAF Test after 45 hrs solo. Passed OK.

Having won his 'wings', Laurie moved on to the SFTS at Kinloss, in Scotland. There he flew twins, as indicated by his diary 'Airspeed Oxford. Splendid instructor'.

6. Pilot Officer H. L. 'Laurie' Whitbread.

25 May: Went solo on Oxford OK. Rough wind.

9 June: Solo, 40 minutes, N6289.

19 June: Definitely difficult to land with a closed throttle. Two bad landings.

22 June: Someone's going to get hurt before long. Oxford aircraft not being maintained in good condition. Petrol gauge and undercarriage lights all wrong. Not good enough.

3 July: Night flying. Suicide, but made perfect first landing. Solo not so hot.

Two months later, Britain and France declared war on Nazi Germany following Hitler's refusal to withdraw his troops from Poland, which he had invaded on 1 September. The world was now at war for the second time that century. On 26 November, Pilot Officer Whitbread's service flying training was considered complete and he was posted to 222 'Natal' Squadron, a new unit based at Duxford. The 222 Squadron was commanded by Squadron Leader H. W. 'Tubby' Mermagen, a Cranwell graduate who had led the Inverted Flying Formation at the 1937 Hendon Air Pageant, and performed solo aerobatics for King George VI. In 1992, I had the privilege of interviewing the now late Air Commodore Mermagen, who remembered:

I formed 222 as a 12 Group night-fighter unit equipped with Bristol Blenheim twin-engined aircraft. As I was previously an AI qualified staff flying instructor at the CFS, to convert pilots to this type I was supplied with a dual Blenheim. Whitbread was one of the earliest postings to the new squadron, straight from FTS. I can remember him as a pleasant, well-mannered, quiet individual. A shortish, stocky, cheerful character whom I instantly liked – a good mixer.

My flying logbook records that on 12 December 1939, at 1200 hrs, I took him up in the dual Blenheim, L6712, for a test/conversion to Blenheim Mk Is. The flight lasted twenty-five minutes and I must have been suitable impressed since, so far as my logbook shows, Whitbread had no further instruction and went solo immediately afterwards. I understand that he had trained on twin-engined Oxfords, but even so he displayed a good standard of flying. The Squadron subsequently conducted a very large number of flying hours and we were soon operational, with no accidents.

Throughout December, 222 Squadron flew monotonous convoy-protection patrols over the North Sea, all without incident. As the winter progressed, flying weather deteriorated, there being none whatsoever during the first nine days of February 1940, due to heavy snow. On Wednesday 14th, Laurie wrote in his diary: 'Narrowest escape to date, nearly spun in while night flying.'

The 222 Squadron shared Duxford with the Spitfire-equipped 19 and 66 Squadrons, which, from the cockpits of their comparatively uninspiring Blenheims, Mermagen's pilots viewed with envy. The 222 Squadron, however, was suddenly ordered to convert to Spitfires, five of which arrived on 9 March. Air Commodore Mermagen:

To our delight, the AOC, Air Vice-Marshal Leigh-Mallory, decided to re-equip us with Spitfires. The already enthusiastic pilots faced this conversion from twins to singles with great excitement. To help me with the conversion of all pilots, I was supplied with a Miles Master dual-training aircraft, N7570. My logbook records that at 1600 hrs on 18 March I took Pilot Officer Whitbread up for forty minutes conversion-to-type flying. I did the same the following day for another thirty minutes and he must have then satisfied me completely because he went solo in a Spitfire with no further instruction immediately afterwards.

There followed an intensive flying-training programme for 222 Squadron, including much formation flying. Laurie's diary:

20 March: Spitfire solo.
24 March: Spitfire. Try guns at Sutton Bridge.
16 April: Practising attacks.
10 April: Buy Wolseley Hornet, 1932. Not bad!
14 April: Squadron formation of 12 aircraft. Height climb 26,000 feet.
15 April: First accident: nose in Spitfire but CO exonerates me from blame.

On 17 April, 222 Squadron became fully operational on Spitfires. The 19 Squadron moved from Duxford to Horsham St Faith, so 222 took over their

7. Group Captain H. W. 'Tubby' Mermagen (centre).

recently vacated dispersals at the aerodrome's eastern end. Squadron Leader Mermagen continued to train his pilots hard, introducing night flying into the programme. Laurie's diary:

21 April: Pilot Officer Vigors almost writes both of us off overtaking at 60 mph, and missed by five!

28 April: Formation flying.

1 May: Formation flying. Bad weather.

3 May: Night flying.

9 May: Squadron scrambles. AOC very pleased. 12 minutes for refuelling and reloading the entire squadron: a record!

On Friday, 10 May 1940, the 'Phoney War' came to an abrupt end when Hitler's forces, with surprise, speed, and ferocity, swept into Holland, Belgium, Luxembourg, and France. The Defiant-equipped 264 Squadron, based at Martelsham Heath in the Debden Sector, was ordered to move to Duxford and anticipate operating from forward basis in support of the Dutch. To make room, 222 Squadron was sent north, to Digby in Lincolnshire. Laurie wrote in his diary: 'At 12 mid-day we are told to go to Digby at 9 p.m.! What a scramble packing. Arrived safely.' Two days later he wrote: 'More formation flying. Oh, to be abroad!'

The 222 Squadron moved from Digby to Kirton-in-Lindsey, also in Lincolnshire, on 23 May. By that time it was clear that the situation on the continent was catastrophic. Before the German invasion, the Belgian King, in a misguided attempt to maintain his country's neutrality, refused to allow British troops into his country, even for reconnaissance. Consequently, the BEF, commanded by Lord Gort, dug in on the Franco-Belgian border; when the shooting started the Belgians called for help immediately, meaning that Gort's men had to pivot forward sixty miles, moving from a prepared to an unprepared defensive line and across unfamiliar ground without stashes of fuel or ammunition. When German airborne troops landed in Belgium and Holland, it was assumed that the *Schwerpunkt,* or main point of effort, would come from that direction, as in the Great War. In fact, *Panzergruppe* von Kliest was cleverly negotiating the supposedly impassable Ardennes, thus outflanking the much-vaunted French Maginot Line and punching an armoured fist into the Allies' soft underbelly. The *panzers* raced towards the coast, and Gort had no option but to fall back, from one river defence line to the next, in order to escape envelopment. Eventually it was agreed to evacuate the BEF from Dunkirk. Incredibly, however, Hitler stopped his tanks at the Aa Canal, for reasons never satisfactorily explained; had the *panzers* kept rolling then the 338,226 Allied troops evacuated could all have been lost. Fortunately, the German armour stayed its hand, and the evacuation has gone down in history as little short of a miracle.

During the Battle of France, Air Chief Marshal Dowding had far-sightedly only deployed Hurricanes to the continent, maintaining his smaller Spitfire force for

8. Pilot Officer Whitbread snapped by Sergeant Reg Johnson at Kirton with Spitfire P9318, the Spitfire Laurie flew on most of his Dunkirk sorties.

9. Sergeant Reg Johnson photographed by Pilot Officer Whitbread. Unusually the Spitfire's rear-view mirror is inside the front windscreen assembly.

home defence. The Hurricane squadrons had taken such a pounding in France, however, that there was now no option but to commit the Spitfire squadrons to battle across the Channel in an effort to provide the evacuation with aerial support. These squadrons found themselves sent south, operating from forward bases such as Mansion and Hawkinge, and tried to prevent German aircraft attacking either ships or soldiers on the ground. Most of the air battles arising were either fought above cloud or behind German lines, unseen, therefore, by watchers on the ground. Some German aircraft did get through and mercilessly attacked the columns of soldiers on the sand, giving the impression to many that the RAF had let them down – badly – although in reality this was not the case. Fighter Command's squadrons flew a total of 4,822 operational hours during Operation DYNAMO, destroyed 258 enemy aircraft and damaged 119, offset against their own losses of eighty-seven machines.

On 29 May, 222 Squadron flew south to Hornchurch in Essex, remaining there for two days. Air Commodore Mermagen:

> At 6.30 a.m. that day I led the Squadron, in fact a wing of several squadrons, on its first patrol over the Dunkirk beaches. The sortie lasted two hours and forty-five minutes, a long flight for a Spitfire. The Squadron carried out several further sorties, ending on 3 June when the wretched evacuation appeared completed – no life could be seen either on the beaches or in the country behind. I lost four pilots killed and one missing during that period. Pilot Officer Whitbread must have taken part in most if not all of these sorties. I know that I had already recognised him as a good, reliable and sound Spitfire pilot.

Indeed, the record shows that Pilot Officer Whitbread did fly on the majority of 222 Squadron's sorties from Hornchurch, in Spitfires P9318, P9360, and P9378. Laurie was a member of 'B' Flight, but 'A' Flight had a very colourful Flight Commander: Flight Lieutenant Douglas Bader, who had lost both legs in a flying accident during 1931. In spite of having mastered 'tin legs' and passing a flying test, King's Regulations did not allow for disabled pilots and so the young Cranwell graduate subsequently left the service. At the time of Munich in 1938, however, Bader offered his services to the Air Ministry and was told that if war broke out he would be given another flying test. After war was declared in September 1939, Bader attended the CFS at Upavon in Wiltshire where he was tested in a dual control, American-built, Harvard training aircraft. All American aircraft of the period have foot-controlled brakes, while British machines had a hand-operated lever on the control column. The Harvard's brakes were therefore foot-controlled, which the legless Bader could not actually operate; at the appropriate juncture during the flying test, therefore, his instructor, none other than a Cranwell contemporary, Rupert 'Lucky' Leigh, dabbed the brakes himself so Bader passed the test. Initially, in February 1940, Flying Officer Bader was posted to fly Spitfires with 19 Squadron at Duxford, which was commanded by his old Cranwell and acrobatic chum Geoffrey Stephenson, but Bader found being his friend's subordinate so difficult that the following month he used old boy connections again to obtain a posting as a flight commander to 222 Squadron; the CO, Tubby Mermagen, was, needless to say, another Cranwell contemporary. It is also noteworthy that Bader's meteoric promotion to Acting Flight Lieutenant and Flight Commander was in spite of having 'bent' a couple of Spitfires in careless accidents. Over Dunkirk, however, the Spitfire pilots would meet the Me 109 for the first time, one of which Douglas Bader destroyed on 1 June.

It was now that the years of practising set-piece Fighter Command attacks against slow-moving bombers that took little or no evasive action would be exposed as useless. Fighter-to-fighter combat was not envisaged by British tacticians between the wars, and the tight and inflexible vic of three aircraft would now be found wanting. Flight Lieutenant Reg Johnson (who sadly passed away during my research for this story) remembered this of that period:

I was posted to 222 Squadron in April 1940 at RAF Duxford. I arrived there only to be told that the Squadron had moved to Digby. I arrived there to learn that 222 had moved to Kirton, such was the level of administration in 1940. On joining the Squadron no one was unkind to me but I was the first RAFVR pilot (recognisable by my badges) to join this regular Squadron. After about a week I was shown the 'knobs and things' by Sergeant J. I. Johnson, an ex-Halton apprentice, and sent solo. After successfully landing, my engine failed and I was collected in a green MG sports car by Flight Lieutenant Douglas Bader.

I was a member of 'B' Flight and soon learned that 222 Squadron was addicted to tight formation flying, for which I had no training whatsoever. A study of the pre-war career of our CO, Squadron Leader Mermagen, might explain this addiction, particularly in flying so tight that our wings overlapped. From Kirton he led us off in squadron formation; three behind three, we looped in formation. We even rolled as a squadron on one occasion! Mermagen was an exceptional pilot but such training was to prove unsuitable for the Battle of Britain that lay ahead, although at the time, of course, he was not to have the benefit of hindsight.

When I joined 222 Squadron in April 1940, Pilot Officer Whitbread was already an established member. During the following weeks and months he proved himself to be a pleasant and friendly young man. We spent many hours together in conversation at Dispersal, and I have a photograph of him beside 'my' Spitfire at dawn readiness, about 4 a.m. on a June morning. We each took each other's picture despite the light at that early hour being poor as we were forbidden cameras so had to take our snaps in secret.

Pilot Officer Whitbread was also a very good hockey player and spent long periods with his hockey stick dribbling around the aircraft and running around bouncing a ball on his stick. We also spent many hours together flying in Squadron training, often wing-tip to wing-tip. He was much more skilled at tight formation flying than I was at that time.

In our Squadron there was definitely an RAF social barrier between officer and NCO pilots. Pilot Officer Whitbread, whom I never knew as 'Laurie' but always 'Sir', overcame this with his natural charm and was at ease with all ranks. He never lost face because of it and we were firm friends. We enjoyed a number of Squadron flying adventures together at Kirton and would later suffer a number together during the Battle of Britain.

Squadron Leader Iain Hutchinson was also a sergeant pilot with 222 Squadron:

In general I remember Pilot Officer Whitbread as an unassuming, approachable person, without affectation. You will understand that during the time we served together in 222 Squadron I was a sergeant pilot while Laurie Whitbread was commissioned. Therefore, there was only a very limited opportunity for an association between each group. Nevertheless, there was less 'side' in Laurie's relationships than there was with other officers. I should emphasise, however, that within the constraints imposed by differences in rank there was still an excellent spirit in the Squadron.

10. Sergeant Iain Hutchinson.

The only incident in which I was involved with Pilot Officer Whitbread occurred on 10 August 1940. An intruder was detected by the forward radar station and he and I were scrambled to intercept. We taxied out at speed, Laurie leading and me following. I was swinging the nose of my Spitfire from side to side, according to the relevant rules, to ensure that I could see ahead as the nose blocked out a large sector of forward view. When I swung the nose right I suddenly saw the tail of Laurie's machine ahead of me, stopped! Despite heavy braking and evasive action I was unable to clear his aircraft and my wing demolished his tail.

I also recall that one night a raider attacked the Scunthorpe steel works and Laurie was sent up to intercept. Unfortunately, the fighter controllers were apparently unable to get their act together and we watched frustrated as we heard the bomber droning on a western approach to its target while Laurie was vectored in the opposite direction.

After the danger and excitement of Dunkirk, the flying at Kirton that August must have been dull, especially with 11 Group's squadrons being so heavily engaged over southern England. By that time, Squadron Leader Mermagen had been sent to command temporarily 266 Squadron at Wittering before being promoted and posted to command RAF Station Speke. His successor as CO of 222 Squadron was Squadron Leader John Hill, to whom it would fall to lead the Squadron during its turn in the combat zone.

On 29 August, an uncharacteristically quiet morning permitted Fighter Command to rotate and rest several squadrons. Among these was 264, a Defiant unit decimated while flying from Hornchurch and whose place in the line was taken by 222 Squadron. The following day, Hill's Spitfires were scrambled to patrol Gravesend. 'B' Flight soon contacted ten Me 109s north-west of Dover. No general combat ensued but Sergeant Hutchinson was shot at from behind and forced to land a mile from the airfield. Reg Johnson:

In the first forty-eight hours that 222 Squadron was at Hornchurch we lost eighteen aircraft and a number of pilots. We proceeded to go into action in tight formation and our losses were heavy. Eventually we evolved a weaving 'Tail End Charlie' section, Green Section, which weaved about above, below, and to the Squadron's rear (still in tight formation). It helped. I was made a permanent member of Green Section, with Pilot Officer Whitbread and one other, and we were given the job to do.

According to the 222 Squadron diary, on 30 August, 'the Squadron was very positively engaged in operations and flew three patrols during the day. Sergeant J. I. Johnson was killed. Flight Lieutenant Matheson and Flying Officer Edridge were wounded.' During the three separate actions fought that day, 222 Squadron lost six Spitfires destroyed and three damaged. In response, Flight Lieutenant Robinson had probably destroyed an Me 109, Pilot Vigors a 110 destroyed, Pilot Officers Davis and Cutts an He 111, and Squadron Leader Hill an Me 109 damaged.

On 31 August, Fighter Command suffered the heaviest losses of any day throughout the Battle of Britain. During the day's first patrol by 222 Squadron, Pilot Officer Whitbread flew Spitfire L1010 and patrolled base uneventfully at 25,000 feet. Laurie flew the same Spitfire on the next sortie, which was flown from the forward field at Rochford: 222 Squadron was vectored to intercept bombers and their fighter escort 26,000 feet over Gravesend. 222 Squadron attacked the 109s; Pilot Officer Vigors claiming one destroyed and another as a probable. Later, Pilot Officer Whitbread and ten other 222 Squadron Spitfires patrolled Canterbury at 20,000 feet. Over Maidstone, twenty-four Me 109s protecting a formation of He 111s were tally-hoed, the ensuing combat concluding very much in the Spitfires' favour: several of the enemy were shot down, against the loss of two Spitfires, the pilots of which were safe. Pilot Officer Whitbread reported his combat, which took place at 1.30 p.m., 16,000 feet over Sittingbourne:

I manoeuvred until the Me 109 appeared in my sights, the enemy aircraft climbing slowly away not having seen me. I fired at about 400 yards and rapidly closed to within 50 yards, when I could see the bullets entering the fuselage from tail to cockpit. The 109 half rolled onto its back and remained at that attitude, flying quite slowly with a little white smoke issuing from it. It eventually nosed down slowly

11. Hornchurch Sector Station, 1 September 1940, showing Spitfires of both 222 and 603 Squadrons, and a steamroller repairing the runway which was heavily cratered the previous day.

when I was obliged to lose sight of it having noticed an aircraft approaching my tail which turned out to be a Spitfire.

This enemy machine was possibly one of 1/JG 77, which crashed between Walderslade and Boxley; the pilot, *Unteroffizier* Keck, baled out and was captured.

The next few days followed an identical pattern, with numerous scrambles and interceptions being made by 222 Squadron. On 7 September, the Germans bombed London round the clock, and by 4.30 p.m. all twenty-one Fighter Command squadrons based with seventy-one miles of London were airborne. Pilot Officer Whitbread later wrote the following of his combat, which took place at 27,000 feet over the capital:

> We engaged an enemy formation of Me 109s. I became separated from the rest of the Squadron so climbed back to my original altitude and flew round looking for a target. I found one in a formation of 25-30 Do 215s which appeared to have no fighter escort. Keeping in the sun I dived down on the last aircraft which was straggling behind some 100 yards at the rear of the formation and flying at 20,000 feet. I carried out a quarter attack from the port side (formation was flying westwards along south bank of the Thames at Dartford). I opened fire at 300 yards, range closing rapidly. The starboard engine set on fire and I broke away, the return fire from the three rear gunners and my closing range making this advisable.

By the end of that day, 306 civilians had been killed and 1,337 Londoners injured. The reader should note that this was long before RAF Bomber Command and the American 8th Air Force pounded German cities, and we must not forget that the Germans had also reduced the defenceless town of Guernica to rubble during the Spanish Civil War. Current German condemnation of Bomber Command's offensive seems conveniently to forget the basic and undeniable fact that it was the *Luftwaffe* which began indiscriminately bombing civilian populations as a legitimate means of waging war.

After the massive enemy assault of the previous twenty-four hours, 8 September was a quieter day and 222 Squadron was not engaged. The following afternoon, however, saw 222 Squadron in action over Ashford. Pilot Officer Whitbread:

> While on patrol over east Kent we sighted a formation of enemy bombers flying west at 20,000 feet, above cloud. It had an escort of Me 109s, flying above and behind at 26,000 feet, and also another formation of fighters flying to one side, at the same height as the bombers. The fighters were engaged. I had a combat with an Me 109. A burst of roughly four seconds from my guns appeared to shoot off the starboard aileron when the 109 went into a spin. It continued to spin downwards into the cloud layer where it disappeared from view. My flight leader stated that he had observed the 109 spin down and also the pilot baling out.

In his diary, Laurie wrote: 'One Me 109 claim. Confirmed by Van Mentz.' The enemy fighter belonged to 6/JG 27 and crashed at Beneden; *Unteroffizier* Georg Rauwolf baled out and was captured.

The pathos of action remained constant over the next few days. On 14 September, Laurie wrote to his mother from the Officers' Mess at RAF Hornchurch:

Dear Mother

Thank you for your letter, received this morning. How nice to have Rex and Doris, and Colin at home together. I am disappointed that I won't be there too. Fancy Ludlow having some bombs!

Everything is going fine down here. We get far less to do now that the weather has broken. There is no sign of us leaving this station yet, so I doubt that I will get any leave until things quieten down again.

I am keeping fit – except that I got a touch of frostbite in the left hand last week. It's better now except from a large blister on the thumb.

Mother, would you see if I've left my RAF navy blue blazer at home? I don't want it but can't find it here. Please tell me in the next letter. I do hope I haven't lost it.

Love to all, Cheerio, Laurie.

The reference to 'frostbite' requires some clarification, as a previously published account states that this was because Pilot Officer Whitbread had been sleeping in his Spitfire (so as to be immediately available at dawn). The truth is, however, that September nights are just not that cold, so the 'frostbite' was actually caused by intense cold while flying at high altitude.

As for 'getting far less to do', the next day, 15 September, has gone down in history as 'Battle of Britain Day', the whole fury and might of the enemy being thrown repeatedly at London. On that great day, Pilot Officer Whitbread's Spitfire, N3023, ZD-R, was unserviceable, necessitating him flying it from Rochford to Hornchurch for repair.

In his diary on 18 September, Laurie wrote 'Seven days leave start?', but none was forthcoming. Instead of travelling home to see his sweetheart Jane, Pilot Officer Whitbread was patrolling over Canterbury in Spitfire P9878. He did not fly the following day, but his usual mount N3023 was serviceable for 20 September.

By this time the back of the German offensive had been broken, although fierce fighting continued. In a few days' time, the He 111 would be completely withdrawn from daylight operations as the German bomber fleet concentrated its efforts on safer night bombing. Enemy fighter sweeps, however, had failed to provoke the required response, RAF Controllers recognising that these incursions were no threat unless fighters were scrambled to intercept, so chose instead to let the Germans waste their fuel. This was a disappointment to the enemy fighter pilots who had for so long been frustrated by having to provide close bomber escort. The opportunity to roam freely, hunting prey, was most welcome, but morale took a further plunge when Göring ordered that one *staffel* in each *gruppe* would re-equip as a fighter–bomber unit. Such a statistic represented a significant one-third of the available German fighter force, and not surprisingly the majority of senior fighter leaders disagreed with such a move given that the force was already too weak to achieve aerial supremacy over England. At operational level, everything had been done to wring extra performance out of the 109s, but, instead of being given the long-range auxiliary fuel tanks requested for so long, SC250 bombs arrived instead. The tactical thinking, however, was that if the fighter formations contained fighter–bombers, which could not be identified by radar, the RAF Controllers would have to consider every sweep a threat and respond accordingly.

On Friday, 20 September, for the first time, twenty-two Me 109 fighter–bombers of II/ LG 2, protected by numerous fighters, took off from the Pas-de-Calais bases, London bound. Between Calais and Dover the Germans climbed to 25,000 feet before swooping down on the capital. Believing the enemy sweep to be no threat, Fighter Command's squadrons were kept on the ground, permitting the fighter–bombers to reach London unmolested. Diving to 22,000 feet and pressing the bomb release switch, the *Jabo* pilots had already turned for home when their bombs exploded in the City of London and on a rail terminus west of the Thames's great bend. Listening to the British radio frequencies, German intelligence reported a great confusion of orders and counter-orders after the 'fighters' had dropped their bombs.

After the first wave of raiders had caused confusion, a second was reported incoming over the Kent coast at 14,000 feet. Unbeknown to the RAF controllers, there were no fighter–bombers in this formation, so the Biggin Hill and Hornchurch Spitfire squadrons were scrambled. The 222 and 603 Squadrons were up from Hornchurch at 10.55 a.m., but as they desperately climbed for height over the Thames Estuary the 109s fell on them. The first Spitfire pilot to fall in action that day was Pilot Officer Whitbread. Reg Johnson:

My vivid memory is that this sortie was a 'B' Flight commitment only, led by Pilot Officer Broadhurst in Blue Section, followed by Pilot Officer Whitbread, myself and another in Green Section. We climbed to the suicidal height of 14,000 feet and stooged around in tight formation with only one pair of eyes available to scan the sky in front, perhaps over 200 degrees. I do not think that we deserved to be jumped, but we were certainly inviting it. We were banking gently to the left, which allowed me at No. 3 to look over the top of No. 1, and I shouted the warning 'Bandits! 2 o'clock above – attacking!' I turned over and dived straight down. There is no way that Pilot Officer Whitbread could even have seen the enemy, formatting as he was on the aircraft to his left and with three-quarters of his head and back to the attackers. When I left it was his right side facing the 109s, which were already in firing range. I can only assume that having received my warning he too rolled to his right, exposing his left side to the enemy and was hit before his dive commenced. It was a tragedy.

Spitfire N3203 crashed at 11.15 a.m. in the garden of Pond Cottage, Hermitage Road. Higham, near Rochester in Kent. The occupant, a Mrs Perry, wrote to Pilot Officer Whitbread's father:

Your son died a great hero. He had three German planes firing all around him and his machine was riddled with bullet holes. It appears he was trying to bale out as he was out of his seat. My husband, who was in the garden, ran to the Spitfire to see if he could be of any help, but the pilot was lying outside the plane. He must have been trying to bale out as the Germans caught him down his left side – he must have then fallen back into the cockpit and came down with the plane as it bumped across the ground, or maybe he got stuck in the plane while coming down. Either way he was thrown clear upon impact. He lay just outside the plane and must have died instantly. He did not suffer, so please tell his mother. I know this is very soon after your great grief but perhaps it will help you with a little relief knowing that he did not linger on and suffer after his injury. Will it help you if I say that if I have to lose one of my own boys then I hope that they go the same way. It would be awful if he had endured weeks of suffering only for the Lord to call. I hope God will give us the means to overcome these murderers. I feel sure that your son will not have given his life in vain. It was an awful feeling when the Spitfire was coming down. It gave me an awful shock especially as I thought that it was coming down on my house, but we felt more than sorry when we found that your son was dead. My husband covered him up until the ambulance arrived to take him to the mortuary. Where we live is between the Thames Estuary and the south-east, so if the Germans try to get to London from either direction we witness the full force of the fighting. We had another plane almost on us today; it crashed in the field in front of our house.

When initially researching this story some years ago, I believed that Pilot Officer Whitbread had been shot down by *Oberleutnant* Hans Hahn, of II/JG 2. More recent research, however, suggests that 'B' Flight of 222 Squadron could equally have been attacked by none other than Major Adolf Galland, *Kommodore* of JG 26 and one of the *Luftwaffe*'s foremost *experten*, who shot down a Spitfire in a diving pass. After the initial bounce, 'B' Flight re-formed only to be attacked again, losing two more Spitfires, although both pilots were safe. In such confused circumstances, involving so many enemy fighters, it is impossible to be absolutely certain who was responsible for bringing Laurie Whitbread down, but Galland does appear to be another strong contender.

12. Me 109 pilots of 4/JG 2. From left: *Oberfeldwebel* Siegfried Schnel, unknown, *Hauptmann* Hans 'Assi' Hahn, who may have shot down Pilot Officer Whitbread, and *Unteroffizier* Rudolf Miese. (Chris Goss Collection).

13. Another contender for shooting down Pilot Officer Whitbread is Major Adolf Galland, *Kommodore* of JG 26.

14. Pond Cottage, Hermitage Road, Higham, near Rochester, Kent, where Pilot Officer Whitbread crashed and was killed on 20 September 1940.

By the time the Me 109s withdrew, only one of their number remained behind in a foreign field. Fighter Command, however, had lost four pilots killed and several wounded. 222 Squadron's Sergeant Norman Ramsay made this observation regarding his personal attitude to losses at that time:

People missing or killed at that stage of the battle meant little or nothing to me. I had joined 222 from 610 at Biggin Hill after we had lost 10, yes *10*, pilots, so I was well used to disappearing faces. Having been shot down myself I had learned to survive, to get the experience necessary for survival.

Pilot Officer Geoffrey Wellum of 92 Squadron adds:

On 20 September 1940, I flew two patrols in Spitfire K9998. After this length of time I can recall nothing of the action, but do remember that during September and October the 109s were always active in the Biggin Hill Sector, and caused problems. I recall that they were always above us as we seemed to be scrambled in time to get enough height. Our climb was always a desperate, full-throttle affair, but we never quite got up to them. I did manage to get a crack at two Me 109s on one patrol, but although I saw strikes I could only claim them as damaged.

It is perhaps characteristic that Laurie Whitbread had arranged that in the event of his death on active service the official telegram arising should not be delivered directly to his mother but to the Revd Hulbert, whose duty it would then be to break the news. On 3 October, 222 Squadron's CO, Squadron Leader John Hill, wrote to Mr Whitbread:

> It is with deep regret that I have to write to you from 222 Squadron and offer our sympathy in the sad loss of your son. He was killed instantly by a bullet from an enemy aircraft when doing his bit in the defence of our country. His passing is a great loss to us; he has been in the Squadron since its formation and always most popular, having a quiet and efficient disposition and charming manner.

Reg Johnson remembered what happened, and why, literally minutes before passing away himself, forty-three years later:

> From my now very senior years, I remember Pilot Officer Whitbread as a brave man of the highest quality. Naturally courageous, he was always prepared to give his life for his country, but it was taken away from him due to the practice of unsatisfactory tactics.

15. Pilot Officer Whitbread's grave on the day of his funeral. He was the first Ludlovian to make the ultimate sacrifice in the Second World War.

For me personally it was a great privilege to be a member of 222 Squadron, with which I completed 101 operational sorties. I was shot down twice and parachuted twice, and was wounded once. From the junior reserve pilot I soon became the senior NCO pilot due to my incredible good fortune.

Reg certainly was fortunate: during the Battle of Britain 222 Squadron lost nine pilots killed in action.

Pilot Officer Whitbread was the first Ludlovian to lay down his life in the Second World War, and that fact hit the small rural community hard. As a mark of respect he was laid to rest in the local cemetery with full military honours. St Laurence's Church, in the town centre, is illuminated in his honour every 20 September, and a road in Ludlow has been named after this gallant twenty-six-year old. To me, Laurie Whitbread epitomises that generation of young men who volunteered to defend their country in its hour of need, all possessed of intelligence and tremendous potential. The world, there can be no doubt, is a poorer place for their passing. Laurie's old schoolmaster, George Merchant, attended the funeral, and it is to him that we give the last word:

So we turned and went back and left him alone in his glory, with his name and rank on the gravestone and proud badge of the Royal Air Force that he had carried through peril to the stars.

For some reason, I think of him as typical of those fifty boys from the school who died in the same way, a kind of symbol of what they were and what they did and why. I hope nobody will think I have singled him out from the others, it does not mean that I regard them as having done anything less or deserving less to be remembered. He was just the kind of boy you noticed first, and remembered afterwards if you saw him talking in a group of his fellows, though he was probably saying less than any of the others. He was the kind of boy one does not forget and is glad to have known.

2

PILOT OFFICER ROBIN RAFTER

Pilot Officer William Pearce Houghton Rafter's story typifies the experience of young replacement pilots, with limited training and experience, pitched into combat during the Battle of Britain. Known by his family as 'Robin', this tragic casualty was born on 17 July 1921, the son of Sir Charles and Lady Rafter, whose home was at Elmley Lodge in Old Church Road, Harbourne, Birmingham. Sir Charles was Chief Constable of the Birmingham City Police and served for thirty-seven years. He died in 1935, being survived by his wife, eldest son Charles, Robin, and the boys' elder sister, Elizabeth. When Sir Charles passed away, Robin was at Shrewsbury School, moving to Cheltenham College the following year. At school he was an enthusiastic sportsman, excelling at cricket, rugby, football, squash, and swimming. His education complete, on 26 June 1939, the eighteen-year-old was given a Short Service Commission in the RAF and accepted for flying training.

Robin's *ab initio* flying training was undertaken on Tiger Moths with 6 CFS at Sywell in Northamptonshire. There he achieved his civilian flying licence before moving on to 12 FTS at Grantham in Lincolnshire on 2 September – just one day before Britain and France declared war on Nazi Germany. Two days after war broke out Robin was transferred to 10 FTS at Ternhill in Shropshire, where he was authorised to wear the coveted pilot's brevet on 3 November. The nineteen-year-old pilot passed his final exam with 64 per cent and was assessed thus: 'Ground subjects a poor average. Navigation and airmanship weak. A safe pilot but lacks polish. A keen average officer.'

It is a fact that between the wars strategic thinking always supported the view that 'the bomber will always get through'. Fighters were considered of limited value, even for defence, and yet the role of army co-operation flying was considered essential. Fighter Command was actually responsible for training pilots to serve in such squadrons, and instruction was provided at the School of Army Co-operation at Old Sarum in Wiltshire, which had existed since the Great War. In 1939, the object was to train replacement crews for tactical

16. Pilot Officer W. P. H. 'Robin' Rafter.

reconnaissance squadrons flying the twin-engined Bristol Blenheim. Shortly after the war started, many of these units were sent out to France with the BEF's Air Component. Anticipating the likely need for replacement pilots, a reserve pool was added to the school at Old Sarum, the combined output of which was seventy-two pilots, thirty-seven observers, and seventy-two air gunners on a six-week course which included forty hours of flying. The school's aircraft establishment was increased to twelve Lysanders, twelve Hectors, twelve Ansons, and fifteen Blenheims. The site at Old Sarum consequently became too small, and the school was therefore divided: single-engine types remaining there while twins went to Andover. Old Sarum trained twenty pilots and twenty air gunners per fortnight on a fortnightly course, while Andover's course remained six weeks.

Pilot Officer Rafter was posted to Andover on 1 February 1940, where he completed the twin-engine course before reporting to Old Sarum on 17 March. Unfortunately, Robin's pilot's flying logbook has not survived, but from the logs of other pilots we know that flying exercises on the Lysander included 'pinpointing ponds, photography and vertical pinpoints'.

Now a fully fledged Army Co-operation pilot, on 26 April, Pilot Officer Rafter reported for duty at Andover, where he was engaged on supply flights until 7 May. On that day, together with Pilot Officers McCandlish, Tuppin, and Walsh, Robin joined his first squadron, 225, at Odiham. Three days later Hitler attacked the west. By 3 June, the French and Belgian armies had collapsed, the British forced to retire on and be evacuated from Dunkirk. On 10 June, 225 Squadron moved to operate from Old Sarum, conducting a significant amount of dawn and dusk flying. Robin Rafter's first operational flight was made on between 2030 and 2230 hrs on 27 June, in Lysander N1315, in company with LAC Howes. This 'coastal recce' of St Albans and Selsey Bill was uneventful except for a destroyer, six miles south of Ventnor, which gave no reply when challenged. On 1 July, the Squadron moved to Tilshead. During that month, Robin flew six more similar patrols, with LACs Howes and Parr, all of which were uneventful, as were the two operational sorties he made in August.

By this time, however, the Battle of Britain was in full swing, and Fighter Command's casualties were a serious issue. The number of replacements required exceeded the ability of OTUs to produce pilots, even though the courses were cut back to the absolute bare minimum in terms of time and content, so Air Chief Marshal Dowding appealed to other RAF commands and to the FAA for help. So it was that on 22 August, Flying Officer Hallam and Pilot Officer Rafter answered the call and left 225 Squadron to fly Spitfires at 7 OTU, Hawarden. Their 6 Course comprised thirty-four officers, six American officers, and four NCO pilots, with three students being re-coursed due to injury.

It is interesting to compare the flying experience of Flying Officer Hallam and Pilot Officer Rafter at this point. The former was aged twenty-three, was commissioned, and learned to fly in 1937. After service flying training Pilot Officer Hallam reported to 2 Army Co-operation Squadron at Hawkinge on 30

April 1938. By the time his unit moved to France on 6 October 1939, therefore, Hallam was an experienced pilot who remained on the continent until his unit was withdrawn in May 1940. In July, he joined, on temporary attachment, the PRU based at Heston, where he was able to gain air experience on such aircraft as the Spitfire, Harvard, Hornet Moth, Wellington, and Hudson. On 7 August, Flying Officer Hallam reported to 225 Squadron, when he met Pilot Officer Rafter. Hallam's logbook indicates that by then he had over 500 hours' experience on single-engined aircraft *alone*. A study of comparable logbooks suggests that Rafter would have had such an amount in *total*. Moreover, Hallam had already logged six Spitfire hours at Heston. For Rafter such an experience at Hawarden would be completely new.

Ian Hallam's logbook indicates that while training on Spitfires at Hawarden, he made fourteen Spitfire flights between 23 and 29 August. These sorties included local familiarisation, formation flying, aerobatics, map-reading, homing practice, No. 1 and 5 Attacks, and firing guns into the sea. Upon conclusion of the course, Flying Officer Hallam had accumulated fifteen hours on Spitfires, so it is reasonable to assume that Pilot Officer Rafter would have achieved a similar amount of flying time. Originally the operational training course was of four weeks' duration, but as the need for replacements increased this was reduced to a fortnight. In reality, pilots were passed out when considered competent on type, which was usually between ten days and three weeks after ten to twenty hours' flying time. Incredibly, those hours did not include any air-to-air firing, owing to the shortage of both time and ammunition, so dire was the hour. All the OTUs were able to do, therefore, was provide conversion experience to operational type.

Who decided, I wonder, which pilots went to which squadrons? What criterion, if any, was used other than that on paper all were qualified to fly the Spitfire operationally? On 31 August, Flying Officer Hallam, who, as we have seen, was an experienced pilot of several years' experience, was posted to 610 'County of Chester' Squadron at Acklington in 13 Group. Based in the north of England, 610 Squadron was absorbing replacement pilots and providing further training, so Hallam was able to record a further 21.05 Spitfire flying hours, before being posted south, to 222 'Natal' Squadron in 11 Group, on 1 October. The inexperienced Pilot Officer Robin Rafter, however, was posted straight from Hawarden into the front line, joining a heavily engaged squadron in the thick of battle. Whose pen, I wonder, made that stroke and would it not have made better sense to send Flying Officer Hallam south from Hawarden and Pilot Officer Rafter north? On paper, though, both were qualified pilots and that appears to have been the only consideration when postings were chosen.

On Saturday, 31 August, just over a week since reporting at Hawarden to fly Spitfires, Flying Officer B. R. MacNamara (also a former Army Co-operation pilot) and Pilot Officers F. J. MacPhail and W. P. H. Rafter arrived at Hornchurch Sector Station in Essex, joining 603 'City of Edinburgh' Squadron. The scene greeting them must have been dreadful: on that day, the *Luftwaffe* had bombed various airfields, the Sector Stations at Hornchurch and Biggin Hill being hit twice. Some of the battered airfields were rendered close to non-operational. The Hornchurch Station Operations Record Book records a vivid picture of events:

> Mass raids continued to be made against our aerodromes, again starting early in the morning. The two attacks were delivered at 0830 and 1030 respectively and were directed at Biggin Hill, Eastchurch and Debden. The third attack was delivered at Hornchurch, and although our squadrons engaged, were unable to break the enemy bomber formation, and about 30 Dorniers dropped some 100 bombs across the airfield. Damage, however, was slight, although a bomb fell on the new Airmen's Mess which was almost completed. The only vital damage, however, was to a power cable, which was cut. The emergency power equipment was brought into operation until repair was effected. Three were killed and 11 wounded. 54 Squadron attempted to take off during the attack and ran through bombs. Three aircraft were destroyed, one being blown from the middle of the landing field to outside the boundary, but miraculously all three pilots escaped with only minor injuries.
>
> The fourth attack of the day was also directed at Hornchurch, and once again, despite strong fighter opposition and ack-ack fire, the bombers penetrated our defences. This time, however, their aim was inaccurate, and the line of bombs fell from them towards the edge of the aerodrome. Two Spitfires parked near the edge of the aerodrome were written off, and one airman was killed. Otherwise, apart from the damage to dispersal pens, the perimeter track and the aerodrome surface, the raid was abortive and the aerodrome remained serviceable. Our squadrons, which had a very heavy day, accounted no less than 19 of the enemy and a further seven probably destroyed. 603 Squadron alone responsible for the destruction of 14 enemy aircraft. Although we lost a total of nine aircraft, either on the ground or in combat, only one pilot was lost.

On what was clearly a particularly bitter day of fighting, 603 Squadron was in action four times, not suffering a casualty until the final sortie. At 6.20 p.m., Pilot Officer 'Sheep' Gilroy was shot down but baled out safely. Unfortunately, his Spitfire crashed into 14 Hereford Road, Wanstead, killing the occupant's pet dog. Over Woolwich, minutes later, an Me 109 of I/JG 3 shot down and killed Flying Officer Waterston. Flying Officer Carbury was more fortunate and returned safely to base after his Spitfire compressed air system was hit by a 109's 20 mm rounds. The enemy fighters were on a *freie hunt*, sweeping over Kent; Flying Officer Carbury, simultaneously with Flight Lieutenant Denys Gillam of Kenley's 616 Squadron, attacked and shot down JG 77's *Staffelkapitän*, *Oberleutnant* Eckhart Priebe, who baled out and was captured near Elham. Fighter Command, however, lost a total of thirty-nine pilots during that furiously contested day.

The 603 Squadron was an Auxiliary unit raised at Turnhouse near Edinburgh in 1925. Having flown Wapiti, Hart, Hind, and Gladiator bi-planes, in

September 1939, by which time the Squadron had been called to full-time service, 603 received Spitfires. The Squadron's pre-war pilots were all wealthy individuals who flew for pleasure at weekends, and personnel comprised both friends and relatives from the local area. After war broke out, 'A' Flight was deployed to Dyce, affording the RN some protection, and 'B' Flight at Montrose, where a vulnerable FTS was based. The Squadron was therefore responsible for defending a great stretch of coastline between the Firth of Tay and Aberdeen. German aircraft, however, faced a long flight across the inhospitable North Sea to attack targets in Scotland, and so these tended to be probing raids by either single or pairs of bombers. The crucial thing to remember, however, is that these raiders were operating well beyond the range of fighter cover and were therefore unprotected. When northern-based squadrons moved south, however, and met 109s, the change in operational conditions could only be described as traumatic. On 27 August, Squadron Leader 'Uncle' George Denholm led twenty-four pilots of 603 Squadron south to Hornchurch: only eight would survive the Battle of Britain.

In Scotland, 603 Squadron had been accustomed to keeping just one section of three pilots at readiness. At Hornchurch, three *squadrons* were kept at this state throughout daylight hours. In their naivety, some of 603 Squadron's young pilots remained exuberant: Pilot Officer 'Broody' Benson wanted to 'shoot down Huns, more Huns, and then still more Huns!' and was certain that 'Now we'll show the bastards!' Shortly after arrival, 603 Squadron was scrambled; by the end of that first day, two pilots, including Pilot Officer Benson, were dead. There would be no let-up, and from the following day onwards half a dozen of the Squadron's pilots would sleep in their dispersal hut as security against a surprise dawn attack. They would rise at 4.30 a.m., on what could well be the last morning of their young and promising lives, and by 5.00 a.m. their Spitfires' engines would shatter the silence as ground crews warmed them up. The first raid usually came in around breakfast time and from then until about 8.00 p.m. the Squadron was continuously engaged. Bacon, eggs, and beans were sent across from the Mess, but pilots ate as and when they could.

Even before 603 Squadron had flown south that fateful August day in 1940, the character of the Auxiliary unit had already started to change. Three RAFVR pilots had joined the Squadron, the pilots of which had previously been exclusively commissioned officers. Among those lowly NCO pilots was Sergeant Jack Stokoe:

> During my Spitfire training at Aston Down, I logged between ten and fifteen flying hours. Fortunately I then went north, to 603 Squadron in Scotland, which meant that I was able further to get to grips with the Spitfire. When we arrived at Hornchurch, I was therefore fortunate to have a total of around seventy hours on Spits. Had I gone straight from Aston Down to Hornchurch I would not have rated my chances of survival very highly.

Jack Stokoe was an aggressive and competent fighter pilot who immediately opened his account against the *Luftwaffe*. On 29 August, he flew on four patrols, damaging a 109 but having his own control wires shot away. The following day, Jack destroyed a 109 and damaged another, but again his own machine was not unscathed: a cannon shell hit the windscreen and the pilot's left hand was peppered with shrapnel. On 1 September, he sent a 109 down in flames over Canterbury, and damaged two more the next day. Jack Stokoe:

> I was attacking an enemy aircraft and remember machine-gun bullets, or maybe cannon shells, hit my Spitfire, followed by flames in the cockpit as the petrol tank exploded. I thought 'Christ! I've to get out of here and *quick*!' I undid the straps and opened the hood, but this turned the flames into a blowtorch. I was not wearing gloves, as during our hasty scramble I had forgotten them, but had to put them back into the flames to invert the Spitfire so that I could drop out (no ejector seats in those days!). I remember seeing sheets of skin peeling off the backs of my hands before I fell out of the aeroplane. I was then concerned regarding whether the parachute would function or whether it had been damaged by fire, but I pulled the ripcord and fortunately it opened perfectly.
>
> I landed in a field, but the Home Guard queried whether I was an enemy agent; but a few choice words in English soon convinced them I was genuine! I was then rushed to into the emergency hospital at Leeds Castle, suffering from shock and severe burns to my hands, neck and face. I was in hospital for six weeks, during which time my parents received a telegram to say that I was 'Missing in Action', such was the confusion of that hectic period. I returned to operational flying six weeks later, on October 22nd.

During those early days of action with 11 Group, 603 Squadron had to learn quickly or be damned. Having fallen prey to the experienced 109 pilots, Squadron Leader Denholm's Spitfire pilots rapidly determined not to let themselves be 'bounced'. 'Uncle George' would fly on a reciprocal of the course given by the Controller, until at 15,000 feet, when he would turn the Squadron about, still climbing. This way 603 Squadron often saw the enemy striking inland below them, and, enjoying the advantage of height, were in a perfect position to intercept. Breaking away from the officially accepted vic of three aircraft, Denholm devised a new system whereby a pair of Spitfires would fly together, offering mutual support. Recent research by John Alcorn (see Chapter 1) suggests that 603 was actually Fighter Command's top-scoring squadron in the Battle of Britain; if this is so, and I for one believe it to be so, George Denholm's tactical awareness and application of original thought must take the lion's share of credit for this accolade. Moreover, unlike many squadron commanders, 'Uncle George' also led his Squadron, virtually without exception, on every sortie during the Battle of Britain, in addition to performing numerous administrative tasks. After an engagement, Squadron Leader Denholm remembered that:

the Squadron would come home either individually or in ones and twos in intervals of about two minutes. About an hour after landing I used to check to see if anyone was missing. Sometimes a phone call would be received from a pilot who had perhaps force-landed elsewhere, or baled out and was safe, which was always news well received. Other times we would be informed by recovery team of the identity of a crashed Spitfire and pilot.

The Oxford undergraduate Pilot Officer Richard Hillary, who had joined 603 Squadron in June 1940, wrote of the attitude towards casualties in his classic first-hand account *The Last Enemy*: 'At the time, the loss of pilots was somehow extremely impersonal; nobody, I think, felt any great emotion as there simply wasn't time for it.'

The day after Sergeant Stokoe went down over Leeds Castle, Pilot Officer Hillary fell victim to *Hauptmann* Erich Bode, *Kommandeur* of II/JG 26, and also dropped from the fight in flames. Miraculously Hillary was thrown clear of his blazing Spitfire and although terribly burned managed to deploy his parachute. Two hours later, he was rescued from the Channel by the Margate lifeboat, close to death. Cared for by the remarkable surgeon Sir Archibald McIndoe, Hillary subsequently became a 'Guinea Pig' at East Grinstead's now famous Burns Unit. Tragically, his suffering and recovery would be for nothing: while training to be a night fighter pilot Hillary would be killed in 1943.

While all of this dangerous drama was going on high over southern England, during the first four days at Hornchurch, Pilot Officer Rafter watched his Squadron scramble time and time again, returning all too often with casualties. In 1989, Air Vice-Marshal Harry Hogan, who commanded 501 Squadron throughout the Battle of Britain, told me that 'some of our replacement pilots were straight from OTUs and these we tried to get into the air as soon as possible, to provide a little extra experience, but we were just too tired to give any dogfight practice at all. They were all very green, youngsters who were often completely bewildered and lost in action.' With 603 Squadron so heavily engaged, however, taking casualties in terms of both pilots killed and wounded, and Spitfires damaged, requiring repair either on-site or at a MU, or destroyed, there were neither experienced pilots available to train new pilots nor aircraft to spare for anything other than operational flying. So it was, therefore, that Pilot Officer Rafter's first flight with 603 Squadron was an operational one.

At 9.34 a.m. on Thursday, 5 September, Squadron Leader Denholm led twelve Spitfires off from Hornchurch, his three new replacement pilots, including Pilot Officer Rafter, in the formation. The Squadron had been scrambled in response to a major threat approaching Dungeness, where two large German formations crossed the coast and set a north-westerly course. Squadron Leader Harry Hogan's 501 Squadron was already airborne from Gravesend, and spotted the raiders while patrolling Canterbury and the Kentish coast: thirty Do 17s escorted by seventy Me 109s, all incoming at 20,000 feet. Hogan's Hurricanes

17. While on leave for the funeral of his brother, Flying Officer Charles Rafter, Pilot Officer Rafter poses adjacent to an imposing painting of his late father, Sir Charles Rafter, a former Chief Constable of Birmingham.

valiantly charged the 109s, but over Maidstone two large enemy formations separated into numerous smaller groups, the progress of which the Observer Corps found impossible to plot. One of these smaller raids struck out for Biggin Hill, thirty Me 109s of II/JG 3 weaving 6,000 feet above the bombers. The *Gruppenkommandeur* himself, *Hauptmann* Erich von Selle, was leading the 109s and in his *Stabschwarm* were two of his main staff officers: *Leutnant* Heinrich Sanneman, the *Gruppe* Technical Officer, and *Oberleutnant* Franz von Werra, the Adjutant.

Squadron Leader Robin Hood's 41 Squadron had been scrambled from Hornchurch at 9.10 a.m. and vectored to patrol Canterbury. When the Germans crossed the coast and headed north-west, the Squadron was vectored south. The Spitfires were flying high, at 27,000 feet, enjoying the benefit of being 1,000 feet above Von Selle. Between Maidstone and Romney a flight of Hood's Spitfires fell on the enemy fighters: Flight Lieutenant Norman Ryder damaged a 109, Pilot Officer Bennions hit another, which he later reported having seen 'streaming glycol and going down about eight miles south of Maidstone', and Sergeant Carr-Lewty watched his victim crash into a wood south-east of Canterbury. Flight Lieutenant Webster hit two 109s, the engine of one bursting into flames, but neither was seen to crash; attacked another 109 which rolled over and went in near Maidstone. Flying Boyle set about another 109 that was attacking two Spitfires, but only Squadron Leader Hood and Pilot Officer Wallens got through to the bombers. Then 603 Squadron arrived on the scene and joined the fray (Flight Lieutenant Norman Ryder of 41 Squadron reported having seen 'XT'-coded Spitfires during the combat).

Just take a moment to visualise this scene: around 100 fighters in total cutting and thrusting, whirling, twisting, and turning in some kind of bizarre but deadly aerial choreography. What could Pilot Officer Robin Rafter's impression of this vivid and incredibly dangerous scene have been as a mere youth with comparatively limited flying experience? Opposing the Spitfires were some of the most experienced combat flyers in the world at that time; unsurprisingly, therefore, Pilot Officer Rafter lasted just a matter of seconds after joining the fray. He later wrote this account of the action in a letter to his mother:

Well, I was over Kent at a little over 25,000 feet on a lovely morning of the 5th September when I sighted a huge formation of Jerries. I very nearly shot a Spitfire down by mistake, but then saw on the starboard side, underneath me, an Me 109. I got all fixed and started my dive onto the Me 109 and was nearing it when I saw in my mirror a couple of Me 109s on my tail. Well, I took what evasive action I could, but found two a bit of a problem. I started to get away from them when my tail must have been damaged as all movement on the control column was to no avail, thus putting my machine out of control so far as I was concerned. Well, by this time I had a little piece of shrapnel in my leg, and probably owe my life to the fact that my machine was out of control, as the Jerries evidently found difficulty in getting their sights on me as my machine was going all over the place. Luckily I was very high up and it then occurred to me to bale out. My oxygen tube had already become detached, but I had great difficulty in undoing the pin of my harness to loosen myself out of my seat. I eventually got the pin out, but could not get out of the aircraft. By this time the Jerries had ceased firing at me, but I had no idea where I was over. The next part of my experience was rather a miracle. The machine's nose dropped violently, thus having the effect of throwing me forward, the force so great that I went: through the canopy, thus unknowingly injuring my head. You can't imagine my surprise! I was then at 15,000 feet and floating about in the air rather like a cork. You will understand why when I explain that instead of diving at 400 mph, I had rapidly slowed down to about 180 mph, as the human body never falls faster, that being the 'terminal velocity'. I then felt so light I had to look to ensure that I was wearing a parachute. Luckily I had given it a slight inspection that morning. I pulled the cord and the chute opened up and I breathed once more.

Now the most terrifying experience happened, I floated down right through the aerial battle that was taking place. I came through it without a scratch, but then I noticed an Me 109 coming towards me, and you've no idea what a damned fool you feel suspended in mid-air with an enemy fighter buzzing around you. Well, he never fired at me, as a Spitfire came along and drove him off; whether he would have done or not cannot be said. Next worry was where I was going to land as there were a lot of trees near. I avoided them and landed in a nice field. My Spitfire, which was new, crashed in a ploughed field some way away. The LDV accosted me with a shotgun as I was wearing my RAF battledress which must have confused them a bit. I was treated by a local first aid post then taken to hospital.

That afternoon they performed a slight operation, stitching up the back of my head, which had a slight cut, and my right cheek, which is invisible now. They also took me the piece of shrapnel from my right leg which entailed a rather deep incision, but I am OK now and had all of the stitches out yesterday. I have been up and about for the last three days. I am coming out at the end of this week and will soon be back to get my own back on the Jerries! There is a saying that you are not a fighter pilot until you have been shot down once. Well, you have nothing more to fret about and you've heard everything there was, and see how simple it all was, and how well I was cared for? I'm still as good as new, with no facial disfigurement. Might even get a few days leave to see you. You must remember that I got off lightly and many more have received worse than me.

It is interesting that only pilots who claimed victories made out after action reports. Those pilots who were shot down, without claiming a kill, did not, and yet their experiences can often be the key to crucial discoveries. Of course, actual combat reports became available to the public during the 1970s, and have provided an absolutely crucial reference for historians. The foregoing account, however, as a personal letter from a son to his mother, although preserved, remained in the family's private hands and so has never been available in the public domain. On that basis this unique evidence – crucial to reconstructing the events of this particular air battle – remained hidden away and denied to researchers until located by myself twenty years ago. Having read the letter I was interested to see if any 603 Squadron combat reports might suggest who drove off the 109 that was circling Pilot Officer Rafter during his parachute descent. Imagine my delight when I found the following report at the Public Record Office, submitted by Pilot Officer Stapleton:

> I was diving to attack them (the bombers) when I was engaged by two Me 109s. When I fired at the first one I noticed glycol coming from his radiator. I did a No. 2 attack and as I fired was hit by bullets from another Me 109. I broke off downwards and continued my dive. At 6,000 feet I saw a single-engined machine diving vertically with no tail unit. I looked up and saw a parachutist coming down circled by an Me 109. I attacked him (the 109) from the low quarter, he dived vertically towards the ground and flattened out at ground level. I then did a series of beam attacks from both sides, and the enemy aircraft turned into my attacks. He finally forced landed. He tried to set his radio on fire by taking off his jacket, setting fire to it and putting it into the cockpit. He was prevented by the LDV.

Pilot Officer Rafter's Spitfire crashed at Marden, in Kent, some twenty-four miles south-east of Biggin Hill. Three Me 109s force-landed in England as a result of damage sustained during the same action, one at Wichling (32 miles east of Biggin Hill), one at Aldington (16 miles south-east of Wychling), and another at Loves Farm, Winchett Hill, Marden. This enemy fighter came down at 10.10 a.m. and very close to where Rafter's Spitfire crashed. That particular Me 109 is known to have been one of Von Selle's II/JG 3 *Stabschwarm*, and the pilot was captured in identical circumstances to those described by Pilot Officer Stapleton. The enemy pilot was none other than *Oberleutnant* Franz von Werra, later to become infamous as the only German prisoner to escape Allied custody.

In 1958, Kendal Burt and James Leaser published their book recounting von Werra's adventures, *The One That Got Away*, this subsequently being made into a feature film with Hardy Kruger starring as von Werra. Burt and Leasor, however, incorrectly accredited von Werra's demise on 5 September 1940 to Flight Lieutenant Webster of 41 Squadron, who reported having attacked an Me 109 which 'turned over and crashed near Maidstone'. Such a description does not suggest a forced landing, which the authors described von Werra as having made that day. Other authors have similarly incorrectly accredited von Werra to Flight Lieutenant Pat Hughes of 234 Squadron, but in reality Hughes is not even a contender given that his action was fought over the Isle of Sheppey, many miles from Marden. Another source correctly credits Pilot Officer Stapleton with shooting down von Werra, but states that the latter's 109 had already been damaged when attacked by the 603 Squadron pilot. Indeed, that damage, it is

18. The infamous *Oberleutnant* Franz von Werra – better known as 'The One That Got Away'.

claimed, was caused by 41 Squadron's Pilot Officer Bennions, who reported attacking a 109 which he subsequently saw 'streaming glycol and going down eight miles south of Maidstone'. From Stapleton's report, however, there is no doubt that von Werra's aircraft was not at all damaged when he attacked it. Moreover, it is extremely unlikely that a pilot would hang around to buzz a parachutist in the middle of a combat had his aircraft been damaged.

My findings were published in 1993, in my third book, *Through Peril to the Stars* (Ramrod Publications), and there can be no doubt that this was the first time the correct sequence of events leading up to von Werra's capture was published. Early in 1994, I traced Squadron Leader Jerry Stapleton himself, who had only very recently returned to live in Britain. Prior to our contact, the Squadron Leader had absolutely no idea that it was he who had shot down the infamous Franz von Werra, but remembered the combat: 'It was right on the deck. I recall having to shoot carefully so as to avoid hitting people working in the fields.' Naturally, Squadron Leader Stapleton was delighted to learn that he had brought down 'the one that got away', and I was pleased to provide him with a copy of the combat report he had last seen over fifty years previously.

As for Franz von Werra, after escaping from Allied custody in Canada he resumed operational flying and significantly increased his score over Russia. In

August 1941, his unit, I/JG 53, was withdrawn to Holland; on 25 October, while leading a *Schwarm* of Me 109Fs on a coastal patrol, von Werra's engine failed, sending 'the one that got away' to a watery grave in the North Sea.

The wounds suffered by Pilot Officer Rafter on 5 September 1940 led to some weeks recovering in hospital. On 2 October, he was transferred from Maidstone to the Officers' Hospital at Torquay, where, on 11 October, came devastating news: his elder brother, Pilot Officer Charles Rafter, had been killed when the wing of his 214 Squadron Wellington hit a hangar shortly after take-off from Stradishall. Robin returned home for the funeral, Charles being buried next to the boys' distinguished father in Birmingham.

On 29 October, Robin Rafter was discharged from hospital and sent home for a week's leave with his bereaved family. On 7 November, he returned to RAF Hornchurch, although still categorised as 'non effective, sick' and unable to fly. He was considered fit on 26 November, however, and reported back to 603 Squadron, which remained at Hornchurch.

The Battle of Britain was now over. By the end of September, the German bomber force had been unable further to sustain such heavy losses, so was withdrawn from the daylight battle. At night, though, the enemy bombers were able to operate with impunity, Blitz claiming many lives that winter. The German defeat in the Battle of Britain was largely due to the fact that the bombers were of a medium capacity only, designed to support the army in a tactical capacity, and lacked the range and payload to achieve a strategic decision. Moreover, the Me 109 was designed and intended as a short-range defensive fighter, not as a long-range escort fighter, and was completely unsuited, therefore, to the role into which it was pressed during the summer of 1940. Given these factors and the onset of winter weather, unsuitable for a seaborne invasion, Hitler had to accept that the opportunity to invade in England had passed. In February 1944, *Hautpmann* Otto Bechtle, the Operations Officer of KG 2, gave a lecture in Berlin regarding the air war against England from 1940 to 1943. Failure in the Battle of Britain was due, he maintained, to one factor: 'the enemy's power of resistance was stronger than the medium of attack.' 'Churchill's Few' had, therefore, given Hitler his first reversal of the war.

When Pilot Officer Rafter returned to active duties, although the crisis had passed, the threat had not. By day German fighters continued to sweep over southern England and, owing to the inclusion of fighter–bombers in their formations, could not be ignored by Fighter Command. The RAF pilots found themselves mounting standing patrols from dawn to dusk, and many survivors recall this period as the most exhausting.

On 29 November 1940, Pilot Officer Rafter made his second operational flight with 603 Squadron. Squadron Leader Denholm led nine Spitfire Mk IIAs south-east at 9.50 a.m. Off Ramsgate the Squadron tally-hoed a lone Me 110 of *Stab/StG I* on a reconnaissance flight. The 603 Squadron's Operations Record Book comments that the Spitfire pilots 'were frustrated as being in search of

19. Pilot Officer Peter Olver of 603 Squadron, who was shocked when Rafter crashed inexplicably.

bigger game'. Denholm's Spitfires virtually used the hapless enemy machine for target practice, its destruction subsequently shared between all nine pilots. The 110 soon crashed into the sea, killing the pilot, *Oberleutnant* Pytlik, whose gunner remains *vermisst*.

After the action, 603 Squadron returned to Hornchurch at low altitude. Flying at 2,500 feet, however, Pilot Officer Peter Olver was shocked to see Pilot Officer Rafter's Spitfire, P7449, suddenly drop from formation and crash in a meadow at Kingswood, Sutton Valence, Kent. There was no parachute. Many years later, Peter wrote and told me that 'I do remember Rafter, mostly I expect because of the horror I felt at him flying to the deck for no apparent reason. In those days, if a pilot failed to return, you could usually be 100 per cent certain that an Me 109 had sneaked up unseen, but during this operation there had actually been no such enemy fighters in the area.' According to Group Captain Denholm, 'I can only vaguely recall Pilot Officer Rafter, probably because he was with us for such a very short time, but I cannot recall his accident. After an action the Squadron rarely returned to base as a cohesive unit, but in ones and twos, so the only witnesses would have been whoever was flying with him. Cases like this were often oxygen system failing, causing the pilot to black out, but Rafter would have had no need to use oxygen at such a low altitude.'

So what caused the crash? Could Rafter's Spitfire have been damaged by return fire from Pytlik's Me 110? This is possible, but had the young pilot known that his machine had been damaged, surely he would have reported this over the radio after the action? Perhaps, then, the Spitfire was damaged without the pilot's knowledge? That being so, and if the pilot was uninjured, why did he not shout up over the R/T that he had lost control of his aircraft? Why did he not bale out? So many questions, but Robin Rafter's (sadly now late) sister, Elizabeth Barwell, believed she had the answer: 'I have always been of the opinion that Robin blacked out as a result of the head injury sustained on 5 September. He was still not 100 per cent, in my opinion, but was so keen to get back to his squadron and into the air again. I will always be absolutely convinced that this was the case.'

Ironically, on the eve of Pilot Officer Rafter's death, 603 Squadron held a dinner party at the Dorchester Hotel to celebrate its successes against the enemy.

The nineteen-year-old Pilot Officer Robin Rafter was buried with his father and brother in Birmingham. In more recent times their graves were seriously damaged in an act of mindless vandalism.

20. The Rafter brothers' grave at Harborne Church, Birmingham.

3

FLYING OFFICER FRANEK SURMA

Francizsek Surma was born on 1 July 1916, at Rybnik, in the Galcowicz district of Poland. His parents, Francizsek and Tekla Surma, were peasant farmers and also had three daughters, all of whom were older than 'Franek' and doted on the baby in their family. A clever boy, Franek won a scholarship to attend the grammar school at Galkowicz, of which the Surmas were justly proud. A model son, even after long days of studying Franek would always help out on the farm. In 1928, he continued his education in Zory, and at that time decided to become a pilot. Eight years later he enlisted in the Polish Air Force and volunteered for aircrew training. According to his personal air force file, Franek Surma was passed as category 'A' fit for duty, and considered 'very physically fit and an excellent mathematician'.

Every Polish service pilot also had to complete basic infantry training, so although Cadet Surma was on the strength of the Air Force Officer Cadet Training School at Deblin, he completed his infantry experience with 4 Company of the Polish Cadet School. That over, Franek started *ab initio* flying training in April 1939 as a Cadet Staff Sergeant. At Deblin his flying instructor was Joseph Szlagowski, featured on the excellent (1980) television documentary 'Churchill's Few'. In July 1939, Officer Cadet Surma received his 'wings', a silver eagle clutching a laurel wreath, and his file at that time records that he was 'well above the average both physically and intellectually. He shows initiative and enthusiasm, and is an example to his comrades to whom he displays maximum loyalty'. Posted to the Krakow Squadron, Surma flew the little P.IIc fighter: a dream had come true.

On Friday, 1 September 1939, after several years of tension, peace was shattered when Hitler invaded Poland with sixty-three divisions, the spearhead of which comprised no fewer than fifteen *panzer* divisions. The Germans enjoyed the benefits of modern technology and tactics while the fifty-six Polish divisions retaliated with the outdated equipment and thinking of 1925. Both

21. Flying Officer Franek Surma

armies were largely horse drawn, but the Poles even had horses in the front line: sabre-brandishing cavalry against steel *panzers*. The struggle would be bitter but brief, and could only end in defeat for the gallant Poles. In the air it was the same: totally obsolete Polish fighters and bombers were decimated by modern enemy combat machines. After two weeks, the Polish Air Force had taken some 90 per cent losses in both aircraft and aircrew, and was consequently unable to continue operations. On 17 September, what Polish aircraft remained serviceable were flown across the border into neutral Romania, and many Polish Air Force personnel also managed to escape. The original plan was to train the Poles in Romania on British aircraft types, but as both German and Russian influence in that country was so strong this proved impossible. Leaving the Romanians to their fragile neutrality, the Poles travelled westwards, the majority by boat and via Constanza, Beirut, Malta, and Marseilles.

In France, Lyons was made the central collecting area for the free Poles, and in March 1940, Polish pilots began being absorbed into French Air Force squadrons. Although the French aircraft types were superior to those in which the Poles had met the Nazis over Poland, they were still inferior to the German machines. Having struck against the west on 10 May 1940, the Germans dominated the battle, both on the ground and in the air. Again, the hapless Poles found themselves on the losing side and were again forced to flee, this time across the Channel to England. No possible means of escape from the continent were overlooked by the Poles, whose only aim was to remain free and eventually to liberate their homeland. In Britain, Blackpool became the central collecting point for the Poles, where slowly administration managed to review the status of escapees and ensure that no 'fifth columnists' were among them. Fortunately, pilots with combat experience, including Franek Surma, had made it safely to England; as Fighter Command's losses increased their services would soon be sorely needed by the RAF.

Franek Surma's route to England in 1940 was via Romania, Syria, and France. He was initially billeted at 51 Pool, Eastchurch, where his combat experience marked him out for immediate posting to 6 OTU at Sutton Bridge. There Pilot Officer Surma of the RAF, as he now was, learned to fly the Hawker Hurricane. The difficulties, however, for these Polish exiles must have been immense, not least having to learn a new language spoken both on the ground and in the air. The language barrier, particularly regarding the Poles and Czechs, was of great concern to Air Chief Marshal Dowding. Although by the summer of 1940 there were two Polish and two Czech squadrons in Fighter Command, albeit with British commanding officers and administrators, the language difficulty stayed Dowding's hand in committing them to the fray. On 30 August, however, Flying Officer Ludwik Paskiewicz destroyed a German bomber while on a training flight, as a result of which his Squadron, 303 based at Northolt, was declared fully operational; the other three foreign squadrons were swiftly added to the board.

22. Surma on readiness at Tangmere, while flying Hurricanes with 607 Squadron during the Battle of Britain.

By that time, the experienced foreign pilots chosen for early RAF flight training were also starting to reach the squadrons. On 20 August, Surma reported to North Weald, where he flew Hurricanes with 151 Squadron, which had already fought determinedly during the Battle of France and early stages of the Battle of Britain. The young Pole's first operational flight was on 25 August, when his Flight was deployed to operate from the forward base at Rochford. Five days later he opened his account against the *Luftwaffe*, claiming an He 111 'probable' over the Thames Estuary. On 1 September, 151 Squadron was taken out of the line, having suffered eleven pilots killed during the Battle of Britain alone, and flew to Digby. After a period of leave it was decided that the Squadron's two Poles, Pilot Officers Surma and Jan Orzechowski, being fresh to the fray, should report to 607 'County of Durham' Squadron based at Tangmere.

The 607 Squadron was an AAF unit and had also fought in the Fall of France, taking heavy casualties since returning to the combat zone a few days previously. Having joined 607 on 10 September, Surma made his first operational flight from Tangmere four days later. The Squadron was making up to six flights a day at this time, which must have been exhausting, and on 17 September he chased an Me 109 off Sergeant Lansdell's tail. Although the Pole managed several quick bursts, the enemy fighter made off into cloud. During that action Pilot Officer Harry Welford was shot down, possibly by *Hauptmann* Neumann of I/JG 27, but although slightly wounded he safely force-landed at Bethersden. Harry remembered 607 Squadron's Polish pilots:

Jan Orzechowski was a short, stocky, and rather serious man. He smoked cigarettes incessantly and used a cigarette holder. The Polish officers tried to strike a certain pose, I suppose, to keep up with us rather casual Britishers. They were extremely good pilots, but quite mad and totally fearless. Surma, who was with me in 'B' Flight, was a bit more relaxed and met us half-way, probably because he spoke more English than the others.

On Thursday 26 September, the Germans heavily bombed Supermarine's Spitfire factory at Woolston. The defending squadrons were scrambled and battle was soon joined. Heavy combat ensued over the Isle of Wight, Portsmouth, and at sea, six to twelve miles south of the Needles, between 3.50 and 4.30 p.m. The 607 Squadron arrived on the scene just as the raiders started bombing. After the initial head-on charge, the Squadron was split up and pilots acted independently. Some fifteen to twenty miles out to sea, south of St Catherine's Point, Surma found 15-20 Ju 88s at 15,000 feet:

> I saw a bomber break away from the enemy formation and tried to overtake him. At the same moment I saw an Me 109 gliding down above and behind the Ju 88s. I followed the enemy aircraft for a considerable distance and when several miles south of St Catherine's Point I made two or three long bursts from 100 to 150 yards on the tail of the enemy aircraft, which immediately went into a dive and crashed into the sea.

Unfortunately, however, the raid on Woolston was a complete success: the Supermarine works were gutted; at least thirty-six civilian workers were killed and sixty seriously injured. Aircraft production at the site was brought to a standstill that September, but the following month, to the great credit of Supermarine's work force, 139 Spitfires were built in October, compared to the August high of 149. Harry Welford:

> I do recall an amusing anecdote concerning Franek Surma and the events of 26 September. We had a very intrepid and garrulous fighter pilot in Jim Bazin's 'B' Flight called 'Chatty' Bowen, who seemed to enjoy continued success in combat. Franek envied Chatty's success and wished that he could borrow some of his luck. Chatty was known to carry a stuffed toy elephant as a mascot, and Franek pleaded with and cajoled Chatty into lending it to him for a sortie. After much argument and persuasion from other members of the Flight, Chatty agreed to lend Franek the mascot to fly with, but only on a sortie he was not flying himself. Franek was instructed to return the mascot to Bowen's Hurricane the moment he landed. Later, Surma returned jubilant as he had destroyed a 109, and as promised he returned the mascot to his rigger, who replaced it in the cockpit of Bowen's Hurricane. Chatty, however, just couldn't find the mascot on his next trip and cursed Surma for not returning it. On that sortie Chatty was shot down and it was assumed that his change

23. Surma, left, playing 'pax' with Flight Lieutenant Charles 'Chatty' Bowen at Tangmere in September 1940. A successful fighter pilot, Bowen wears a German lifejacket, probably a coveted trophy taken from an enemy flier he shot down.

24. The Supermarine factory at Woolston, gutted after KG 55's raid on 26 September 1940.

of luck was due to Surma not having returned the toy elephant. The twist to the tale is that when the salvage team recovered the wreck of Bowen's Hurricane from the Isle of Wight, they discovered the elephant in the cockpit; it was believed that the mascot had fallen from the gunsight and jammed the rudder pedals!

The time that Franek and I were together in 'B' Flight was extremely short – only six days – but the loss of life occurred so rapidly that the experiences of a lifetime could be crammed into less than even that short time. Franek was the sort of chap who was immediately popular, and when we had a beer in the evening he would teach us how to say 'Nostravia!', which means 'Good health' in Polish. He impressed me. The story about the mascot I probably got second hand off a Squadron chum while I was in Ashford hospital, as the incident occurred after I was shot down, but the story is certainly true to the characters of both Chatty and Franek. Before I was wounded, Franek was trying to borrow the mascot, and used to infuriate Chatty – who was, after all, a senior pilot while Surma was very junior – beyond all reason by calling him his 'Lovelee boy'!

On 11 October, 607 Squadron was pulled out of the line, having lost eleven pilots killed that summer. On 17 October, Pilot Officer Orzechowski was posted to the new all-Polish 306 Squadron, while Pilot Officer Surma went to another RAF fighter squadron, 46, at Stapleford. He arrived on 18 October, along with several other replacement pilots, but three days later was posted to 257 Squadron at North Weald. The 257 had only been formed at Hendon the previous June. Initially equipped with Spitfires, these were soon exchanged for Hurricanes. During the early stages of the Battle of Britain, the Squadron flew from Northolt and suffered heavy casualties. This led to a change in command, and the charismatic Squadron Leader Robert Stanford-Tuck revitalised the Squadron. Reg Nutter was a sergeant pilot at the time, and remembers Tuck:

I found him to be a very charismatic leader and this, combined with his exceptional combat record, immediately gave one a good deal of confidence in him. His style of leadership contrasted greatly with that of his predecessor, Squadron Leader Harkness. Tuck would make suggestions to the Ground Controller as to how we might be better placed to intercept, but Harkness would follow all instructions explicitly. There is no doubt that before Tuck's arrival the Squadron's morale was at a low ebb: under his leadership, however, there was a tremendous improvement. In many ways he was an individualist, but he would nevertheless go out of his way to give sound advice to other pilots.

On 28 October, Surma engaged an He 111 in an inconclusive combat over Romney and Folkestone. The enemy bomber was credited as a 'probable', but the following day Pilot Officer Surma was not so lucky. That afternoon the Me 109 fighter–bombers of II/LG 2 attacked North Weald at low level, supported by JG 26 Me 109 fighters. Flight Lieutenant Peter Brothers was at tea in the

Officer's Mess when the raiders struck: 'We all dived under the table! My car, an open 3-litre Bentley, was parked outside and I was livid to find that a near-miss bomb had filled it with soil, which took forever to clean out!' As the raid came in, twelve Hurricanes were actually taking off. Sergeant Goodwood's aircraft left the ground but was then slapped back down by a bomb blast; the pilot was burned to death. Flight Lieutenant Blatchford got up safely and engaged, but was hit by a 109 and forced to crash land back at North Weald. The 257 Squadron Intelligence Officer, Flying Officer Geoffrey Myers, described what happened to Pilot Officer Surma:

> Red 2, Pilot Officer Surma, saw the bombs falling as he was taxying over the aerodrome. A bomb exploded on his left-hand side as his aircraft was running up. The explosion jerked him, but he took off satisfactorily. He noticed four enemy aircraft flying over our hangar between 4,000 to 5,000 feet, and also saw many planes on his right, which he took to be Hurricanes.
>
> When he climbed to about 3,000 feet he heard an explosion in his cockpit, which filled with white smoke. His plane went into a spiral dive, he no longer had control, so opened the Perspex. After a moment the Hurricane came out of its dive and levelled out, but soon began diving to starboard. After trying to bring it out of this second dive without success, he attempted to bale out. By this time he had lost height to 1,500 feet. After struggling to get out of the cockpit he baled out at about 1,000 feet and made a safe parachute descent, landing in a treetop near an inn at Matching. After quickly convincing the Home Guard that he was Polish and not German, he was given two whiskies and driven back to the aerodrome. He had lost both of his flying boots when jumping out of the plane, received a black eye, but was otherwise unharmed.

Pilot Officer Surma had been shot down by *Hauptmann* Gerhard Schöpfel, *Kommandeur* of III/JG 26. Shortly before he died, in 1987, Wing Commander Stanford-Tuck commented that: 'Of course I knew Franek Surma very well and there are many stories I could tell you of him. He was a wonderful little chap – but wild! He was also a loyal and thoroughly trusty wingman.' The Poles held their CO in similarly high esteem: Surma presented Tuck with a miniature set of Polish 'wings', which his Poles asked him to wear on his tunic; this he did, until shot down and captured in 1942.

Characteristically, after his lucky escape on 29 October, Pilot Officer Surma was flying again on 2 November. By that time, the Battle of Britain was over, but the opposing fighter forces would continue to clash over the Channel and southern England until the following February, and the night blitz continued apparently unchecked.

On 11 November, the Italian Air Force sent fifty aircraft to attack a convoy off Lowestoft. The 257 Squadron intercepted and decimated the Breda 20 bombers and CR42 bi-planes. Although Surma was not involved, another Pole, Pilot

Officer Carol Pniak, actually forced an Italian bomber to surrender and made it land at Woodbridge in Suffolk!

November 1940 continued with more convoy patrols from Martlesham Heath. December saw little activity, the weather causing problems. On 6 December, Sergeant Bennet's Hurricane was tipped on its nose by high winds while taxying, and Surma, in V7052, stalled on approach to Clacton, landing in a field short of the runway. The verdict was that he had misjudged the wind strength, which was over 40 mph

On 16 December, Pilot Officer Surma was posted to 242 Squadron, flying Hurricanes again, at Martlesham. This largely Canadian squadron was commanded by Squadron Leader Douglas Bader, who had been given the task of improving morale following the beating suffered by 242 in France. This he did, and subsequently led the Squadron throughout the Battle of Britain. During the winter of 1940/1, however, 242 was also providing aerial cover for Channel convoys, Surma flying seventeen such patrols. Of the young Polish fighter pilot, Squadron Leader Bader reported that he was 'A very competent fighter pilot who understands English well on the R/T'.

On 14 March 1941, Pilot Officer Surma took leave of 242 Squadron to join a Polish unit, 308 'City of Krakow' Squadron, equipped with rather old Hurricanes, at Baginton, near Coventry. Unit 308 had been formed at Speke in September 1940, moving to Baginton later that month to afford some protection to both Coventry and the Armstrong-Whitworth factory, which was adjacent to the airfield. The Poles' first kill was a lone reconnaissance bomber on 24 November, which was appropriately celebrated during the Squadron's Christmas bash at Leamington Spa's Clarendon Hotel. By March 1941, combat-experienced Polish pilots serving in British squadrons were identified and posted to Polish units, as was the case with Pilot Officer Surma. Joining him in 308 would be other veterans of 1940, including Flight Lieutenant Marian Pisarek and Pilot Officer Jurek Poplawski, who became a particular friend. Many years later, Wing Commander Poplawski wrote to me from his home in Argentina:

Franek Surma and I were close friends. We were both veterans of the Battle of Britain, although he was a much more distinguished pilot than me, and we were of a similar age. He was a rather deep person, perhaps even a little reserved. Perhaps we were all like that, trying not to think of tomorrow. It would be wrong to say that we were not afraid, after all we were just ordinary human beings, and as such we all knew what fear was. But we also had an unwritten code of conduct in our lives, a sense of duty that helped us control our fear. That code was possibly the most important influence on our lives. Franek and I discussed it a lot.

Because the night blitz was reaching its zenith, enemy reconnaissance aircraft were regularly active over the Midlands during daylight hours. At 11.25 a.m. on Wednesday 26 March, Pilot Officer Surma led Pilot Officer Bozek and Sergeant

Kremski off from Baginton to intercept one such intruder. The Ju 88 was sighted over Leamington and attacked, the German pilot immediately jettisoning his bombs. Much to the delight of 308 Squadron, the combat progressed until it was over the airfield at 3,000 feet, but the raider somehow escaped, albeit trailing smoke. The Poles were credited with a third of a probable each.

On 2 April, the Poles received great news: their Hurricanes were to be replaced with Spitfires! These were not the new Mk Vs, however, or even Mk IIs, but obsolete and tired Mk IAs of Battle of Britain vintage. Two days later the CO, Squadron Leader Jan Orzechowski, took two other pilots to Kirton-in-Lindsey and collected three Spitfires from 65 Squadron. On 6 April, the Poles tried out their new aircraft, the Squadron diary commenting that the 'pilots take to new machines at once. Very manoeuvrable and lighter to handle than the Hurricane'.

At 1.40 p.m. on Sunday 11 May, Pilot Officer Surma and Sergeant Widlarz were scrambled to investigate a 'bogey' at 27,000 feet over Kidderminster in Worcestershire. No aircraft were found, however, and the Poles were informed by Ground Control that the radar plot had transpired to be a friendly Blenheim. It was a perfect day for flying, with excellent visibility, and so the two Spitfires continued on patrol, the two pilots no doubt enjoying the sheer thrill of flight.

Over Malvern, the engine of Pilot Officer Surma's Spitfire, R6644, suddenly burst into flame. Having shut off the fuel supply to minimise the risk of fire spreading, the pilot checked his instruments and noted a severe drop in oil pressure. Standing Orders dictated that in such circumstances the pilot should make a forced landing and save the aeroplane, and it is likely that Surma, an experienced pilot, intended to do just that – until his windscreen became covered in oil, obliterating his essential forward vision. Smoke also started pouring into the cockpit, making it clear that the wisest course of action would be to abandon the Spitfire over rural Worcestershire. Waiting until the aircraft was clear of the built-up area of Malvern below, Surma inverted the aircraft and dropped out, leaving R6644 to its fate. The parachute opened safely and as the pilot descended he saw his Spitfire crash in an open field east of Malvern Link. Not surprisingly, in sleepy wartime Worcestershire, the high drama over Malvern had attracted great interest. Schoolboy Harry Cleaton:

I was walking along the main Worcester Road in Malvern, between Great Malvern and Link Top on the Malvern Hills. I had just reached the leather craft factory and sat down on a low stone wall to admire the view. I could see a Spitfire over Malvern Link, flying towards Worcester, but it was trailing a thin plume of black smoke and losing height rapidly. This was an astonishing sight; and then the pilot baled out! I ran all the way to North Malvern Police Station, in Newtown Road, but when I arrived, breathless, the local bobby, PC Jack Calder, was just leaving on his pushbike to find the crash site.

Mr Davies, Malvern's Chief Air Raid Warden, was walking his dog along Pickersleigh Road when R6644 passed over him, trailing smoke. He ran to the nearest house, No. 9, and called Malvern Police Station, giving the Station Officer a running commentary of events until the aircraft disappeared from his view. Schoolboy Jimmy Thomas:

> We had been playing an early season game of cricket on Malvern Link Common and were walking home when we saw the Spitfire. When the pilot baled out we just couldn't believe it! The Spitfire pitched down vertically, and we reckoned that both plane and pilot would make landfall in the Madresfield area. We immediately jumped on our pushbikes and pedalled off furiously in that direction!

25. Land Army girl Vi Probert – first on the scene when Surma landed by parachute at Hawthorne Lane.

These pages: 26 and 27. Surma pictured at Bosworth Farm, Madresfield, while awaiting transport back to Baginton after baling out of Spitfire R6644 on 11 May 1941.

Bill Pritchard, a twenty-one-year-old milkman working for Bennett's Dairy of Worcester:

I was driving my milk truck down Jennet Tree Lane, which leads from Malvern Link to Callow End, and knew nothing of the crashing Spitfire until there was an explosion in the field to my right, near the junction of Jennet Tree and Hawthorn Lanes. Naturally I was absolutely startled and stopped immediately. Good job I did, as a length of aluminium three feet long hit the road directly in front of me; had I still been driving it would have gone straight through my windscreen! I realised then that it was an aircraft and not a bomb that had caused the explosion, so I climbed over a newly laid hedge and hurried to the crash site, although I realised that if the pilot was still in the plane he would be beyond any help. As I made across the field I was puzzled by someone shouting at me, but looking around there was no one else on the scene but me. Then I looked up and saw the pilot coming down on his parachute, shouting at me to keep away from the burning wreckage because of dangerous exploding ammunition. The parachutist drifted over me, towards the cottage at the junction of the two lanes, so I returned to my truck, picked up the piece of aircraft in the road, and took it home as a souvenir.

Inside the nearby cottage, Mrs Probert was having lunch with her daughter, Vi, who was enjoying a rare weekend off from her work in the Land Army, and two evacuees. Vi remembered:

We were startled by the explosion and all four of us dashed outside to investigate. We could see a pall of smoke rising and assumed a stray bomb to be the cause. As we turned around to go back inside we were amazed to suddenly see a parachute disappearing over the back of our cottage! We ran into the adjacent field and watched an airman land before gathering up his parachute. Our instinct was to go to him and help, but then we had second thoughts as he could have been a German! I can't remember what was said between us but I do recall that he had a foreign accent which sounded a bit German.

Having collected up and removed his parachute, Pilot Officer Surma walked across the lane and looked at the wreckage of his Spitfire, which was burning fiercely in a small crater while other debris was scattered on the surface over a wide area. By now literally hundreds of people were arriving, by various modes of transport, from the directions of both Malvern and Callow End. Local lad Neville Grizzell had just enough time to give the pilot a Woodbine before the Pole was ushered away by a doctor and PC Calder. Hurrying to the scene along Hawthorn Lane was a group of airmen from a searchlight site, who took charge of the situation and confirmed Surma's identity.

The area was farmed by the Page family, who took the pilot to Bosworth Farm where he was made most welcome until transport arrived to return our hero to

Baginton. The airmen and police then had to fend off souvenir hunters. Young air cadet Ken Davies, son of the Chief Air Raid Warden, was rapidly on the scene and managed to purloin a much-coveted piece of Spitfire wreckage. Harry Cleaton was not so fortunate, as en route his pushbike suffered a puncture, meaning that he could not get to the crash site until the following day. By then the site was so well guarded, the recovery team being on site, that the young schoolboy was unable to acquire a souvenir. These events, however, would remain indelibly etched upon the memories of all who had witnessed the drama take place.

Shortly after Pilot Officer Surma and Spitfire R6644 parted company over rural Worcestershire, 308 Squadron moved from Baginton to Chilbolton in Hampshire. There the Poles exchanged their Spitfire Mk Is for Mk Vs, and undertook gunfiring practice at Chesil Beach with 118 Squadron. On 24 June, 308 Squadron moved again, this time to RAF Northolt, the home of 1 Polish Fighter Wing. Flying from Northolt the Squadron provided cover to convoys off Portland Bill, Swanage, and Bournemouth but, more importantly, Northolt was within striking distance of enemy-occupied France; it was in that direction that the Polish Wing would be engaged.

Two days before 308 Squadron arrived at Northolt, Hitler invaded Russia. No longer were the Nazis' territorial ambitions aimed westward, at Great Britain, but eastwards. This meant that although the prospect of any renewed attempt to invade Britain that year was unlikely, the British government was under pressure from the Russians to open a second front. Moreover, there was a new offensive attitude prevalent at Fighter Command HQ: Dowding's successor, Air Chief Marshal Sholto Douglas, being keen to 'Lean into France'. The idea was that small formations of medium bombers would attack various targets in north-west France in daylight, escorted by huge numbers of Spitfires which would take on smaller numbers of enemy fighters and destroy them. The initiative would be called the 'Non-Stop Offensive', and in readiness for this undertaking Fighter Command had reorganised itself into 'wings' of three squadrons, each with a dedicated Wing Commander (Flying) and based at Sector Stations. The squadrons had also been largely re-equipped with the Spitfire, it having been recognised as the superior British fighter of the period. For the Spitfire pilots it was to be a hectic 'season'.

On 27 June 1941, 308 Squadron flew its first sweep over France, during which Pilot Officers Surma and Szyszka shared the destruction of an Me 109 while strafing the *Luftwaffe* airfield at St-Omer. The Poles were in action daily, either sweeping or supporting bombers in complex Circus operations involving hundreds of aircraft. Although there were combat successes, there were casualties too: on 12 July, Flying Officer Stanislaw Wielgus, one of 308 Squadron's original members, was shot down and killed over the Channel; the following day, amidst torrential rain and thunder, his body was washed ashore on the south coast. On 17 July, 308 Squadron's new CO, Squadron Leader Marian Pisarek, ran

28. Spitfire Mk Vs of the Polish Fighter Wing take off from Northolt on an offensive operation in 1941.

into 'pretty big trouble': 306 and 308 Squadrons had taken off together but became separated over France. North of St-Omer, Pisarek's twelve Spitfires were jumped by sixty Me 109s, probably of III/JG 26. Pisarek ordered his pilots into a defensive circle before resuming formation, with weavers, and zigzagging back to the coast. Owing to repeated enemy attacks, defensive circles had to be resumed several times, but somehow the Poles kept together and fended off the Germans. Three 109s were claimed destroyed and two probables, but two 308 Squadron Spitfires, having taken off late and straggling behind the main formation, were missing. Pisarek keeping his tiny force intact, however, while scoring victories against an overwhelming enemy force, is the stuff of legends. The two missing pilots, Pilot Officer Maciejowski and Sergeant Hegenbarth, courted disaster by flying alone over France and paid the price: the former was captured, the latter killed.

On 22 July, 308 Squadron participated in a sweep of Dunkirk, St-Omer, and Gravelines. Enemy aircraft were shot up on the ground at St-Omer and Guines, and on the return flight Pilot Officer Surma destroyed a 109E which he caught attacking a Spitfire between Guines and the French coast. The combat took place at just 200 feet, and the Spitfire pilot clearly saw the 109 crash into the ground. On 26 July, 308 Squadron's pilots were released for twenty-four hours, the Squadron diary commenting that 'the pilots will soon be engaged on a sweep of a different kind!' Throughout August 1941, the Squadron would be further engaged, claiming more victories and suffering further casualties. On 29 August, Squadron Leader Pisarek led 308 Squadron as top cover on a Circus to Hazebrouck; over the coast, the Poles were attacked by 'Masses of Jerries'. Once more, skilful leadership kept the Spitfires together and got them home safely without loss.

In early September 1941, 308 Squadron upgraded its Spitfire Mk IIs for the newer Mk VB, which boasted a more-powerful Merlin and two 20 mm cannons. Some of 308 Squadron's Mk IIs were cannon-armed 'B's, but the engine was the same as that which powered the purely machine-gun-armed, and therefore lighter, Mk IIA. The improved performance of the Mk VB, therefore, was most welcome and would become Fighter Command's workhorse until the Spitfire Mk IX arrived in 1943, just in the nick of time, to counter the FW 190 menace. On 16 September, Pilot Officer Surma made his first flight in a Spitfire Mk VB, AB930, ZF-J. That day, 308 Squadron's 'A' Flight (six Spitfires) engaged thirty Me 109Fs over Gravelines. Surma, by now promoted to Flying Officer, was leading Red Section and destroyed a 109 which his wingman, Sergeant Warchal,

29. The tail unit of Spitfire AB930, damaged in action with Sergeant Jan Okroj at the controls on 20 September 1941. Flying Officer Surma was subsequently reported missing in this machine on 11 November 1941.

confirmed as destroyed. Surma's friend, Pilot Officer Poplawski, claimed a kill in unusual circumstances by forcing a 109 down into the sea without firing a shot!

On 20 September, the Polish Wing flew as escort cover wing on Circus 100, to Rouen. Over the target Surma and his wingman, Sergeant Jan Okroj, became separated. The latter was flying Surma's usual AB930 and was attacked by three Me 109s. From long range their cannon shells damaged his tail unit but somehow Okroj outran his assailants and force-landed at Thorney Island. The Spitfire was so badly damaged, however, that it was sent to Heston Aircraft Limited for repair. During that sortie Flying Officer Surma destroyed two more 109s, both of which crashed in flames, before engaging a third enemy aircraft:

> As I was too low to rejoin the Squadron I flew low to the Channel. About 10 miles out to sea I caught sight of the bombers – they were on my starboard side. As it was quiet I managed to join a squadron on the port side, by which time I could see the English coast, and saw an Me 109F making off after attacking a Spitfire. Behind the Me were three Spitfires in line astern. I manoeuvred to cut off the Me's escape but the Spitfires abandoned their quarry for some unknown reason. The enemy aircraft climbed and I tried to get on his starboard side and into the sun. At that moment the German turned to port and looked back and as I was at the same height he saw me. This Me had its under surfaces painted in the same blue as our Spitfires, and the upper surfaces were camouflaged in green and brown, as our aircraft used to be, no doubt to confuse us.

> The German pulled over on his back, I followed and got him below me. We started a dogfight but he kept on circling and made several attempts to reverse our positions. The Me was superior in engine power and climbed away very easily. My only possible tactics were to turn either to port or starboard to cut in on him. All this time the enemy aircraft was gaining height and attempting to shoot me down, but his ammunition was wasted as I took care to keep out of his axis of fire. I was unable to fire at him as I was unable to get into a sufficiently favourable position to do so. As the position became a stalemate we both broke off at the same time.

This combat is of particular interest, because I doubt that Flying Officer Surma engaged an Me 109F; more likely it was another Spitfire, as German pilots did not paint their machines to represent Spitfires. Also, could that explain why the three Spitfires broke off their pursuit? Did the pilot Surma attacked realise that his assailant was another Spitfire, I wonder, or did he too assume this to be a 109? 'Friendly fire' was an understandable mistake in the heat of battle, especially at this time when the Me 109F was still a comparative newcomer to the action and so dissimilar to its predecessor, the angular Me 109E, being more like the curvaceous Spitfire. Such a scenario was not uncommon, even for experienced and successful fighter pilots.

On 27 September, Flying Officer Surma probably destroyed a yellow-nosed Me 109F during a Circus to Amiens, and Poplawski destroyed another, which the latter reported as 'burning nicely as it crashed into a row of houses west of Amiens'. The 109, however, had previously riddled the Pole's Spitfire with bullets, damaging it so badly that Jurek had to crash-land at Biggin Hill.

On Circus 107, which took place on 12 October, the Northolt and Kenley Wings escorted bombers attacking St-Omer, 308 Squadron flying as forward support at 24,000 feet. Flying Officer Surma:

> I was leading the right-hand four aircraft. Having been warned over the R/T that our aircraft had been engaged by 109s, we wheeled round, re-crossing the French coast south of Le Touquet. Over the Channel I saw two Me 109s flying far apart in line astern, as though following a combat. I took evasive action by flying into the sun and the Me's passed below, unaware of my presence. I dived on the tail of the second Me and fired three short bursts into its tail from above at 100–150 yards range. The leading Me took evasive action and dived out of sight. My victim turned over onto its back and I fired another burst from about 80 yards. While it was in that position white smoke poured from the Me 109, which then went into a steep dive. Bright flames then came from the Me as it crashed into the sea.

The following day saw Pilot Officer Poplawski notch up 308 Squadron's fiftieth victory when he destroyed a 109 between Mardyck and St-Omer. Another important occasion occurred on 28 October when Flying Officer Surma was awarded Poland's highest gallantry decoration, the Virtuti Militari, Vth Class. He was now an 'ace' fighter pilot, having destroyed five enemy aircraft, probably destroyed two more, damaged another, with a third share in a damaged Ju 88. In an impressive ceremony at RAF Northolt, the twenty-five-year-old Pole received his medal from General Sikorski, leader of the Polish people in exile.

During the first week of November 1941, 308 Squadron flew on several Ramrod operations, supporting 'Hurribombers', and a Polish Wing sweep to St-Omer on 7 November. By now the season was drawing to a close, as winter weather set in, but the tempo of operations remained fairly constant. The next operation was a highly complicated Circus, No. 110, to bomb the railroad repair facility at Lille. The Polish Wing's squadrons were designated top (308), medium (315), and close (303) escort. At 11.05 a.m., the Polish Wing Leader, Wing Commander Rolski, led the Wing off from Northolt, completing an orbit of the airfield before setting off to rendezvous with the bombers over Manston. The 308 Squadron was the first to arrive and started an orbit while waiting for the other Spitfires, and the Blenheim bombers, to arrive. On cue, the two other Polish squadrons arrived simultaneously with the bombers and all set course for France. Unfortunately, while completing their turn, 308 Squadron had been blinded by the bright sun and lost sight of the 'beehive'. Wing Commander

Rolski could see that 308 was turning the wrong way, but was unable to communicate via R/T owing to the essential requirement for silence at this stage of an offensive operation. Instead, the Wing Leader violently rocked his wings to attract attention, but to no avail. Eventually, Squadron Leader Pisarek had no option but to break radio silence and inform Ground Control that his Squadron had missed the rendezvous. 'Ops' then vectored Pisarek towards the bombers, and 308 Squadron set off in hot pursuit.

The main formation soon crossed the French coast west of Dunkirk, passing over Bethune before hitting the target and turning for home over Arras. Covering the bombers' withdrawal were five 10 Group Spitfire squadrons; although these units were in their correct position while the bombers were outward bound, they were ahead of their prescribed co-ordinate on the return journey, throwing the bombers and escorting squadrons into confusion. The Blenheim's passage over France had already attracted accurate flak and, after leaving the target, eight 109s were spotted beneath the Allied formation. Although the Germans repeatedly attacked from below and behind, all of the Blenheims were brought home safely. Also in the air were a further seven 11 Group fighter squadrons and one from 12 Group and between them claimed four Me 109s and one FW 190 destroyed, three 109s damaged, and a 190 damaged.

Fighter Command also suffered casualties, however. 308 Squadron, unable to locate the main formation after missing the rendezvous, was vectored to patrol from Dunkirk to Calais, between 16,000 and 25,000 feet. Towards the end of their patrol time, when fuel reserves were a consideration, the Squadron was jumped from above by a large force of Me 109Fs from I/JG 26. The Poles were immediately split up and obliged to disengage and head back across the Channel. After losing their attackers, 308 Squadron's pilots, in ones and twos, found and joined the main formation, also travelling home.

Back at Northolt, Pilot Officer Poplawski reported as follows:

I went to the assistance of a Spitfire that was being attacked by an Me 109F. I got on the Me's tail and from 200 yards above I gave a short burst from my cannons. I saw an explosion in the starboard wing and the Me turned onto its side with the starboard wing down. I fired another burst from both my machine-guns and cannons. Volumes of black smoke appeared from the Me which started to dive down sideways. As four Me 109s were approaching to engage me, and were higher, I decided to join a formation of our aircraft in the distance.

Pilot Officer Stabrowski:

I saw a Spitfire being attacked by an Me 109F and went to its assistance, engaging the enemy aircraft from above and astern. I gave it a burst of fire from both cannon and machine-gun at 300 yards. The Me wobbled badly and I knew that I had hit it. I followed up my attack and fired three more bursts. The Me quivered and wavered more and more, thick black smoke pouring from the underside of the fuselage. It dived towards the sea near the French coast. Being short of ammunition and petrol, and a long way from base, I could not chase the Me and so returned to England.

The only German fighters lost that day were two FW 190s, the pilot of one of which was killed. Three more enemy aircraft were damaged in crash-landings, which could have been combat related, and one of which may even have been the 109 clearly damaged by Poplawski and Stabrowski, who appear to have attacked the same enemy aircraft simultaneously but independently.

Circus 110 was a disaster for Fighter Command, which lost fourteen pilots, including three squadron commanders and a wing commander. From the Polish Wing, Squadron Leader Szczesniewski was captured. The only other Spitfire failing to return to Northolt was AB930, flown by Flying Officer Surma, who was posted 'Missing'. The Squadron's diary summarised the day as 'very depressing'. Franek Surma's body was never found. The gallant Pole is not forgotten, however, and his death was far from the end of this inspirational story.

In May 1985, forty-four years after Franek Surma baled out of R6644 over Malvern, I was working at Malvern Police Station, a twenty-three-year-old police officer with three years' experience. By coincidence, although I did not know it at first, I lived in the Police Authority-owned property that was formerly North Malvern Police Station, and from which PC Jack Calder had hurried to Madresfield on that far-off Sunday lunchtime. Fascinated by wartime aviation my whole life, and extremely moved by the sacrifices made by young airmen during the Battle of Britain in particular, a friend's chance remark, shortly after I moved to Malvern, that a Spitfire had crashed at Madresfield and that the pilot was a Polish Battle of Britain veteran, changed the course of my life.

The friend who first told me about the Surma crash was eighteen-year-old local aviation archaeologist Andrew Long, with whom I had researched on a casual basis for the previous four years. Andrew had collated the basic details of the crash, and knew in which field it had happened. I became so fascinated by the whole story, however, that we soon traced eyewitnesses via the local media and were piecing together a detailed story. Moreover, the Spitfire's Form 78, detailing the units with which it served, provided us with the basic data required to undertake further research at the Public Records Office. A list of pilots who had once flown R6644, which had an impressive total of 266 flying hours, was subsequently obtained and research commenced to trace any survivors, or the relatives of casualties. The story of Franek Surma himself particularly interested me as I was so moved by the fact that he had no known grave. Over the next year, our project grew enormously, and we received permission from the MOD, the landowner, Madresfield Estate, and the tenant farmer, Mr Nugent at Lower Woodsfield, to excavate the crash site of R6644. From that point on the project became bigger and more ambitious still!

Crop rotation dictated that the site could not be excavated until September

These pages: 30 and 31. Pilot Officers Jurek Poplawski (Pl. 30) and Tadek Stabrowski (Pl. 31) who went to the assistance of a Spitfire being attacked by an Me 109 on 8 November 1941. Forced to break when almost immediately attacked by more enemy fighters, the Spitfire the pair tried to help is believed to have been flown by Flying Officer Surma.

1987, so in October the previous year Andrew and I co-founded the Malvern Spitfire Team to undertake the project. We also decided to make the excavation a public one, to raise money for the RAF Association's Wings Appeal, and involved the local branch. Significantly, we all wanted to provide a marker to Franek Surma, a more personal one than the imposing Polish Air Force Memorial at Northolt, on which his name was inscribed. We decided to build a cairn of granite, hewn from the nearby Malvern Hills, in Jennet Tree Lane, near to where Pilot Officer Surma landed by parachute. Needless to say, there was a complex and typically inefficient paper chase by the local authorities before permission was granted, but we persevered and got there in the end. Support was also forthcoming from the local ATC Squadron, 1017, and the MOD Participation Committee approved a fly-past by the Battle of Britain Memorial Flight and a Tornado GR1 of 65 Squadron (with which unit R6644 had flown). The icing on the cake was when the Polish Air Force Association in Great Britain honoured us by accepting our invitation to unveil the memorial. It was a privilege indeed to learn that two Polish Battle of Britain veterans, both of whom remembered Franek Surma, would perform the honours: Squadron Leaders 'Gandy' Drobinski and Ludwik Martel.

My research priority was to try and ascertain what had happened to Flying Officer Surma on 8 November 1941. I was very pleased indeed when Jurek Poplawski was traced to his home in Buenos Aires; protracted correspondence developed between us, and in 1987 the Wing Commander had this to say of Circus 110 and Franek Surma:

> The whole flight lasted one hour and fifty-five minutes. I believe that it was Franek's Spitfire being attacked by at least one 109. The German attack was both sudden and shocking in its ferocity. We tried to assist the Spitfire but I soon had a warning of 'Break left!' from Squadron Leader Pisarek, which I did. Apparently there were even more 109s coining down to attack and so, as I was also short of fuel, I couldn't hang around. Therefore I did not see what ultimately happened to either Franek or the 109 that I had attacked.
>
> I also remember that there was another 109 between me and that which was shooting at the Spitfire, but that is really all I can remember of that action, which was fairly early on in my operational career. I flew throughout the war, and so much happened later, in Normandy and Germany, for example, that it is difficult to recall that fleeting moment in 1941 with any more clarity.

Sadly, Squadron Leader Pisarek was killed later in the war when leading the Polish Wing, but his wingman on Circus 110, a new pilot, Pilot Officer Kazek Budzik, was found very much alive and well in Nottingham:

> That was my first operational flight and Pisarek told me to stay close to him, which I did. As Pisarek shouted 'Break!' to Poplawski, then I must have been with him in

the area that Surma was killed, but I must admit that as I was so inexperienced and concentrating so hard on staying with Pisarek that I didn't see much of what was going on around me. I do remember a 109 flashing across my windscreen and Pisarek yelling at me to fire. Of course, Surma was an experienced pilot, an ace. I hardly knew him but I remember thinking at the time that he had been very unlucky to be killed like that.

Another 308 Squadron combatant was Sergeant Jan Warchal, who I met by chance at the Spitfire Jubilee Air Show at Duxford in 1988, although he was unable to recall anything of the combat. Sadly, all of the other 308 Squadron participants had either been killed during the war or had died since 1945.

The 308 Squadron's combat report mentions a parachute seen in the area of Dunkirk, but the time does not correspond with Poplawski and Stabrowski's combat reports. If Pilot Officer Surma baled out but was not picked up, it is possible that his body was washed up on either the French or British coast and subsequently buried as an unknown airman. Team members scoured CWGC and cemetery records on both sides of the Channel but no likely contenders could be found. On that basis we must assume that Pilot Officer Surma went to his death in the English Channel, imprisoned in Spitfire AB930.

So who shot down Franek Surma? German combat records indicate that the enemy pilot responsible was *Hauptmann* Johannes Seifert, the twenty-five-year-old *Kommandeur* of I/JG 26. Seifert was an *experte*, already decorated with the *Ritterkreuz*, he would be killed in action against American Lightnings in 1943. It was the end of another mystery.

'Operation Spitfire', the recovery of Spitfire R6644 and the unveiling of the Surma Memorial, took place on Saturday, 11 September 1987 and remains one of the most moving experiences of my life. It seemed that the whole of Worcestershire had turned out to support us, and a significant amount of cash and publicity was raised for the 'Wings' Appeal'. The excavation indicated that the Spitfire had hit a layer of very hard clay and granite just a few feet below the surface, shattering all major components. Indeed, the recovery team in 1941 had done a very good job! Nevertheless, many small artefacts were found, the biggest being a piston and liner, the most impressive being the tiny de Havilland badge from the extreme front of the aircraft's propeller spinner cap. All of the finds were laid out for display on a long table while team-member Bob Morris, an engineer with 66 (Spitfire) Squadron during the Battle of Britain, identified the artefacts for our 100 special guests and innumerable members of the public.

Malvern Hills District Council hosted a civic reception for our Polish and other VIP guests, whose number included many former Spitfire personnel, in a marquee at the crash site. It was a poignant occasion, made more so when the Council Chairman, Mrs Lyn Norfolk, explained that her own father remained missing in action from the Second World War. Squadron Leader Martel spoke on behalf of the Polish delegation and, moved close to tears, described how honoured he was

32. *Hauptmann* Johannes Siefert of I/JG 26 who undoubtedly shot down Flying Officer Surma. The German was himself killed in action during 1943.

33. Bob Morris (right), an engine fitter with 66 Squadron during the Battle of Britain, shows Polish Battle of Britain Spitfire pilots Squadron Leaders 'Gandy' Drobinski (left) and Ludwik Martel parts of Spitfire R6644 recovered by the Malvern Spitfire Team.

to have been invited to such a unique event, and how indescribably moved both he and his colleagues were that so many people had turned out to remember a young Polish flier whom they had never met. 'Perhaps', he said, 'the motto of the Malvern Spitfire Team is true: "The Legend Lives On".'

Although bad weather grounded the Battle of Britain Memorial Flight at St Athan, Jennet Tree Lane was absolutely packed when the time came for Surma's memorial to be unveiled. The two Polish pilots walked with the team and the guard of honour, provided by the local ATC squadron, the few yards to the memorial. It was incredible to see the huge crowd of people part ahead of us, and I will never forget the words that Squadron Leader 'Gandy' Drobinski said to me that day: 'In 1945 we Poles were not invited to participate in the great victory parade, such was the situation with Stalin, and we could not even go home. Britain gave us a home and, all these years later, you have now given us our victory parade. It was worth the wait.'

Around the cairn were clustered journalists and television cameras, and during the dedication service Revd Eric Knowles said that 'Flying Officer Surma's sacrifice is an example to us all of how to serve our country, our friends and our God.' Squadron Leaders Drobinski and Martel solemnly stepped forward and removed the Polish Air Force ensign from the memorial. The atmosphere was incredibly charged, the crowd silent as wreaths were laid by the Polish Air Force Association, RAF Association, and the Malvern Spitfire Team. As the last wreath was set down a strong gust of wind suddenly shook the tree beneath which the memorial was built; in the prevailing atmosphere it was easy to imagine that this was Franek Surma's spirit coming to rest. I certainly hope it was.

In June 1988, the artefacts recovered from R6644's crash site became the centre-piece of a major exhibition featuring the Malvern Spitfire Team's research at Tudor House Museum in Worcester. The opening event was attended by numerous Battle of Britain pilots and other VIPs, but the ribbon could only be cut by one man, so far as we were all concerned – Kazek Budzik, Squadron Leader Pisarek's wingman on Circus 110. The exhibition was a huge success, attracting 10,000 visitors in just a few months. Consequently the time allocated to our exhibition was extended, and it then became a travelling show, seen at numerous aviation and cultural centres across the United Kingdom.

Efforts to trace the Surma family had so far failed, but early in 1989 I enlisted the help of Polish Spitfire enthusiast Kryzstof Choloniewski, who placed an appeal on my behalf in the Krakow newspaper. Out of the blue, in February 1989, a letter arrived in my post which remains the most moving piece of correspondence I have ever received; it was from Franek Surma's two surviving sisters, Elzbiete Morcinek, aged eighty, and Otylia Paszek, aged seventy-six:

We were delighted and extremely moved to learn of your project, the knowledge of which affected us considerably. At last we will learn the whole truth regarding the fate of our dear brother. We are the only surviving family of Franciszek Surma

34. The memorial erected at Jennet Tree Lane, Madresfield, Worcestershire, in honour of Flying Officer Surma by the Malvern Spitfire Team in 1987.

and came from a long line of peasant farmers, 'Franek' being the youngest child. We all adored him, as did everyone who knew him. He was a very good child, very obedient and hard working. At school in Zory he passed his exams and decided to become a pilot. On this issue he opposed his parents' wishes for the one and only time. None of us agreed with his plans, for we considered joining the air force to be a very dangerous affair and so were afraid for our little brother. Our concern made no difference as he was decided and would not consider any alternative. We do not regret that we did not succeed in changing his mind as we now know that he was a hero. Two of our family, in fact, were killed by German pilots: the Germans bombed a school in Wieszniowice in Czechoslovakia and hit a house on the opposite side of the street where our sister lived and who was killed instantly.

After Franek completed his education at Zory he moved to Krakow and joined the air force. At this time he wrote about attending a course at the Reserve Officers Cadet School for infantry at Rozane. He also attended cadet schools in Rawicz and Deblin.

We were always delighted to see Franek when he was on leave and our parents would organise parties. He looked wonderful in his uniform. He was an extremely cultured, intelligent, and gallant young man. We were all very interested to learn of his flying exploits and listened to his stories with bated breath. On one of his few visits he even brought home a parachute to show us how safe it was to jump.

Two days before war broke out he made several acrobatic and low passes over every house occupied by a member of our family. We remember running out of the house in a state of great excitement! We all knew that this was Franek but we were scared to death by his aerobatic antics! In Galkowice there stood a large oak tree and this shook violently as Franek passed overhead, so low was he. We understood that this was a sign to say that our little brother was going away.

During the war we received a letter from Franek via Holland. He let us know about the dispatch of two other letters and some money. Only one of those letters reached us. Via Portugal we received parcels from him, known as 'Signs of Life', containing tins of sardines. Our joy was not for the food but the knowledge that the sender was still alive. Can you imagine our great joy? Those were the only happy moments in those cruel days. After the war ended we received another parcel, which made us happy because we assumed that Franek was still alive. But we waited in vain for him to come home. Finally we asked the Red Cross to try and discover whether he was still alive. Eventually we received confirmation that our dear brother had failed to return from an operation in 1941 and was probably killed in the cold waters of the English Channel. We also received his medals and photographs. The news of this tragedy drove us all to the utmost depths of despair.

Since that time, more than forty years have now passed and we are happy that Franek's memory is alive, not only with us. At our 'Memory Room' in Gadawe his photograph is displayed in a place of honour. Also you, in far away England, have not forgotten him. We are so proud of our brother. We are also astonished at your achievements as such a young man, and want to shake your hand for all you have done. Kindly express our gratitude to everybody who has contributed to the commemoration of Franek Surma. We are most grateful to his friends, the chaplain, and the people of England. It is hard to express our thanks in words; there are no words that could adequately express the feelings of two old people who have kept alive in their hearts the memory of their dear brother.

Through your project you have awakened our memories and shown how wonderful people can be. Many special thanks go to you and we will be praying for your success in life, prayers for someone now very dear to us. May God take care of you and your organisation. We are so happy that there is still someone to light a candle for Franek on All Souls' Day. We are happy because the memorial erected to him serves as his grave, a symbol he can see from heaven. We have always worried about Franek having no known grave, but now we are at peace, thanks to you.

4

PILOT OFFICER ROGER BOULDING

I was commissioned as a regular officer in 1938, and learnt to fly at Sywell with Paddy Finucane, later to find great fame and success as a fighter pilot before going missing over the Channel. When war broke out I was flying Fairey Battle light-bombers with the AASF in France, but when things turned a bit sour over there I managed to escape and fly back to England in a Tiger Moth, landing at Hawkinge.

Of course, during the summer of 1940, the RAF needed fighter pilots to make good losses suffered in France and already during the Battle of Britain, which started in July. I therefore answered the call and, much to my delight, converted to Spitfires. In August 1940, I was posted to 74 Squadron, the famous 'Tigers', at Wittering. The Squadron had already seen much action both over Dunkirk and from bases in southern England that summer, and our CO was the highly successful fighter pilot and leader 'Sailor' Malan. Flying from Wittering I damaged a Ju 88 north of Ipswich on 14 September and a Do 17 near Sherringham ten days later. On 5 October I got a Do 215 and on 12 December, by which time we were operating from Manston, I got my first Me 109. We got into a scrap over Margate with some more 109s on 7 May 1941, I got one and damaged another but was shot up myself in the process. My Spitfire's petrol tank and coolant system were damaged, so I crash-landed back at base.

By that time the Germans were bombing our cities, particularly London, very heavily by night. Nocturnal defences were poor, radar, etc. embryonic, and so desperate was the hour that even Spitfires were pressed into a night-fighting role. The Spitfire, however, is not a good aircraft to fly at night, and indeed it was never intended to be by the designer. Visibility was poor because the bank of exhausts on either side of the nose and in front of the pilot glowed red-hot and ruined night vision. The narrow track undercarriage, coupled with the fact that when landing the pilot's view of the airfield below was virtually nonexistent, also made night flying pretty dodgy.

On 10 May 1941, the Germans made their heaviest attack on London, starting some 2,000 fires. One thousand Londoners were killed and 2,000 injured. At that

35. Pilot Officer Roger Boulding of 74 Squadron pictured at Gravesend in 1941.

time we were operating from West Malling, the general idea being that, over the full moon period, the ack-ack guns were restricted to their shells exploding no higher than 12,000 feet over Central London. Over Outer London they could fire up to the maximum, and outside the barrage night-fighters operated under close control. We day fighters were sent up to the Central Area at intervals of 500 feet to patrol individually.

I had been on patrol for quite a while, in Spitfire Mk IIA, P8380, coded 'ZP-Q', throughout which time Central London appeared to be at the base of a huge pyramid of flame. I hadn't seen a thing, except the flames, shell bursts, and the odd aircraft in flames over the outskirts. Didn't really expect to see anything with two great rows of glowing exhaust ports ruining my night vision! So when I began to have a bit of a problem controlling the revs, I headed for base and called control. Almost immediately, I saw this large twin-engined thing in front of me, going the same way! I had only to line up on him and press the button – it obviously wasn't one of ours! I hit him underneath and the effect was of an enormous burst of sparks, which I perforce flew through. It was a *Heinkel* 111, which stuck its nose down and headed for the deck, meaning that it was difficult to see against the earth's dark background, but, of course, his rear-gunner could easily see me silhouetted against the moonlit sky. He opened up on me every time I got into position to give him another burst, and very adjacent he was too!

36. The He 111 of 5/KG 53 destroyed by Pilot Officer Boulding on the night of the extremely heavy raid on London, 10/11 May 1941.

37. 74 Squadron pilots and RAF intelligence officers inspect the He 111 at Kennington, Ashford, Kent.

38. Pilot Officer Boulding (right) on readiness at Biggin Hill in early 1941 with the Polish Pilot Officer Henryk Szczsney (centre) and an unknown pilot.

39. 74 Squadron pilots at readiness, Biggin Hill, 1940. From left: Pilot Officer Roger Boulding (and 'Sam'!), Pilot Officer Henryk Szczsney, Flight Lieutenant John Freeborn and Pilot Officer Harbourne Stephen.

40. 74 Squadron personnel off duty at Gravesend, 1941. From left: Flight Lieutenant Mungo-Park DFC, Pilot Officers Boulding and Baker, next two unknown, Pilot Officer Bob Poulton.

We carried on like this until the German pilot was indulging in some rather fancy low flying across Kent. I don't think that I hit him again. Eventually I lost sight of him so circled the area and obtained a radio fix from base, which established my position, and returned to West Mailing. There we found minor damage to my Spitfire, such as to the oil cooler debris guard, indicating that I had flown into small pieces of debris. When my radio fix coincided with the discovery of an He 111 on the ground, it was credited to me; the rest of the Squadron had stooged around all night but seen nothing!

After that it was a case of flying sweeps over France during daylight hours. On 17 June 1941, I was on such a sweep, flying a Spitfire VB, W3251, and leading a section of four 74 Squadron Spitfires. Sailor Malan led the Wing, 74 Squadron in the van, and we were flying top cover. Having dived onto some Me 109s, in accordance with the standard drill of that time we didn't follow them all the way down but attempted to re-form, climbing towards the sun and weaving. I was following Sailor and another Spitfire was following me. After a while Sailor came on the radio telling someone to 'Look out behind!' I quickly did so and saw the chap still behind me, and screwed my head around some more, still looking for the trouble. Then I saw Sailor below me, violently rocking his wings. Suddenly there was an almighty bang on the armour plating behind my seat and it became rather obvious that the chap behind me had been replaced by someone rather less friendly! With controls gone I had to jump out and floated down from 12,000 to 15,000 feet in broad daylight. Naturally I found a substantial reception committee waiting. And that was that, as the Germans kept on saying 'For you ze var is over!'

5

SERGEANT PETER ROSE

Peter Garratt Rose was born on 17 May 1916 at Burton-on-Trent in Staffordshire. His father, John Frederick Rose, had served in the local county regiment during the Great War, after which his services were retained to assist with administration on the continent. There Major Rose was joined by his family, which remained with him in France until he left the army in 1920. Back in England, Peter Rose became a pupil at Burton Grammar School, where he was an accomplished member of the school rowing club. In 1930, Peter was coxswain and steered the school crew, in which his elder brother John rowed at stroke, to victory in the Burton Regatta, winning the Leander Challenge Vase. In 1932, Peter rowed at bow and was again in the winning team. That year he left school, joining both his father and elder brother at the local brewing company, Bass, Ratcliff & Gretton Limited. Major Rose was the company accountant, and spent fifty years of his life there. John worked in the Engineering Department while Peter was a clerk in the Bottling Department.

Peter Rose had always wanted to fly, so, much against his mother's wishes, he joined the RAFVR in 1936, learning to fly at Burnaston, near Derby. Unfortunately this meant that the close rowing relationship he and John enjoyed had to end, so much did flying training interfere with practice on the River Trent. On 13 June 1939, Peter was called up for full-time service as Britain prepared for the inevitable war with Nazi Germany.

After 'square-bashing' and ground schooling at 3 ITW, Sergeant Rose's service flying training was successfully completed before he reported to 7 OTU, Hawarden, to fly Spitfires. By this time the Battle of Britain was drawing to a close; when Sergeant Rose reported to his first operational fighter squadron, 65, the unit was resting at Turnhouse after being heavily engaged flying from Hornchurch. He then flew with 65 Squadron at Tangmere, moving with the Squadron to Kirton in February 1941. There 65 rested again and trained replacement pilots while providing convoy protection patrols. Such was the monotony, however, that Peter transferred to 1 PRU, based at Benson, 'to escape the boredom of patrolling the east coast'.

41. Sergeant Peter Rose

The PRU started out as the PDU, the first flight of which was made by Squadron Leader Sidney Cotton on 10 March, this being a sortie in a Lockheed Hudson to photograph Mannheim. The unit operated Blenheims before receiving Spitfires in October 1939. The weight of camera equipment and full fuel tanks, however, dictated that these Spitfires were unarmed, relying upon height and speed for protection. All equipment deemed superfluous was stripped out, empty gun ports blanked off and panel join lines were even filled with plaster, thus ensuring a completely smooth finish – these alterations increased the Spitfire's speed from around 362 to 390 mph. Cotton also developed a special duck-egg green paint called 'Camotint', in which all PDU aircraft were painted. With wing-mounted cameras fitted, the first Spitfire photographic reconnaissance flight was made to the German city of Aachen on 18 November 1939. During the Battle of France in May and June 1940, PDU Spitfire pilots flew 557 sorties, losing twelve aircraft. After Dunkirk the unit re-formed at Heston as 1 PRU, finding the Spitfire a superb aerial reconnaissance machine when fitted with long-focal-length oblique cameras. Indeed, the Spitfire remained in service as a photographic reconnaissance machine until long after the cessation of hostilities in 1945, by which time it had undergone numerous adaptations throughout the spectrum of marques. Clearly, however, the PRU pilots' role was a very dangerous (not to mention unsung) one – flying unarmed aircraft deep over enemy territory and returning with essential intelligence.

Saturday, 3 May 1941 dawned cloudless, remaining fair with good visibility. Throughout the day, 1 PRU carried out a number of sorties to photograph the industrial Ruhr Valley. Two Spitfires failed to return.

Sergeant Rose was making only his second trip since having transferred to Heston less than three weeks previously. At 1 p.m., a Spitfire was seen in difficulties over the village of Soumagne, near Liège, in Belgium. The aircraft concerned was R6805, flown by Peter Rose – whose Merlin engine was heard by eyewitnesses on the ground to be running very roughly. The aircraft was then seen spinning and the pilot baled out.

The village policeman, Leonard Melon, rapidly donned his uniform, stepping outside his front door and watching a parachute drifting south-west. In that direction he could see the Spitfire's funeral pyre billowing high in the sky. Melon immediately set off on pushbike, pedalling furiously to the scene. En route the policeman was stopped by excited villagers confirming that the aircraft had crashed near the hamlet of Maireux, in a field owned by the Demollin-Spronck family. There a crowd had already gathered and the officer saw that a single-engined aircraft had buried itself deep in the sloping field. In an orchard some distance from the blazing wreckage he found the body of a young aviator. Eye-witnesses told him that as the parachute descended both wings had suddenly been torn from the aircraft, one of these scything through the parachute's shroud lines. The hapless pilot then plunged to earth, his descent unchecked.

42. 65 Squadron pilots at Kirton, March 1941. Back row, from left: Pilot Officer Rathie, Sergeants Hewlett, Johnson, and Mitchell, Pilot Officer MacPherson. Bottom row, from left: Flight Lieutenant Grant, Sergeants Rose, Oldnall, Stillwell, and Foulgar.

Dr Robert Berlemont was also at the scene and pronounced life extinct. Beside the body lay a collection of keys and two identification tags: one stated 'RAF No. 748692 P Rose', the other 'Do Not Remove. No. 58849'. German troops soon appeared and seized the items as Leonard Melon covered the corpse with a blanket. The Germans ordered Melon to remain at the crash site and guard it while they examined the body and picked through the smouldering debris of Sergeant Rose's Spitfire. Later, Melon was joined by his colleague from the nearby village of Melen, and with the help of German soldiers they loaded the pilot's body onto a cart and went to the mortuary. Melon then returned to the crash site and mounted an overnight guard with police officers from neighbouring Olne. On Monday, 5 May 1941, Sergeant Rose's funeral took place in the village church at Fecher. For some reason the Germans refused permission for burial in the local cemetery, so some 2,000 patriotic Belgian mourners accompanied the cortège to the crash site. Three hundred students from Liège University were in the congregation, carrying wreaths in both Belgian and British national colours.

43. The crash site of Spitfire R6805, Soumagne, Belgium, 3 May 1941 (Patrick Vierstraete).

44. The crash site of Sergeant Rose's Spitfire today (Patrick Vierstraete).

45. Sergeant Rose's grave at Soumagne, Belgium (Patrick Vierstraete).

The coffin was draped in a Union Flag, and covered in floral tributes. At that point truckloads of Germans suddenly appeared, broke up the gathering, and confiscated the coffin.

After the mourners had dispersed, the body was returned to Leonard Melon to bury. Instead of doing so at the crash site, however, and as instructed by the Germans, the policeman interred Sergeant Rose, by cover of darkness and in secret, in the Spronck family plot at Soumagne Cemetery.

In 1948, Major and Mrs Rose visited Soumagne and were told the full story by Monsieur Spronck, who presented the grieving parents with their twenty-five-year-old son's flying helmet. Later, the CWGC decided that Sergeant Rose should be exhumed and re-buried at a new communal war cemetery some distance away. Both the villagers and Major Rose protested, and eventually the Commission agreed that Sergeant Rose could remain at Soumagne providing he was given his own grave. The villagers then erected a memorial to their own war dead, burying the young pilot nearby. A kerbstone surround was paid for by the village, and the Commission erected Sergeant Rose's headstone, inscribed with the words 'This Was a Man'. John Rose observed, 'How well they chose their words; how adequately they describe a most lovable brother.'

In October 1988, John Rose and his family arrived unannounced in Soumagne and were moved to discover fresh flowers on Peter's immaculately kept grave. Each successive generation of children in Soumagne are told the story of 'their' young pilot, whose courage and sacrifice represented hope in those terrible days of occupation.

The inscription on Sergeant Rose's headstone comes from Shakespeare's *Julius Caesar*, Act V, and is both a poignant and moving epitaph to this tragic young man from Staffordshire:

His life was gentle, and the elements
So mix'd in him that Nature might stand up
And say to all the world, 'This was a man!'

PILOT OFFICER VIC LOWSON

Victor Lowson was born on 22 January 1920, at 3 Cardean Street, Dundee, the son of John, an engineer employed at the local gas works, and Helen Lowson. When Victor's younger brother Jack arrived, Mrs Lowson soon had her hands full with two energetic youngsters. Victor was educated at Glebelands Primary School and the Morgan Academy, both in Dundee. He was a brilliant scholar and a committed member of the Boys' Brigade. A keen sportsman, in adult life this clean-living and Christian Scot touched neither tobacco nor alcohol. After leaving school he joined the office staff of Jute Industries, and on 27 May 1939 Victor joined the RAFVR, volunteering for aircrew.

Having been called up for full-time service upon the outbreak of war, Sergeant Lowson completed his service flying training before learning to fly Spitfires at Hawarden, starting his course there on 22 September 1940. On 6 October he reported to 54 Squadron at Catterick, but was posted again, just five days later, to 65 Squadron at Turnhouse. While there, Victor became a member of the 'Caterpillar Club', membership of which was open to airmen whose lives had been saved by Irvin parachutes. This adventure occurred on 26 November; Sergeant Lowson was patrolling over the Firth of Forth, between May Island and North Berwick, with the great ace Pilot Officer Paddy Finucane and Flying Officer Szulkowski. The Section patrolled the estuary for some twenty minutes, crossing from north to south and returning before flying up river towards the bridge and back. Sergeant Lowson later reported:

> The order was received to patrol Crail, and immediately afterwards the Ground Controller contacted with a 'pip-squeak-zero', so I then switched on the Contactor. When the Section reached Crail we were ordered to 4,000 feet, which entailed flying through a layer of cloud. From the conversation on the R/T I understood that we were trying to intercept an enemy aircraft. As instructions came through we changed course and height frequently, never flying one course for very long.

46. Pilot Officer Victor Lowson.

After some time the order to 'pancake' was received, and immediately we started losing height through cloud down to 500 feet. When we emerged from the cloud bank I saw that we were over water. I could see no land in any direction. Immediately the Section Leader requested a homing bearing but got no response except the order to 'pancake' being repeated. The Section Leader continually tried to obtain a homing from Ground Control but without success.

In the meantime I noticed that we were flying due west and did so for about ten minutes before a coastline was sighted, although I was unable to identify our position. We then followed the coastline in a northerly direction while still trying to contact the Ground Station. By this time it was quite dark and ground detail was invisible, except for the coastline. The Section Leader then asked me to try and contact the Controller, but I was likewise unable to get a reply.

At this point I dropped behind the formation, and the Leader, seeing this, and taking into consideration our shortage of petrol, ordered me to climb to 4,000 feet and bale out. I left the formation and climbed through cloud until I reached 5,000 feet, when I turned and flew south before turning west, the idea being to get over land before I jumped. On seeing a break in the clouds below me I went down to find a landmark, but although I could confirm being over land I was unable to identify my position. Thereupon I climbed to 8,000 feet, still heading approximately west, and abandoned the aircraft.

47. A Spitfire Mk IA of 65 Squadron at Kirton sometime between December 1940 and January 1941.

Sergeant Lowson made a safe parachute descent; his Spitfire, X4233, which had seen action flying from Hornchurch in the Battle of Britain, was destroyed. The pilot's report, however, paints a vivid picture of just how basic flying was in those days: unreliable communications, no in-cockpit GPS or computerised fly-by-wire technology!

On 29 November, 65 Squadron flew south to Tangmere and another tour of duty in the hot zone. Shortly afterwards Sergeant Lowson saw the enemy for the first time when he came close to a Ju 88, firing his first shot in anger although the intruder disappeared into cloud. In February 1941, 65 Squadron was rested again, moving to Kirton. From there the Squadron operated on various sweeps as part of the 12 Group contribution to the 'Non-Stop Offensive'. On 24 July, Sergeant Lowson damaged an Me 109 at 20,000 feet above St-Omer. In October the Squadron returned to the Tangmere Sector before moving to Debden in December. The previous month had seen Victor Lowson commissioned for the duration of hostilities, so he was now a Pilot Officer.

By May 1942, 65 Squadron was commanded by Squadron Leader Tony Bartley DFC, a Battle of Britain veteran who later married the actress Deborah Kerr. On 23 May, Bartley led twelve 65 Squadron Spitfires on a sweep over France, as part of the Debden Wing. Between Lumbres and Calais, Red Section, led by Pilot Officer Lowson, attacked three FW 190s. Victor fired at and damaged one of them with an eight-second burst of machine-gun fire, watching his bullets strike home before the 190 dived away, out of control; he was the only RAF pilot successfully to engage the enemy on that day. On 21 July, 65 Squadron was in action again, as the Squadron diary records:

48. 65 Squadron pilots in jovial mood at Tangmere, early 1941. From left: Sergeants Victor Lowson and Ron Stillwell, Flying Officer Tommy Smart, Squadron Leader Sammy Saunders, Pilot Officer Robin Norwood, Flying Officer Paddy Finucane. What the 'For Sale' sign is all about is unknown.

49. 65 Squadron at Kirton, June 1941. Front row, from left: Sergeants Humphrey Baxter, Hugh Chalmers, Victor Lowson, Ron Stillwell. Second left standing: Pilot Officer MacPherson, fourth: Pilot Officer Robin Norwood, centre: Squadron Leader Sammy Saunders.

50. A 65 Squadron Mk II at Tangmere in early 1941. The aircraft has the de Havilland airscrew, the blades of which were made of duralumin.

51. A section of 65 Squadron Spitfires taxying for take-off at Tangmere, early 1941.

52. Sergeant Ron Stillwell in the 'office' and preparing for take-off.

During the afternoon, 65 Squadron participated in a Debden Wing mass Rhubarb. Twelve Spitfires, led by Squadron Leader DAP McMullen DFC took off from Great Stamford at 1616 hrs and, together with other Debden squadrons, set course for Blankenberg. The 65 flew directly over Blankenberg and turned left, re-crossing the coast in the vicinity of Zeebrugge. Very-intense light flak was experienced almost continually while over enemy territory. Targets attacked included numerous gun posts, a military car park, a light railway engine, a factory building opposite Zeebrugge railway station, two searchlight posts, two barges, two aircraft (believed to be dummies) on an aerodrome, and a light bridge over a canal. Eleven pilots returned safely to Great Stamford by 1750 hrs, all having attacked ground targets. Eight of our aircraft had been hit by light flak. The machines of Squadron Leader McMullen and Sergeant Hearne were write-offs, and Sergeant Tinsey's Category 'B'. The other five were all Category 'A'.

Pilot Officer Victor Lowson, flying as Red One, was seen to be hit by machine-gun fire shortly after crossing the enemy coast. He succeeded in getting back across the enemy coast but, about two miles out to sea, prepared to bale out by climbing from sea level to approximately 1,500 feet and turning on his back. The machine then plunged vertically into the sea and the pilot was unable to fall clear. Warrant Officer RL Stillwell circled the spot several times where Pilot Officer Lowson had crashed but nothing more was seen of him. Pilot Officer Lowson was one of the Squadron's most senior members and his loss is deeply felt.

The loss was no doubt particularly 'deeply felt' by Vic Lowson's friend Ron Stillwell. The pair had been sergeants together in 65 Squadron, and had lived and flown with each other for what was, in those days, a very long time. The next day, Squadron Leader McMullen wrote to the missing pilot's parents:

> It is with the greatest regret that I have to write and tell you that your son, Pilot Officer Victor Lowson, is missing as a result of operations yesterday afternoon. I am allowed to tell you in confidence that he was taking part in a low-flying attack against enemy troops and gun positions on the coast of Belgium, near Zeebrugge. While shooting up gun positions his Spitfire was hit and crashed into the sea about two miles off the Belgian coast. I am very much afraid that there is little chance that he survived.
>
> He was one of our best pilots, a Section Leader and potential Flight Commander. In fact, during this flight he was leading a Flight into attack. He always showed exceptional promise as a pilot, an officer, and a leader. It has come as a great blow to me personally that he is now missing.

53. A 65 Squadron Mk II at Tangmere in early 1941. This aircraft has the Rotol airscrew, the blades of which were laminated wood covered in 'jablo'.

54. Ron Stillwell pictured when a Flight Lieutenant with the DFM to his credit and with a 65 Squadron Spitfire Mk IX.

55. Pilot Officer Vic Lowson in a Spitfire Mk V shortly before he was reported missing.

Vicky was the best-loved lad on our Squadron, his quiet steadiness of purpose and gentle wit having endeared him to us all during the long time that he has been with us. He will always remain in the hearts of the rest of the Squadron as one of the very best.

Another letter followed on 8 August, this time from the 65 Squadron Intelligence Officer, Flight Lieutenant Hugh Tarrant:

I regret that we have received no news of Victor. Should we hear anything at all in the future I will notify you immediately. I hope you will accept my personal sympathy. As an Intelligence Officer I am naturally older and more experienced than the pilots in my Squadron; I would like to assure you now that Victor was quite the finest boy that I ever met in the Service. I am happy to think that he liked me and looked upon me as a friend. I miss his companionship in this Squadron very deeply.

On 14 February 1943, the Air Ministry confirmed that as nothing further had been heard of Pilot Officer Lowson since the day he crashed in Spitfire W3697, he must be 'presumed dead for official purposes'. He is remembered on Panel 170 on the Runnymede Memorial, the Commonwealth's tribute to 'missing' airmen.

While researching Victor Lowson's story, I traced Jack Lowson, still living in Dundee and who still felt his elder brother's loss deeply. Among the family's treasured artefacts were Victor's Caterpillar Club badge, made into a brooch and worn proudly by his sister-in-law. Most poignant of all was Victor's diary, a four-leaf clover still pressed into the pages. Sadly, however, the twenty-three-year-old pilot's luck ran out that fateful day in 1942 over the Belgian coast, another intelligent, sensitive, and articulate young man whose potential was enveloped by the cold and dark North Sea.

7

WARRANT OFFICER PETER FOX

On 28 June 1941, Sergeant Fox joined 234 Squadron at Warmwell to fly Spitfires. Warmwell, located slightly inland of Weymouth and again in the West Country, well positioned the Spitfires for sweeps of the Cherbourg peninsula and to provide protection for convoys. It was on such duties, during the Fighter Command Offensive, that Peter found his new squadron engaged. However, Sergeant Fox soon became yet another casualty of the so-called 'Non-Stop Offensive':

It was not long after the CO of 234 Squadron, Squadron Leader HM Stephen, told me that he would hold back his recommendation for my commission by two weeks (because in a fortnight my Flight Sergeant's crown would be due which meant that if I was commissioned thereafter it would be not as a Pilot Officer but as a Flying Officer) that things started to go wrong. About time! I first missed being commissioned at 1 ITW, Cambridge, due to a posting; then, at 8 FTS Montrose, a post with telephone wires interfered with the process, and then, in 1940, while serving with 56 Squadron at Boscombe Down, I was flown into a haystack. One may think that a haystack would be soft enough, but it was three and a half days later that I woke up again with a broken back. Meanwhile, the commission passed by once again!

However, it was a lovely morning on 20 October 1941, at Warmwell airfield in Dorset, and everything seemed to be going well – my back had mended, I was twenty years of age, my commission was on the boil again, and I was poised to go home to Oxford on leave.

In one pocket of my best uniform was a signed leave pass, and, in another, a snapshot of some of the pilots, including myself, standing round the squadron transport with '234' painted on the windscreen. My parents would have been interested to see it in a few hours' time after I had been flown to Kidlington in the station Magister. I was also intending to show my parents the identity disc with 'Rissole' on one side and '234 Squadron, F/Lt Mortimer-Rose' on the reverse. My Flight Commander, 'Morty', had only recently given me the dog.

56. Peter Fox pictured while a sergeant flying Hurricanes with 56 Squadron during the Battle of Britain.

57. Spitfire pilots of 234 Squadron at Warmwell in 1941. Peter Fox is standing, third from right.

58. More 234 Squadron pilots. Those identified are, top row, second right: Flight Lieutenant Mortimer-Rose. Middle row, from left: Sergeants Sapsed, Walker, Macleod; Pilot Officer Burchill, unknown, Sergeant Broad. Kneeling, from left: Sergeants Fox, Shepherd, and Nankeville.

There was also my invention! I had drilled a small hole in the lever of the CO_2 bottle which, when pulled, inflated the Mae West. A piece of cord was then passed through the hole and was tied with a bow to the buoyant cushion which, on top of a parachute, formed a seat for the pilot. This would give automatic inflation of the Mae West, whether or not the pilot was conscious, having baled out over the 'drink'. It was just necessary to remember to untie the bow before getting out of the plane at base.

It was lunchtime and the squadron was about to be 'stood down'. 'It won't count off your leave!' was the CO's response to me volunteering for a 'nuisance' raid over France. Sergeant Sapsed volunteered as my No. 2. The sortie was to locate and blow up an ammunition dump sited just inland and to the east of Cherbourg. Another volunteer pair were to strafe an aerodrome to the west of Cherbourg.

Wind was blowing from west, so a course was calculated from Portland Bill to a bay east of Cherbourg. All four Spitfire Mk VBs, each armed with two 20 mm cannons and four machine-guns, were ready to go. Take off on Warmwell's grass runway, with wind from the west, meant taxying away from dispersal, the full length of the aerodrome and then turning into wind. Peter applied his brakes to turn into wind for take-off and a tyre burst! Undo harness, undo bow to CO_2 bottle and out; run the length of the aerodrome and into another Spitfire, AZ-H, AD203, in place of 'C726' which I usually flew and which was now standing empty at the far end of the field with its burst tyre. No revolver or Verey pistol in the pocket of the new Spitfire!

Over Portland Bill, course set, and no sign of the other pair, just 'Sappy' following me, flying just above sea level across the Channel. What appears to be the correctly shaped bay appears in just under half an hour; cross the coastline and what seems to be a single machine-gun opens up – a thud and the oil pressure gauge drops to zero; I tell Sappy over the R/T 'I've had it!', but the R/T doesn't work, probably damaged by the same bullet. No revolver or Verey pistol with which to destroy the Spitfire, so must turn back to sea to dump it, hoping to then swim back to land. Engine now objecting to running without oil, and sounding very rough. I fired a short burst of my guns in anger until I noted the poor cows scattering in the field ahead. Coast in sight, engine stops, speed drops, and I hit a telegraph pole with one wing. The aircraft slews round and gently tips on its nose and then settles back. Quite a gentle crash really. Must try and escape – undo harness, jump up – up blows Mae West, can't get out! Bags of fumbling, a great raspberry as the Mae West pressure drops, out I get, run across a couple of fields, and dive under a hedge where the cover is good and thick.

I was in the hedge quite deep, at the junction of hedgerows, and had time to take off my Mae West, undo my escape kit, take off right shoe and sock and place money, maps and compass under the instep before replacing sock and shoe. Voices come closer, a male French voice shouts 'Come out, boy. He see you or he shoot!' Two shots ring out, although I do not know whether fired into the hedge or air. After some quick thinking I decide that discretion is the better part of valour, and crawl out hands up to face a small crowd of civilians and a German soldier armed with a rifle on the farther side of a fence to another field. Mae West thrown over fence, two hands on top of fence, a great leap and I am in their field. I well remember the civilians' applause for my athletic prowess! In an endeavour to convey my sadness at not having been able to destroy my plane, and my knowledge of the German language being schoolboyish in the extreme, I point to my Spitfire, klaxon blaring, in the centre of the adjacent field. I placed my hand on the German soldier's rifle. Our conversation in German must have been absorbing as he let go of it! A moment later a couple of German officers appeared – one slapped the soldier's face, snatched the rifle from me, and returned it to the soldier. Life returned to 'normal'. Salutes having been exchanged, we all walked across the field to a road. There a soldier ran out of a building to take my photograph. I will never know why on earth I raised my arm over my face to prevent the photograph being taken, as such a photograph could have been used to show a 'Terror Flieger' – ashamed.

We then went off to Maupertus aerodrome near Cherbourg where I met some Me 109 pilots of I and II/JG 2. Most of the pilots spoke English, but I considered it wise not to tell them that on 26 August my squadron had strafed this airfield – I had blown up a petrol bowser! We enjoyed considerable good-humoured banter, but they would not let me fly an Me 109 to formulate a comparison! While playing table tennis with one of the pilots a very different type of uniformed officer abruptly stopped the game and it was a hard bed in a small cell for me for the rest of the night.

Immediately on arrival at Maupertus I had been searched; my Mae West, photographs, leave pass, English money and dog-tag were stuffed into a bag and parcelled up with no inspection of any item having been made! All was neatly tied up, a label on the parcel's outside duly filled in and an official stamp applied.

Off next day by car and train, via Paris, to a POW camp called *Dulag Luft*, near Frankfurt. The Me 109 pilots had kindly pooled their weekly chocolate ration and gave it to me in a small box. It was all British chocolate, presumably captured during the evacuation in 1940. I only had to carry this small box, until my guard decided that the much larger parcel of confiscated items could best be carried by his prisoner.

Off the train in Paris, into a taxi to a building to the south. Here my guard bade me a temporary goodbye while he went off for food, leaving me in a room with three new guards and my parcel. The window was fully open, about ten feet off the ground, and I could see planes taking off and landing at a nearby aerodrome. There was general friendly conversation between us all, plus boredom on the guards' part. To pass the time I opened my parcel and showed the guards my Mae West – making sure that my leave pass, photograph, and dog-tag went into my pocket before re-parcelling it!

Then a forlorn hope, a striped sentry box was at the gateway entrance to the buildings about thirty yards from the window. On the opposite side of the internal roadway was a narrow building running the full distance. I worked out that if I jumped out of the window and ran three paces, the guard would have to run a full twenty yards before he could get a shot at me. At the bottom of the garden was an even shorter distance and woods lay beyond that to the airfield. A nursemaid with

Above: 59. Spitfire Mk II, P8046, 'City of Worcester II', paid for by the 'Faithful City's' Spitfire Fund. On 26 August 1941, 234 Squadron attacked Maupertus airfield near Cherbourg, Sergeant Fox destroying a petrol bowser. Sergeant Clifford Jacka, however, was hit by machine-gun fire over the enemy airfield and crashed P8046 into the Channel.

Left: 60. Sergeant Clifford Jacka. Sergeant Fox went to visit the Jacka family at their Bournemouth guest house and performed the unenviable duty of informing his friend's parents that their only son had been killed in action.

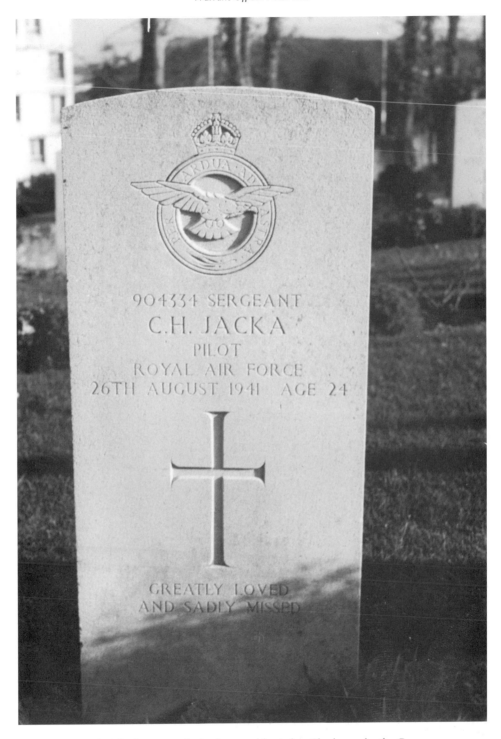

61. Sergeant Jacka's body was washed ashore and buried at Cherbourg by the Germans.

a baby in a pram was chatting to the sentry, the light was fading, and with it the possibility of the window closing and blackout.

I tore up the leave pass, replaced it in my pocket, chewed up the photographs in true spy-drama style; guards all sitting down, thoroughly bored at having had English money explained to them at length, wander over to the window, and OUT! Quick recovery, onto my feet, over the road, down the narrow side of the building – and there is the sentry already, rifle sighted, 'HÄNDE HOCH!' The sentry had not run towards me, but along the road for four or five paces where he had a full view of the bottom of the garden. I was later aware of complaints from the guards about my double-cross after our friendliness earlier, but fortunately they did not harm me.

Then off again in a taxi through Paris for the train to *Dulag Luft*. The taxi window was open and somewhere in some Parisian road were thrown a dog's name tag, a leave pass in little pieces, and a chewed up photograph. Having bought me grapes en route during the long train journey, the guard left me with my Mae West parcel at *Dulag Luft* after wishing me well on my next escape attempt! Sadly those good wishes were of no avail, as I was to make five more abortive escape attempts – earning a total of six and a half months in solitary confinement with bread and water.

Five main POW camps plus three working party camps and three and a half years behind barbed wire had elapsed before I was home again in England and able to read in my logbook the entry: '20 OCTOBER SPITFIRE H203 MISSING – SHOT DOWN BY FLAK OVER LA MAZERIE'.

8

FLIGHT LIEUTENANT HUGH CHALMERS

I enlisted in the RAFVR on 15 March 1939, at Glasgow, my weekend flying training subsequently being conducted at Prestwick on Tiger Moths. Between 19 March and 5 August, I, Sergeant 745344 Chalmers, recorded twenty-five flying hours in my logbook. Having gone solo, the adjutant collected five shillings from me for a licence for cross-country flights. It was never issued, but after the war, having completed some 1,100 hrs and still fit, I applied for said licence, but it was refused. It was necessary to have a medical and there was so much red tape that I rebelled. I thought that if I wanted my money back then authority would reconsider. But no! I later received a postal order for five shillings!

I was mobilised on 1 September 1939, and thereafter had first to report daily, then twice weekly, and then just weekly to Glasgow Town Hall. Finally, the RAF said, 'Don't call us, we'll call you.' Eventually, on 2 December, I was posted to No. 3 ITW at Hastings. Elementary flying training was then undertaken at Burnaston, Derby. The threat of invasion, however, was constantly in mind. Old cars were pushed, sometimes driven, all over the airfield after each day's flying as an anti-parachute landing measure. Each of us was issued with a rifle and five rounds. It was at the time of Dunkirk and although I never experienced any violence, there was expressed a feeling of anger by returning soldiers at the apparent absence of the RAF over the beaches.

At Burnaston, we had learned to fly the Miles Magister monoplane, but then took a step backwards to fly Tiger Moths again, although this time at night (dual), on the Pre-Fighter Course. The Harvard was used as a fairly high performance monoplane trainer as a prelude to Spitfire or Hurricane flight, and I flew Harvards at 15 SFTS at South Cerney. There we were able to practise solo night landings in that type. Eventually we arrived at 7 OTU, Hawarden, where I was passed in the dual environment of the Miles Master, before at last reaching my goal – to fly a Spitfire!

The undercarriage of the Mk Is that we were flying had to be pumped up by hand, and the fore and aft movement of the aircraft controlled on take-off by the other. I can vividly recall therefore my first solos! I only managed about seven hours on the Spitfire there as the weather was poor.

62. Flight Lieutenant Hugh Chalmers pictured in 1942.

Well done Dilip:
Kind regards,
Hugh Chalmers
65 Sqdn. in 1940.

63. Sergeants Hugh Chalmers (left) and Peter Rose of 65 Squadron pictured late in 1940.

On 28 October 1940, I reported to fly Spitfires with 65 'East India' Squadron at Turnhouse in Scotland. Previously the squadron had been heavily engaged during both Operation DYNAMO and the Battle of Britain. On 8 December 1940, 65 Squadron moved south, to Tangmere in Sussex. It was a relatively quiet period with more or less uneventful patrols and the odd offensive sweep with little opposition. My Flight Commander was Gordon Olive and he noticed just how little flying time I actually had on Spitfires and so pushed me on, especially on dusk patrols and night flying. This opportunity to gain extra experience undoubtedly enhanced my chances of survival later on. On 26 February 1941, we were relieved at Tangmere by 616 Squadron, and we swapped over aircraft, 616 taking our Mk IIs and we their tired Mk IAs. We then flew to Kirton.

My new 'A' Flight Commander was Stanley B. Grant. Although again in the front line, 65 flew a lot more from Kirton. It was at the time of Fighter Command's Offensive and 65 would sometimes stand by at Duxford or Fowlmere or join a practice sweep. More often than not it was to West Mailing – sweep – then refuel and return to Kirton well after dark (more night flying practice!). Sam Saunders was our CO, the other Flight Commander was Tommy Smart. I was still an NCO pilot along with MacPherson, Oldnall, Stillwell, Mitchell, Hewlett, Baxter, and Rose.

I shall never forget one scramble as Stan Grant's No. 2. An intruder over Hull. Cloud was at 1,000 feet and I had to close in. We climbed to 19,000 feet and were still in thick rain cloud. No. 1 suggested to the Controller that as he could see nothing

64. Sergeant Hugh Chalmers at Kirton early in 1941. Note the non-regulation sheepskin flying gloves!

then neither would the intruder. We were recalled but I had to stick with him all the way back as I figured that it would be safer two together than alone. We got back to the circuit and Stan landed on the flare path which was two poles with red, orange, and green lights and a string of lights into wind. The strain on my eyes must have upset my judgement because I smacked the left-hand post with my port wing and trailed a whole string of lights up the grass. The interesting and comforting thing was that although the wooden post was snapped like a matchstick, not a mark could be found on the wing's leading edge!

On 9 October 1941, 65 Squadron moved to Westhampnett [now known as Goodwood]. Being closer to the continent, shipping patrols and offensive sweeps were the order of the day. After one low-flying squadron sweep and return, Squadron Leader Saunders' aircraft was found to have a small-calibre bullet passed right through the fuselage – about a foot behind the cockpit, luckily for Sam. I was given the task of ferrying the Spitfire to Hamble for repair. I was so concerned with the barrage balloons round Southampton that I landed with the wheels up. I remember it as one of the softest landings I ever made, but I felt a proper fool! Thankfully the Supermarine rep there was very considerate and put it down to enemy action. I heard no more about it.

65. 65 Squadron's pilots pictured at Tangmere in February 1941. They are in best blue because bad weather permitted a rare day off; just about to leave for a 'sweep' of Chichester's pubs, the press arrived and 'borrowed' the pilots! Left to right: Sergeants Orchard (killed in action the following day), and Chalmers, Flying Officer Finucane DFC (killed in July 1942), Flying Officer Wigg, Sergeant Rose (killed in 1941), and Sergeant Mitchell (killed in 1944).

66. From left: Sergeants Chalmers and Mitchell; standing on wing: Sergeant Rose, Intelligence Officer, Flying Officers Finucane and Wigg, and Sergeant Orchard.

By 23 December 1941, 65 Squadron was based at both Debden and Castle Camps. We were training almost exclusively for night flying and to co-operate with the searchlights now that the German day offensive had dwindled. How strange it was to fly to Castle Camps in the afternoon then sit in dispersal wearing dark glasses (CO's idea!) and long seamen's woollen stockings (pilots' idea, as it was dashed cold in the December night air in our unheated cockpits!). The Spitfire was definitely not suited to night take-offs. When the throttle was opened, flames, sparks, etc., shot past at eye level blinding the pilot who had to 'eyes down' quickly and use instruments. Latterly we found we could safely get off with zero or even negative boost. The Hurricane's configuration, however, made it a better bet for night flying, as I later found out. In January, our CO, Humphrey Gilbert, who had taken over from Sam Saunders, killed himself in a Spitfire and Tony Bartley then took over. My last flight with 65 Squadron was with Ron Stillwell. With snow on the ground we took the squadron Magister and followed the railway line up to Kirton and returned with as many eggs as the farmer could spare. He had been as kind when we had previously been stationed there.

On 25 February 1942, five other pilots and myself left Mount Batten in a Sunderland flying boat (L5798, KG-B), stopping at Gib before carrying on to Malta, arriving at Kalafrana at 0700 hrs. The captain was very keen to get rid of us and get on his way. Later on I realised why! Even as we travelled in the pickup to Hal Far we saw two Me 109s in formation just offshore, going round the island. That was the morning patrol, we were told. No wonder the Sunderland pilot was keen to get en route for Cairo!

Because I had been night flying on Spitfires I was sent on to Takali to join 1435 Flight MNFU with Hurricane Mk IICs. Only a few nocturnal patrols were undertaken, however, as aircraft were drained away to the day boys at Hal Far. Squadron Leader Westmacott was the CO, but latterly a Pilot Officer Oaks was left in charge. Eventually only one Hurricane was left and after the toss of a coin Sergeant 'Timber' Wood went on an intruder flight. In that aircraft, BE347, he was shot down and killed over Sicily on 26 April 1942. Night-fighter Beaufighters started to arrive on the island and I was duly appointed Ground Control Pilot at Luqa. Wing Commander 'Jumbo' Gracie was in charge at Takali. He allowed airmen to draw rifles and ammunition to shoot at E/A attacking our returning fighters. By this time, batches of Spitfires were coming out from Gibraltar. The last line of one of Gracie's memos was 'Don't shoot wildly, don't panic, don't shoot at a Spitfire!'

On 10 July 1942, I arrived back in the United Kingdom and on 30 July reported for instructor duties at 56 OTU, Kinnell, Dundee. There I instructed on Masters and Hurricanes. I was commissioned on 5 October, and after the usual OTU tour of six months was posted to 501 Squadron flying Spitfires in Northern Ireland. Only one exercise from that period stands out in my mind, a Fighter Night over Belfast. The whole Squadron was deployed with gaps of 1,000 feet between each aircraft. It was not funny when a Spitfire slid right across my canopy with only feet between us. Thank goodness that we suffered no casualties but the exercise was never repeated. Shortly afterwards the Squadron moved back to England and Westhampnett.

On 10 May 1943, I was suddenly posted to 277 ASR Squadron, 'C' Flight, at Shoreham, Sussex. My Flight Commander was an Australian, Dicky Vere, and CO was a Squadron Leader Brown. My ten-month or so stay with 277 was extremely pleasant – much like the camaraderie I had found in 65 Squadron. The only real worry was the long over-sea trips with just one 'fan'. I flew three trips on D-Day but had no customers. There were so many ships in the Channel that no one could have landed in the sea anyway!

On 14 January 1945, I left 277 ASR and went to 55 OTU, Aston Down to learn to fly Typhoons, which were a completely different proposition from the sleek Spitfires and even Hurricanes – more like driving a bus than a racing car! The CFI was Ron Stillwell DFM DFC, my old NCO mate from 65 Squadron days. After converting to Typhoons, the idea was that I was to join a 2nd TAF squadron in Holland, but for some reason I was posted to Karachi, India. Whether this was due to my efforts, Ron's influence, or my inaccurate attempts at releasing rockets and bombs in the Channel I don't know, but there I was in a Sunderland once more, this time flying from Poole.

In India, on 6 May 1945, I joined a drogue-towing flight: Hurricanes, Vengeances, and Defiants were in use. The Defiant had the gun turret removed and a winch installed. Later I moved to take over the Flight at Poona. Although things in Europe were still dicey for our aircrew, we knew that the horror was coming to a close. We just had to press on, but not as regardless as before. For us, however, both VE and VJ Days were most depressing. Authority had thought that there would be a break out of celebratory violence and all side arms were withdrawn – even the rotors of motor transports were removed. However, I think that we all felt then so far from home and family that even the celebrations on the steam radio deepened the depression.

My total war flying hours were 1,100, including 600 on Spitfires and 160 on Hurricanes. The Spitfire was my favourite of course. I am proud to have served in some fine units, especially 65 Squadron, alongside some absolutely first-class individuals like Paddy Finucane and Ron Stillwell. Those were the days!

9

SERGEANT CEDRIC STONE DFM

I learned to fly before the war, one hour per month. I went solo after ten hours dual. When I joined the RAF it took eleven hours for me to shake off the instructors! I was nearly thrown off my advanced training course by senior instructors. Was it luck or fear of a high casualty rate that persuade powers that be to keep me on?

As a Sergeant Pilot I flew my first 72 Squadron Spitfire, RN-N, on a patrol of Gravesend, Manston, Maidstone, Tonbridge, etc. Squadron Leader Desmond Sheen DFC was CO. Flight Lieutenant Clark was 'B' Flight Commander. Many of the Squadron boys, including myself, went to Squadron Leader Sheen's wedding. Max Aitken DFC, 'Sailor' Malan DSO DFC, Al Deere DFC and Brian Kingcome DFC were all pilots among us when we became a part of the Biggin Hill Wing. I remember on one occasion Sholto Douglas (Lord Douglas of Kirtleside) and Air Chief Marshal Leigh-Mallory visited Biggin Hill. They later joined an Officers' Mess party where Douglas was debagged! Cedric Masterman took over 72 Squadron in about October 1941. Bocock was then 'B' Flight Commander, with whom I paired frequently. My own 72 Squadron Spitfire was a presentation aircraft paid for by the South Africans of Basutoland. In this aircraft I often flew *day* escorts to Stirling bombers, sometimes as close escort; sometimes we went over France as the bombers were leaving. On one occasion I came out of France in a Spitfire Mk V to the Seven Sisters, the famous white chalk cliffs in Sussex; The radar fixes on me, both sides of the Channel, were said to indicate that I crossed the Channel in ONE MINUTE! This is actually unlikely, but if fixes were taken five miles to sea from each coast, then my ground speed would have been 600–700 mph. Thank God for the Spitfire!

In fact, on that particular sortie, our job was to relieve the squadron who had escorted the bombers to France. We were deep in France and in tight formation when suddenly, from 7 o'clock behind us, we were about to be attacked by a unit of Me 109s. Desmond Sheen was leading us and he turned sharply. I was his No. 2 inside the turn. To avoid collision I had to throttle back to keep station, and tighten my turn. There was nothing for me to do but stall, and in the unexpected stall I lost height quickly, in a spiral spin. By the time I had recovered and sorted out the spin, I

67. Sergeant Cedric Stone DFM.

68. Spitfires of 72 Squadron preparing for a sortie from Biggin Hill in 1941.

realised that the Squadron was too far away for me to catch up. I was in the middle of nowhere, very vulnerable, 20,000 feet up or so, with no cloud cover, a long way from home in a very hostile environment and over territory that I did not recognise. My only hope was to return to England as soon as I could.

The next question was where was the French coast and English Channel? My compass was slow to settle down after the spin and recent turmoil. Slowly, however, I could see north and recovered my bearings. Heading north I seemed be the only aircraft in the sky. It was a moment or two later that I saw a speck on the horizon. I kept an eye on that speck. I weaved to enable me to see the horizon all around me. The speck came nearer and nearer and seemed to divide into two specks. Then I could see: they were each a pair of aircraft heading towards me. I took my time. I prepared my sights and turned my gun button to 'fire'. I examined those two specks again. They were aircraft. They were 109s. I prepared for action. Fine pitch and a re-check. I was ready for a fight. I must keep firmly seated as otherwise the gunsight, including range finder, would be distorted.

The second pair was now positioning itself. I had one pair on each side of me so that I could be attacked one after the other from two sides. I could not play cat and mouse with them because there were no clouds in which to hide – my only move was to climb to gain the advantages of height. With a half roll and shuddering in a violent tight turn I felt gravity drain the blood from my knees. I levelled out to a point where I regained full sight of one. Then in another turn I knew that only a superhuman, fitter man than I could undertake an even tighter turn. Therefore it was unlikely that anybody could tighten his turn to jet a 'bead' on me. I then suddenly came out of the turn with my gun platform to pocket my first victim, immediately rolling in the opposite direction while also performing a barrel roll. I felt flushed and sweating but determined. My engine was purring marvellously, even though it was being overworked. I offered a gentle prayer as I felt two 109s had been put out of action. I did not see the next to leave, I just knew there were only two left in the ring, and they'd not felt a bullet in me yet! As they made another effort, I got one of them on a beam attack. I had no more ammunition left! As the third went down I turned again for the fourth. He, however, headed for home but I was fully prepared to collide with him rather than be his victim. However, he was shy and left me to gather my wits and reconsider where I had got to. I could do no more: I had no more ammunition, so home I must go.

As soon as I had sighed my relief, I looked down at my instruments. My goggles were misted. I was wet with perspiration. I could see nothing in the dark floor of the cockpit. It took a moment or two to reorganise myself, to find north, to find a mark on the French landscape to which I could relate on my map. Then, with another check for bandits, the sky appeared clear. I put my nose down for home, checked the fuel, pitch of the propeller, and revs of the engine. My speed was too high for a German to catch me up! I reached the French coast, and then the greatest sight of all was the white Seven Sisters of England's coastline. I had survived – four Germans had

69. Spitfire! An aircraft of 72 Squadron has its cannons harmonised in the gun butts at Biggin Hill, 1941.

strategically arranged themselves and attacked, but had now to lick their wounds. I returned safety.

If my memory serves me well, on one occasion we were patrolling at 30,000 feet over the English Channel in a cloudless, sunny sky. The Spitfire Mk VB cruised at about 250–300 mph. Wing Commander Robinson (later to become an Air Vice-Marshal) was our Section Leader, and Jamie Rankin was his No. 2. I was 'Tail-end Charlie' in our section of three aircraft. No other aircraft were visible, although we had been vectored to the patrol area in anticipation. R/T silence had been observed throughout our flight and patrol. Suddenly a message from base informed of E-Boats in the Channel. Our instructions were to 'seek out and attack!' Wing Commander Robinson answered 'Roger' and we went nose down at full throttle. We gained speed rapidly. The Air Speed Indicator needle went beyond the dial figures and ceased to record! The Altimeter showed a very rapid descent. The aircraft vibrated badly and I throttled back to save the engine which was already well over maximum permissible revolutions per minute. I became conscious of our No. 2 aircraft having problems holding station. Suddenly his Perspex canopy flew off and nearly hit me. The later post-mortem indicated that 'Robbo' had fired his guns. An empty cartridge case hit Jamie's canopy and damaged a Perspex panel which allowed the air to enter. That in turn created a surge of pressure in the empennage, blowing the rivets on the panels so that the canopy broke away completely. I had followed, but fortunately avoided the shower of debris, although it felt like riding a bicycle on corrugated iron sheets. Our speed was probably the speed of sound, i.e. almost twice the normal maximum for which the Spitfire was designed!

We three landed safely, but the flying characteristics seemed different from normal. All three Spitfires were recorded as unserviceable until checked. In fact the wings had been bent to a permanent set of some 8 degrees. Luckily they did not break off, another accolade to the designers and manufacturers of this superb fighter! The three aircraft were all stripped down and rebuilt, never to fly again in their distorted state. I was not informed whether the E-Boats had been hit!

I was posted overseas at the end of January 1942, joining 73 Squadron in North Africa, flying Hurricanes – an awful comedown!

10

FLIGHT LIEUTENANT
PETER HOWARD-WILLIAMS DFC

Peter Ian Howard-Williams was born at Cowes on 27 December 1919. In April 1939, he entered the RAF College, Cranwell, as a flight cadet. He was commissioned in March 1940 and posted to 19 Squadron at Duxford in May. Although non-operational during Operation DYNAMO, Pilot Officer Howard-Williams served throughout the Battle of Britain. It was later, during the 'Non-Stop Offensive', however, that he rose to prominence:

I made my first flight on 30 April 1933, in a de Havilland Moth. The pilot was my father, Wing Commander E. L. Howard-Williams, and the flight lasted twenty minutes. It is recorded in one of the old-style small RAF logbooks which my father obtained for me and my brother Jeremy. In the 'Remarks' column, father has written 'The first juggle', as he always referred to flying as 'juggling with death'. He was a Great War pilot and won the Military Cross with the Royal Flying Corps. He eventually retired as an Air Commodore. Towards the end of the war he became Air Correspondent on the *Daily Telegraph*. Both Jeremy and I followed in his footsteps and joined the RAF. My brother became a successful night-fighter pilot and also won a DFC. This same logbook also indicates that on 6 September 1936, I flew in a Heston Pheonix, and in the 'Remarks' column wrote, 'Record speed: 145 mph'. Later that year my father flew my mother, my brother, and me to Baghdad in a de Havilland Dragonfly. We had no radio and map-read all the way – and weather forecasting was almost nonexistent. Quite a trip!

The problems of a new pilot joining a squadron like 19 were many. First, we usually took off as a squadron across the grass. A new pilot was either positioned at the extreme right or left of the formation, which consisted of four tight vics of three aircraft. This made it very difficult to keep up and meant a lot more throttle was required than used by the leaders. Secondly, after Dunkirk, a few new aircraft arrived which were fitted with automatic undercarriages. These aircraft were naturally flown by the leaders, so their undercarriage (u/c) came up quickly while we poor new boys were hand-pumping like mad and at the same time trying to keep up with the leaders

70. Wing Commander Peter Howard-Williams DFC.

71. Flight Lieutenant Peter Howard-Williams before a local flight (note that he is not wearing a lifejacket) pictured with his ground crew. The photograph was taken at Fowlmere in late 1940, whilst serving with 19 Squadron.

who already had their u/c up. More throttle, thus more fuel used up. When airborne, we finally got into battle formation, tight vics in line astern, i.e. one vic immediately behind another. The new pilots were given the job of weaving to and fro at the formation's rear, keeping a lookout for trouble, but again almost at full throttle and so burning up more fuel. As we later discovered, it was a crazy formation which was eventually changed to the 'Finger Four'. The Germans had already learned this basic lesson in the Spanish Civil War.

After the Battle of Britain, I went to 118 Squadron which had recently formed at Filton. We were then stationed at Ibsley where we became a Wing with two other squadrons. On 3 September 1941, I flew Spitfire Mk VB AD210 when we beat up a 400-ton ship off Cherbourg. Later the same day, flying AD209, we went to have another look and found a big convoy off the Cherbourg peninsula. We were not allowed to attack a convoy. Flying west we passed through a rainstorm. When west of the peninsula the weather cleared and there was the most magnificent E-Boat flying a large swastika flag. I remember that John Robson was with us and we must have been six or eight Spitfires. I led the attack on the E-Boat, and it was rapidly stopped in the water. We all made two attacks and it was soon a right mess, with smoke pouring from it when we all set course for home. We were shot at from the convoy and from the Channel Islands, so someone was on the ball. Now for the odd

72. Flight Lieutenant Peter Howard-Williams with an unidentified pilot and 118 Squadron's scoreboard at Ibsley, Hampshire, in 1941.

73. An interesting diversion for the Ibsley Wing's pilots in 1941 was certain scenes of the morale-boosting propaganda film 'First of the Few', about R. J. Mitchell, were filmed there. The pilots of 118 and 501 Squadrons did all the flying involved in the film and can be seen at the start of which clustered around the pilot's hut – among them is Peter Howard-Williams, seen here in discussion with Flight Lieutenant John Robson and Leslie Howard, who both directed the film and starred as Mitchell.

74. Leslie Howard on set.

75. Flight Lieutenant Howard-Williams discussing a forthcoming flying sequence with Leslie Howard.

76. Flight Lieutenant Howard-Williams taxying past the film set – having returned safely from an operation over France.

bit. Later the Germans announced that the Commander-in-Chief of all the western defences had been killed at sea. We put in for one German Field Marshal destroyed! Later we got a message from the Air Ministry saying that there was no proof, and in any case a Hampden squadron had successfully attacked a convoy that night off the Frisian Islands.

I can see that E-Boat now. It was a really super-looking ship, and a mess when we had finished with it. I am still surprised that it had no fighter cover, as Maupertus, near Cherbourg, was only a few minutes' flying time away. Despite what the Air Ministry said, I remain convinced that the General was on our E-Boat. I cannot think what he would have been doing off the Frisian Islands at night; more likely he was on an inspection of ack-ack defences on the Channel Islands. The ack-ack guns on Alderney and elsewhere were very quick to open fire. Against my argument is that there was no fighter cover when Maupertus was so close, and of course the Germans knew that we regularly flew around the area.

On 30 September 1941, I did a shipping recce in clear weather flying Spitfire Mk VB AD209. The flight lasted fifty minutes. I spotted two flak ships well to the north of France. An attack was laid on with Hurricane Mk IICs, each armed with four 20 mm cannon. I led four aircraft from 'A' Flight and John Robson led four of 'B'.

We were to act as escort to the Hurricanes. The ships were fifteen miles north of Cherbourg, much to our surprise, stationary and stopped together to form an L-shape. I thought that the Hurricane attack was pathetic – as they came in low their shells fell across the ships in one line. So they got very few hits. They then turned for home. I called up Robbie on the R/T and climbed to 500 feet, so that in a dive I could be sure of every shell hitting the ships. I broke off just over the masts. Robbie and his section did the same. My No. 2, Geoffrey Painting, was shot down. He was aged only seventeen, which of course we didn't know at the time. There was a lot of publicity in the press about it. I also remember that Robbie was pretty shot up when he got back. We were later informed that one of the ships (600 tons) sank.

On 9 November 1941, I flew twice to beat up tanks on Salisbury Plain as a demonstration for munitions workers. By coincidence, one of the tank commanders was an old friend, Major Johnnie Aird. He later became secretary of the MCC at Lords. He told me a few days after the exercise that we had actually taken off several of the tank aerials!

Distilleries were another of our targets while flying Rhubarbs. On 15 November 1941, flying W3943, 118 Squadron attacked four distilleries. I attacked that at La Meuffe and the target furthest south was at Saint-Lô, which was attacked by David Fulford's section. There were three Spitfires in each attack. It was a Fighter Command-organised attack and many other squadrons were involved. A few weeks later I received a report from the French Underground that our attack had been successful. In the late 1950s, I went to La Meuffe and could still see where our cannon shells had hit. Apparently the attack had been co-ordinated for when all of the distilleries were full of alcohol.

On 17 January 1942, we patrolled Swanage as Winston Churchill was there, or at least that is what we were told. I was airborne for one hour and twenty minutes. There is an interesting story about when 'Widge' Gleed took over our Wing. He had commanded 87 Squadron for much of the Battle of Britain and was an ace. However, after the Battle of Britain 87 Squadron had been re-equipped with Turbinlite Havocs and Hurricanes for night-fighting, so he was a bit out of practice at day operations. However, he insisted on leading the Wing on our first sweep over Cherbourg since his arrival. It was a pure fighter sweep as I remember it. Apparently the Germans had got a little fed up with the way we almost considered the peninsula as home territory, and this day lay in wait. They used the Maupertus Wing and called in the Wings from St-Omer and Abbeville. The idea was to clobber us good and proper. Widge, however, made an error somewhere, so instead of hitting the coast just east of Cherbourg to make a sweep inland and out west of Cherbourg, we ended up west of Alderney near the Casquets lighthouse. To divert a moment, the lighthouse keeper always gave us a friendly wave and we often made a low pass around the light. Widge decided on this particular trip that there was no point going east to Cherbourg as fuel would soon get critical, so he wheeled the Wing round and we set off for home. It was an interesting journey back as when we had gone about twenty miles, Ground Control came on saying that there were twenty-plus bandits fifty miles astern of us, then thirty-plus, and then even a third group of Me 109s. We sped up a little and I think that Tangmere was scrambled in support. We didn't see any Me 109s as after ten minutes they turned for home. Great relief all round. We always said that Widge

Gleed's cock-up had saved us as someone reckoned that there were 100 Me 109s
waiting to pounce from above!

In November 1941, Peter had been awarded the DFC and the same year also
appeared briefly with the other Ibsley Wing pilots in the film 'The First of the
Few'. During that time he also flew escort to the He 111 bomber that the film
company had used as an air-to-air camera ship. Fortunately, Peter was a keen
photographer and took many snapshots of the Spitfires and the stars during the
making of the film.

On 2 February 1942, Flight Lieutenant Howard-Williams DFC flew Spitfire
AA964 on 'Rhubarb 87', an attack on the alcohol distillery at Eroudeville. His
No. 2 was Pilot Officer Ted Ames. Red Section took off from Ibsley at 1120 hrs
and set course for France. When twenty miles north-east of Pointe de Barfleur,
with cloud 8/10ths at 1,000 feet, at just 100 feet over the slate-grey sea Red
One turned slightly west. The Spitfires bobbed along in line-abreast formation
just twenty-five yards apart. Five miles further on, at 1150 hrs, the Spitfires
were bounced by four Me 109Fs of III/JG2 that 'swept out of the cloud taking
our aircraft completely by surprise'. Red Two took evasive action by climbing
to 800 feet. Three hundred yards ahead an Me 109 overshot and passed across
Red One's nose from east to west. Peter immediately snapped off a quick burst
at the fleeting target but without result. He then dodged into cloud seeking
sanctuary, but upon emerging was immediately attacked from behind by two
Me 109s. Turning tightly to the right, he managed to get on the tail of one of his
assailants, firing a five-second burst of both cannon and machine-gun fire from
200 yards range. Descending, the Spitfire pilot saw an aircraft crash into the sea
and believed that it was the 109 which he had attacked. Suddenly, however, Peter
was hit from behind, a 20 mm Oerlikon cannon shell entering the fuselage and
smashing the wireless set and cutting some of the machine's control wires. A 7.9
mm machine-gun bullet also struck the Spitfire adjacent to the pilot's throttle
hand, but fortunately did not penetrate the cockpit and harmlessly ricocheted
off. Peter again managed to reach the protective envelope of some 7/10ths
cloud, but was again attacked upon emerging. He then had a 'general dogfight'
with four Me 109s, during which he hit two of them. By this time the wind had
carried the combatants far to the south. Being out of ammunition, and with a
seriously damaged aeroplane, Red One found protective cloud and set course
for base.

Research indicates, however, that JG 2 did not lose any Me 109s in the combat,
a fact perhaps confirmed by Peter himself when stating that he again fought four,
the total number which originally attacked, when he emerged from cloud the
second time. *Oberleutnant* Bottcher and *Unteroffizier* Minche each claimed a
'P36' destroyed west-north-west of Cherbourg, but these claims undoubtedly
tally with Peter Howard-Williams and Ted Ames, the latter pilot being lost over
the sea. It seems, however, to be yet another example of the speed and confusion

77. A shaken Flight Lieutenant Howard-Williams showing damage sustained by Spitfire AD209 when bounced by Me 109s on Rhubarb 87.

78. A gaping hole in the aluminium fuselage of AD209.

79. With the access panel open and a small section of fuselage blown away, the pilot examines the damaged control wires. Extensive shrapnel damage from the exploding 20 mm round is clearly evident.

80. That was close: a bullet hole adjacent to the cockpit. All of Peter Howard-Williams's Spitfires were called 'Sheila', after his wife of that time, although the significance of the labrador's head is unknown. Sadly the Wing Commander passed away in 1995.

of cloud cover deceiving the human eye, as Peter must have surely seen his No. 2 crash into the sea and not an Me 109 as he thought.

Peter's return journey was somewhat eventful:

It is always difficult to recall the details of so long ago, but I always remember the trip back. I have written some notes but in fact the actual experience was probably more hairy and frightening than I have been able to convey! Certainly the weather was bad across the United Kingdom and over the French coast. I think that it was even marginal for a Rhubarb.

I started off in cloud, climbing after a while, and found that I was flying between two layers of cloud. My radio had been shot up so I was unable to obtain a homing bearing. I continued to steer due north over 10/10ths cloud with no idea where I was. Suddenly I nearly hit a barrage balloon – not the wire but the balloon itself which suddenly loomed up out of the haze. Visibility was very poor even between the cloud layers. I thought that it was either from a coastal convoy or part of the Portsmouth barrage. I turned on to a course west, and after a while descended to try and ascertain my position. After getting down below 1,000 feet I decided that this was getting dangerous and climbed again until I was clear of cloud. I flew north for about five minutes before finally making the decision to out. I opened the hood and side door and undid my straps. I decided to climb onto the wing.

Looking out I suddenly saw a small gap in the cloud and a green field. I quickly resumed my seat, did up my straps, and started to circle, descending into the hole. At about 500 feet or less, I found myself below cloud in poor visibility, flew around for a few minutes and saw a golf course. Just the place for a wheels-up landing, I thought, and selected one of the fairways. I made a couple of passes hoping to clear the golfers away, but they just stood and waved! I returned to cloud base and suddenly saw that Bournemouth was nearby. It was then a simple matter to fly along the coast, turn left to Christchurch, and follow the River Avon to Ringwood and Ibsley. Cloud base was still low so I waggled my wings in a low pass past the control tower and prepared to land.

I knew that my rudder and elevator trim wires had been shot away, so I had to be especially careful when landing. The wheels and flaps came down, and in spite of the lack of trim controls I made an ordinary landing. I taxied in, but in view of the time that I had been airborne people were getting a little worried, especially as control had been calling me on the R/T but receiving no response.

I went into my Flight Commander's dispersal hut, but in spite of sitting in front of a fiercely blazing log fire I could not stop shaking. There was only one cure. That evening we all went to Christchurch, to the Kings Arms, where I consumed more than my fair share of beer. Mary and Sidney Barker, who ran the famous inn, let me have a room for the night, even supplying pyjamas and a toothbrush. Next morning I drove back to the airfield and resumed normal flying.

I only ever shot up one airfield on the Cherbourg peninsula, which happened on another Rhubarb. After one pass with all guns blazing, one of the other Spitfire pilots called me up: 'Red One, take another look at the aircraft.' I turned and realised that it was a dummy airfield with dummy aircraft! It was about twenty miles inland from Cherbourg. I never went to Maupertus which was heavily defended.

In 1943, I was with 610 Squadron flying Spitfires again after an eight-month rest job commanding 2 Delivery Flight at Colerne near Bath. A super job! The 610 were at Westhampnett as part of the Tangmere Wing when I joined them, later moving west to Bolt Head near Salcombe, and afterwards to Perranporth in Cornwall for a month. There we did all the usual jobs flying with the Exeter Wing, but we also had some odd jobs too.

A fishing boat would come out of the Helford River in Cornwall and we would escort it south until it was dark, flying very low the whole time. A day would go by, and the following morning we would try and pick it up in mid-Channel, again keeping low. On landing we would say a code word down the telephone, and immediately be connected to someone in London who wanted to know how many were on board and various other questions. The fishing boat had joined the Brest fishing fleet and gone into harbour either with or to pick up agents. We were always the squadron who did this job so far as I know. I have vivid recollections of the fishing boat.

We would also do the same thing with Navy MTBs. Two would leave Dartmouth, towing small landing craft. We would take them until last light, and be up next morning to pick them up again. Sometimes they would be without one of the landing craft, presumably having beached it and the tide gone out, I presume that they were small Commando raids. Anyway, it was interesting for us to do something different.

It may interest you to know that I did 294 operational trips lasting 306.55 hours, so the average trip was an hour about. Often though, one would be scrambled, and after being airborne for fifteen minutes would be recalled as the bandits had returned home.

Peter Howard-Williams remained in the post-war RAF until 1958, when he retired as a Wing Commander. I traced him during 1988 while I was researching 19 Squadron during the Battle of Britain, the subject of my first book, *Spitfire Squadron*. Peter was from the outset extremely helpful and offered great encouragement. I had the enormous pleasure of meeting both Peter and his wife Pamela at the RAF Museum on 13 May 1990, when *Spitfire Squadron* was launched, and on which occasion we were privileged to have present every surviving 19 Squadron Battle of Britain pilot resident in the United Kingdom. Sadly, however, Peter was a cancer sufferer and eventually succumbed to his illness in 1993, at the age of seventy-three. In the final weeks of his life, Peter, a colourful character, full of fun, wrote many letters to me, and the foregoing has been largely extracted from that correspondence. He also discussed his treatment and operations but always appeared both cheerful and optimistic. As he said, 'I used to gamble as I had no shoes until I met a man without feet ... .' I believe that my friend knew that he was dying and wished to record his memories before it was too late. My only regret is that he did not live to see the publication of this book, with which I know he would have been thrilled.

11

WING COMMANDER DOUGLAS BADER DSO DFC AND SQUADRON LEADER 'BUCK' CASSON DFC AFC

The name Douglas Bader will be forever inspirational for, though no less flawed than any other human being, here was a *real* hero. A public schoolboy captivated by the thought of powered flight, and whose uncle was adjutant of the RAF College, Cranwell, Bader was commissioned into the RAF between the wars. He achieved his ambition and became a fighter pilot. A gifted sportsman – Bader had not only played cricket to a high standard but also was expecting to play rugby for England – it became apparent that the young pilot had a natural aptitude for aerobatics. Although a member of the RAF Aerobatic Team, such daredevil flying proved his undoing. Having disregarded various warnings from his Flight Commander, Harry Day, against low flying, Bader crashed at Woodley aerodrome, near Reading, attempting a slow roll at virtually zero feet. The reckless manoeuvre was executed for no other reason than to show off to civilian pilots. As Bader himself later said, 'Made a balls of it, old boy; that's all there was to it!' Indeed he had: the young pilot's legs were so badly crushed that both were amputated and he lingered near death for several days. But the incredibly tough Bader spirit could not be crushed. Remarkably, he recovered and not only mastered comparatively primitive and clumsy artificial limbs, but amazingly passed a flying test! Unfortunately, King's Regulations failed to provide for disabled pilots, so, rejecting the offer of a desk job, Douglas Bader, aged twenty-three, left the service he loved so much, in 1933.

That very year, however, saw Adolf Hitler achieve power in Germany, starting the countdown to the Second World War. Bader, working in the office of the Asiatic Petroleum Company's aviation department, recognised not only that war was inevitable, but that England would soon need trained service pilots like himself. The RAF would not back down, however, and refused to offer Bader a flying appointment. Undeterred, Bader maintained pressure on the Air Ministry, until, on 31 August 1939, Air Vice-Marshal Portal, the Air Member for Personnel, confirmed that in the event of war he would be reinstated to flying duties. Three days later Britain and France declared war on Nazi Germany.

81. Wing Commander Douglas Bader DSO DFC at Tangmere during the 'season of 1941'.

82. Squadron Leader L. H. 'Buck' Casson DFC AFC

Having passed a medical and a flying test, Douglas Bader was re-commissioned as a Flying Officer and pilot. After a refresher course at the Central Flying School, Bader joined 19 Squadron at Duxford on 7 February 1940. At last he was flying Spitfires! When Hitler attacked the west, however, on 10 May, Air Chief Marshal Sir Hugh Dowding far-sightedly preserved his Spitfire force for home defence, committing only Hurricane squadrons to the losing battle being fought in France. By then Bader had been promoted to Flight Lieutenant and was a flight commander in 222 Squadron, still flying Spitfires. When the BEF was left with no option but to retire on and be evacuated from Dunkirk, Spitfires were at last deployed and clashed with Me 109s for the first time. On 1 June, Bader scored his first aerial victories when he destroyed an Me 109 and damaged an Me 110 over the French coast.

On 24 June, Bader was promoted to Acting Squadron Leader and left 222 Squadron to command 242, a demoralised unit of largely Canadian Hurricane pilots who had been badly mauled during the Fall of France. Leading by example, Squadron Leader Bader soon demonstrated that he was no disabled passenger and whipped his new squadron back into shape. Based at Coltishall in 12 Group, however, Bader soon became frustrated as the forward squadrons of 11 Group bore the brunt of the Battle of Britain. His energetic personality did not permit an idle role, and Bader was unable to understand the (sound) concepts of Dowding's System of Home Defence, in which 12 Group's role was to protect 11 Group's airfields while their fighters were engaged, and not otherwise sally forth southwards against the enemy. On 30 August 1940, 242 Squadron was ordered to reinforce 11 Group and intercept a German raid on aircraft factories to the north-west of London. Bader's Hurricanes fell on the unescorted enemy bombers and, he believed, alone executed great damage. This led Douglas Bader to believe that had he been commanding more fighters in the air then even greater losses would have been inflicted upon the enemy. This was, however, a fallacy, as contemporary combat records prove that a number of 11 Group fighters, both Spitfires and Hurricanes, were successfully involved in the same engagement which was not, therefore, the solo 242 Squadron execution that Bader believed.

Squadron Leader Bader already enjoyed a unique relationship with Air Vice-Marshal Sir Trafford Leigh-Mallory, the Air Officer Commanding 12 Group, who, amazingly, had never been either a fighter pilot or leader. 'LM', however, saw merit in Bader's suggestion that he should lead several squadrons forward over 11 Group and against the enemy, even though this was contrary to the System. That System, which was tried and tested, was, it must be remembered, created by two of the RAF's most experienced fighter leaders, Dowding and the AOC 11 Group, Air Vice-Marshal Keith Park. Both men had significant experience of flying fighters during the Great War, and Dowding also possessed a terrific scientific understanding which had enabled the early harness of radar into the System. That Leigh-Mallory and the very junior officer Acting Squadron

Leader Douglas Bader should challenge the thinking of Dowding and Park was insubordinate to the extreme. But so it was that the ambitious Leigh-Mallory, and ever impatient but enthusiastic Bader, saw the 'Big Wing' concept as a means of ensuring that 12 Group played a fulsome role in the Battle of Britain, which would no longer be the private concern of 11 Group.

On 7 September, Squadron Leader Bader led the Hurricanes of 242 and 310 (Czech) Squadrons, and the Spitfires of 19, into action as a 'Wing' over London for the first time. Bounced by 109s while climbing over the Thames Estuary, the engagement was not the great success that both Leigh-Mallory and Bader had hoped for, but as the days went on the Wing's perceived success increased. This led Leigh-Mallory to deploy two further squadrons to fly with the 'Big Wing', namely the Spitfires of 611 and the Hurricanes of 302 (Polish). The evolving tactics led to the higher performance Spitfires taking on the German fighter escorts, while the Hurricanes attacked the bombers. The Big Wing's claims were subsequently impressive, and led to many congratulatory signals being received by Squadron Leader Bader. Unfortunately, no one seems to have checked these claims against the actual German aircraft lying wrecked across southern England. Had they done so, a massive discrepancy would have become immediately apparent. The fact of the matter was that ambition and enthusiasm concealed the truth: the more fighters are in action, the more confused a battle becomes, and thus several pilots can simultaneously attack and claim the same aircraft destroyed. These claims were made in good faith, however, the speed of combat having deceived the human eye and each pilot being unaware of the presence or involvement of other friendly fighters.

Unfortunately, Leigh-Mallory had friends at the Air Ministry, whereas Dowding and Park had neglected such politics in favour of defending the country. People in high places began taking notice of the Big Wing's claims, and became convinced that such tactics were better than those of Park's, which carefully employed penny-packet formations. The adjutant of 242 Squadron was also an MP who had the Prime Minister's ear, and this officer was responsible for betraying his Commander-in-Chief at top level. Although the Battle of Britain was won by Dowding and Park, towards its close they were both called to account for their tactics at the Air Ministry. The meeting was unprecedented, and what was virtually a kangaroo court heard evidence from the exponents of both tactical doctrines. That having been said, Squadron Leader Bader was the most junior officer present, and vigorously expounded his Big Wing theory, while Dowding and Park were not invited to bring along one of their many squadron commanders, any one of whom had far more combat experience than Bader.

The result of the 'Meeting of Infamy' was that the two real architects of victory in the Battle of Britain were shamefully treated. Dowding was sacked as Commander-in-Chief of Fighter Command and Park was moved into Training Command. His place at the helm of prestigious 11 Group was taken by Leigh-Mallory, and Sholto Douglas, a Leigh-Mallory and Bader supporter, took over from Dowding. And so it was that the fundamentally flawed Big Wing prevailed, and convinced high RAF commanders that the Wing, of three squadrons, should become the basic fighter formation in both attack and defence. Strangely enough, shortly after the Battle of Britain, a simulated exercise took place in which Big Wings responded to a recreated German raid that had actually taken place during the summer of 1940. The result was a disaster: confusion reigned, and the enemy successfully bombed all targets.

After the change at the helm of Fighter Command, the outlook shifted from the defensive over to the offensive. The idea was to 'reach out' and take the war to the enemy over occupied France. The concept was simple: wings of Spitfires would sally forth across the Channel and engage German fighters, which would be destroyed en masse. A new operational command post was created, that of 'Wing Commander Flying'. Following on from Douglas Bader's role at Duxford in 1940, experienced fighter squadron commanders were promoted to be Wing Leaders and appointed to various Sector Stations. Naturally, Bader himself was a top choice, and his old friend Leigh-Mallory even gave him a choice of venue for the coming season: Biggin Hill or Tangmere? The dedicated Bader decided that Biggin Hill was too close to the distractions of London for his young pilots, and so opted for Tangmere, nestling near the south coast near Chichester. And so, in March 1941, Wing Commander Douglas Bader took leave of his beloved 242 Squadron and became Wing Leader at Tangmere.

83. Pilots of 222 and 92 Squadron pictured at Hornchurch during Operation DYNAMO. Flight Lieutenant Bader is at centre, to his left is another soon-to-be ace, Flight Lieutenant Bob Stanford Tuck.

84. Douglas Bader, who lost both legs in a flying accident before the war, playing golf while leader of the Tangmere Wing in 1941.

85. Wing Commander Bader exits his Spitfire after a sortie. Although his Wing Commander's pennant can be seen, it is not known whether this is Spitfire Mk IIA P7666, which he flew many times from Tangmere, or Mk VA W3185 – the aircraft in which he was brought down over France on 9 August 1941.

86. The *inner sanctum*: from left: Squadron Leader Billy Burton DFC, CO of 616 Squadron, Pilot Officers 'Johnnie' Johnson (who became the RAF's official top scorer) and Hugh 'Cocky' Dundas, Wing Commander Douglas Bader and Sergeant Alan Smith.

On the south coast Bader found 616 Squadron (commanded by Billy Burton, another Cranwell graduate and the 1937 Sword of Honour winner), with which he was already familiar: during the closing stages of the Battle of Britain, 616 had reinforced the Big Wing. Burton's squadron was at Westhampnett, which was shared with the Spitfires of 610 Squadron, led by former 616 Squadron Battle of Britain stalwart, Squadron Leader Ken Holden. At nearby Merston was the Wing's third Spitfire squadron, 145, commanded by the indomitable Canadian Stan Turner, who had flown with Bader during the Battle of Britain. Bader soon chose to lead the Wing at the head of 616 Squadron, and took a young Sergeant pilot from the Volunteer Reserve stable as his wingman. Alan Smith remembers that day:

Wing Commander Bader came stomping into the dispersal hut, and looked around at we pilots gathered therein. He already knew Cocky Dundas and 'Johnnie' Johnson, so said to me 'Who are you?' I nearly jumped out of my seat! 'Smith, Sir,' I replied, 'Sergeant Smith.' 'Good,' said Douglas, 'I want you to fly as my Number Two.' I just couldn't believe it: it was like God asking me to keep an eye on heaven while he popped out for a minute!'

The Wing Leader's initials, DB, were painted on the fuselage of his personal Spitfire, and Bader's radio call sign therefore became 'Dogsbody'. His leading section of four Spitfires inevitably became 'Dogsbody Section'. Soon the Tangmere Wing was frequently flying fighter sweeps over France, regularly engaging the enemy. These sweeps were not necessarily successful, however, as the Germans knew only too well that a fighter is only going to cause damage if another fighter is sent to intercept. So, the *Luftwaffe* very sensibly chose either to remain on the ground, the RAF fighters just wasting time and fuel, or carefully chose to attack only when the tactical situation was entirely in their favour. Interestingly, this was a reversal of the Battle of Britain situation, the RAF pilots facing a two-way sea crossing on a single engine and fighting over enemy occupied territory. Moreover, and most importantly, the Spitfire, designed as a defensive fighter and in which capacity it excelled, was being used as an offensive fighter, for which it was possessed of insufficient range. The Me 109, however, now found itself fighting the defensive battle for which it was designed, as opposed to having also been pressed into an equally unsuitable offensive role during the Battle of Britain. Clearly, the Fighter Command 'Non-stop Offensive' of 1941 was not going to be the pushover that the RAF's optimistic high commanders expected and required.

During the Battle of Britain, RAF fighter controllers had likewise not responded to German fighter sweeps over southern England, but were forced to do so when fighter–bombers, indistinguishable from normal fighters on the radar screen, began to be included in the enemy formations. After bombs had unexpectedly rained down on London during the morning of 20 September

87. Wing Commander Bader exclusively led the Tangmere Wing at the head of 616 Squadron. He is pictured here at front right with pilots of that squadron at Westhampnett in the summer of 1941. The other pilots are, from left: Flight Lieutenant Denys Gillam DFC (who was visiting the Squadron, with which he had flown during the Battle of Britain), Sergeant McCairns, Pilot Officer Heppell, Sergeants West and Brewer, Squadron Clerk, Pilot Officer Johnson. Seated to Bader's right is Squadron Leader Billy Burton DFC.

1940, Fighter Command had not only been forced to respond to every enemy incursion, but had to mount standing patrols over the south coast. The tables were now turned, however, and the RAF started sending small formations of light bombers to attack certain targets in north-west France. These raiders, which the Germans could not ignore, were escorted by wings of Spitfires and it was hoped that this tactic, the 'Circus' operation, would help achieve the required end result. In reality, however, there were no targets in France that were crucial to the German war effort and which would therefore generate the kind of reaction hoped for by Sholto Douglas and Leigh-Mallory. Although the Germans started to respond to these nuisance raids, they still chose when, where, and how to attack. The initiative was completely theirs, and do not underestimate the fact that the German day fighter force at that time possessed some massively skilful and experienced *experten*.

Down at Tangmere, however, Bader's Spitfire pilots had observed the German fighters flying, as 'Johnnie' Johnson later put it to me, 'in this lean-and-hungry-looking formation'. Flying Officer Hugh 'Cocky' Dundas of 616 Squadron discussed this with Wing Commander Bader, and persuaded him that it was worth

88. A section of Spitfires forms up after take-off from Westhampnett for a sweep over France during the summer of 1941.

an experiment to emulate the enemy *Schwarm*. So it was that one morning in May 1941 found four Tangmere Spitfires stooging up and down the Channel, imitating the German formation, and hoping to get bounced. Sure enough, the 109s took the bait, but Bader timed the break into fighting pairs slightly wrongly and Dundas was shot down, crash-landing at Hawkinge. But the experiment had convinced Bader that the 'Finger Four' was the best tactical formation. From then on the Tangmere Wing practised the method until the Spitfire pilots got it right. Ron Rayner, who joined the Wing when 41 Squadron relieved 145 at Merston in July 1941, told me that 'the "Cross-over" or "Finger Four" was absolutely brilliant. It made such a massive difference which cannot be emphasised enough'.

While the Spitfire pilots' experience increased with the improving weather, so too did the tempo of the air war over France: on 22 June 1941, Hitler made a surprise attack on Russia, Operation BARBOROSSA, and soon the Soviets were clamouring for Allied support. As with Poland two years earlier, the Western Allies were unable to provide direct military assistance, so the only option was to try and tie down *Luftwaffe* units on the Channel coast. The sweeps and circuses, supplemented by rhubarbs and ramrods, continued unabated that fateful summer, but RAF losses were high and the Germans continued to defend the west with just two fighter groups, JG 2 *Richthofen* and JG 26 *Schlageter*.

89. Group Captain 'Woody' Woodhall, Station Commander and 'Boss' Controller at Tangmere.

90. From left: Sergeants West, Brewer, and Mabbett with Pilot Officer Heppell, all of 616 Squadron and posing with Wing Commander Bader's Spitfire Mk IIA. Note the caricature of Hitler being kicked in the backside by a flying boot – identical to the nose art previously appearing on Bader's 242 Squadron Hurricane.

As can be imagined, Wing Commander Bader ensured that the Tangmere Wing was kept busy and in the thick of the press. But, by August 1941, he was tired. Other Wing Leaders had already been rested, but, characteristically, Bader had refused all such offers, preferring instead to see out the 'season' at Tangmere. His pilots had christened the Wing 'Bader's Bus Company', and morale was high. The RAF fighter pilots, operating over France in large numbers, had submitted grossly exaggerated combat claims, the majority of which were allowed by Intelligence Officers without any accurate means of verification (due to the combats having taken place over France or the Channel and there not being access to any wrecked enemy machines). The Spitfire pilots believed, therefore, that they were doing well, blissfully unaware of the actual German losses and combat claim ratio which was, in fact, in the enemy's favour by a ratio of two to one. Churchill and the War Cabinet knew the truth, of course, through ULTRA decrypts, but could not permit the facts to become common knowledge. And so it was that the 'Non-Stop Offensive' continued unabated, but became known by the Germans as the 'Non-sense Offensive'.

By this time, Douglas Bader had been decorated with both the DSO and bar, and the DFC: he was a celebrity. Naturally the media had capitalised on the morale-boosting story of the legless fighter 'ace', and so Douglas Bader's contribution to the war effort was not only from the cockpit of a Spitfire but also via the propaganda war. The public eagerly read the newspapers, listened to the wireless, and watched the cinema news reels for news of their heroes. Uppermost among the august were fighter pilots: as in the Great War the public saw in their knightly deeds something romantic and noble, and so the exploits of the 'aces' were enthusiastically followed. Douglas Bader became a household name.

On the morning of Monday 9 August 1941, the teleprinter clattered away at Tangmere as the Form 'D' came through from 11 Group HQ, detailing the Wing's task for that day. This was another complex Circus, No. 68, involving many aircraft to Gosnay. The Tangmere Wing was to provide Target Support. Directives issued that August stipulated that the Target Support Wing's role was to:

> clear the road to the target area, also to cover the withdrawal of the bombers and escort Wings. There are usually two Target Support Wings, one being routed the same direction as the bombers, to arrive over the target three minutes earlier, and the other is given a different route, but also arriving three minutes in advance of the bombers.

For Wing Commander Bader and the Westhampnett Spitfire squadrons, 616 and 610, Target Support was a routine sortie, although not, of course, without the usual hazards. Although Squadron Leader 'Elmer' Gaunce DFC's 41 Squadron had arrived at Merston just two weeks previously, the Squadron had already flown numerous practice sweeps when based at Catterick and at least

91. This is believed to be Wing Commander Bader's Mk IIA at Tangmere, on which the nose art can be seen.

92. Another photograph of Wing Commander Bader's Mk IIA which clearly shows the nose art. The aircraft is having the first colour cine-gun camera fitted at Westhampnett.

one offensive patrol over France from Redhill. Circus 68, therefore, represented nothing other than a typical sortie and was not beyond the capabilities of any of the Tangmere Wing's three Spitfire squadrons.

Sergeant Alan Smith, Wing Commander Bader's usual 'Dogsbody 2', had a head cold and so was unable to fly. Imminently to be commissioned, and as his name was not 'on the board', Alan prepared to go into London to buy a new uniform. His place as the Wing Leader's No. 2 was taken by a New Zealander, Sergeant Jeff West, a pilot with one-and-a-half Me 109s destroyed and one damaged to his credit. Clearly, West was not without experience: frequently that summer he had flown No. 2 to Flight Lieutenant E. P. Gibbs, until that officer was shot down over France on 9 July 1941. For this Target Support sortie to Gosnay, 'Dogsbody Section' therefore consisted of:

'Dogsbody': Wing Commander Douglas Bader.
'Dogsbody 2': Sergeant Jeff West.
'Dogsbody 3': Flight Lieutenant Hugh Dundas DFC.
'Dogsbody 4': Pilot Officer 'Johnnie' Johnson.

Also leading 'Finger Fours' within the 616 Squadron formation of three sections would be the squadron commander, Squadron Leader 'Billy' Burton (Yellow Section), and the 'B' Flight commander, Flight Lieutenant Lionel Buck Casson (Blue Section). Across the other side of the airfield, Squadron Leader Ken Holden DFC and 610 Squadron also prepared for the morning sortie.

Take-off came at 1040 hrs, 'Dogsbody Section' leading Westhampnett's Spitfires for yet another sortie into very hostile airspace. High over Chichester, Squadron Leader Holden swiftly manoeuvred 610 Squadron into position above and slightly to port of 616. As Target Support, the Wing had no bombers to meet prior to setting course for France, although the Spitfires were still routed out over Beachy Head. As the Wing left Chichester, however, there was no sign of 41 Squadron.

The Beachy Head Forward Relay Station recorded the Tangmere Wing's R/T messages that day. As the Wing neared 'Diamond', 41 Squadron had still not appeared. Group Captain Woodhall, at Tangmere, was the first to speak, making a test call:

'Dogsbody?'
'OK, OK'.

Bader then made R/T test calls to the commanders of both 610 and 41, using their Christian names as was his usual practice:

DB: Ken?
Ken Holden (KH): Loud and clear.
DB: Elmer?

There was no response from Squadron Leader Gaunce which provoked an acerbic remark from the Wing Leader to 'Woody'. Unable to wait, 616 and 610 Squadrons set course for France and Gosnay, adopting their battle formations in the process. Still climbing, Wing Commander Bader waggled his wings insistently, indicating that 'Dogsbody 3', Flight Lieutenant Dundas, should take the lead. Dundas slid across, tucking his wing tip just two or three feet from Bader's. From this close proximity, Dundas saw the Wing Leader mouth two words: 'Airspeed Indicator', meaning that the instrument on Spitfire Mk VA W3185 was unserviceable. The Wing had to climb at the right speed to ensure Time on Target at the appointed time, which was crucial. Dundas gave a 'thumbs up' and moved forward to lead the Spitfires to France. On the rear of his hand he had fortunately written the time at which the Wing was due over the French coast in addition to the speed which had to be maintained. The twenty-one-year-old Flight Commander then 'settled down to concentrate on the job'.

Sir Hugh Dundas later recalled that the 'sun was bright and brilliant, unveiled by any layer of high haze or cirrus cloud'. Realising that the white cumulus cloud below provided a background which would immediately reveal the silhouettes of any aircraft, Dundas correctly anticipated that under such conditions 'Dogsbody' would wish to climb as high as possible, and so adjusted both his throttle setting and rate of climb accordingly, taking the Spitfires up to 28,000 feet. Then, more radio messages:

DB: Ken and Elmer, start gaining height.
KH: Elmer's not with us.
Unidentified, garbled voice on the R/T, believed to be Squadron Leader Gaunce.
DB: Elmer from Dogsbody. I cannot understand what you say, but we are on our way. You had better decide for yourself whether to come or go back.

Following the last radio transmissions, at least the Wing was now aware that more Spitfires were bringing up the rear, even if some distance away. The Spitfires cruised over the Channel, towards France, with 610 Squadron above and behind 616. Dundas led the Wing over the French coast right on cue (although there is conflicting evidence regarding whether the coast was crossed south of Le Touquet, known as the 'Golf Course', or Boulogne, slightly further north). This crucial timing observed, Bader accelerated ahead and informed 'Dogsbody 3' over the R/T that he was resuming the lead. The Spitfires' arrival over the coastal flak belt was greeted by dangerous little puffballs of black smoke which made the formation twist and turn. 'Beetle' then called 'Dogsbody' informing that the/beehive itself was 'on time and engaged'. As the Spitfires forged inland, therefore, some distance behind them the bombers and various cover Wings were now bound for France and action.

Slightly below the condensation trail level, a 610 Squadron pilot reported seeing contrails 'above and to our left'. Squadron Leader Holden consequently led the squadron higher still while 'Beetle' (B) reported:

B: Dogsbody from Beetle. There are twenty-plus five miles to the east of you.

DB: OK, but your transmitter is quite impossible. Please use the other.

B: Dogsbody, is this better?

DB: Perfect. Ken, start getting more height.

KH: OK, Dogsbody, but will you throttle back? I cannot keep up.

DB: Sorry Ken, my airspeed indicator is u/s. Throttling back, and I will do one slow left-hand turn so you can catch up.

KH: Dogsbody from Ken, I'm making smoke [contrails] at this height.

DB: OK, Ken. I'm going down very slightly.

Beetle then advised Dogsbody of more bandits in the vicinity. The 616 Squadron's Flying Officer Roy Marples saw the enemy first.

RM: Three bandits coming down astern of us. I'm keeping an eye on them. Now there are six.

DB: OK.

B: Douglas, another twelve-plus ahead and slightly higher.

RM: Eleven of them now.

DB: OK, Roy. Let me know exactly where they are.

RM: About one mile astern and slightly higher.

B: Douglas, there is another forty-plus fifteen miles to the north-east of you.

DB: OK Beetle. Are our friends where they ought to be? I haven't much idea where I am.

B: Yes, you are exactly right. And so are your friends.

RM: Dogsbody from Roy. Keep turning left and you'll see 109s at nine o'clock.

DB: Ken, can you see them?

KH: Douglas, 109s below. Climbing up.

By this time, 616 and 610 Squadron had progressed into a very dangerous French sky indeed, Beetle having already reported some seventy-two bandits, representing odds which outnumbered the Spitfires by nearly three to one. Clearly, this was not to be an uneventful sortie. Tension mounting, the Spitfire pilots switched on their gunsight reflectors and gun buttons to 'Fire'. Anxiously they searched the sky, an ever-watchful eye being kept on the 109s positioned 1,000 feet above the Wing, waiting to pounce. Bader himself dipped each wing in turn, scrutinising the sky below for the 109s reported by Ken Holden.

DB: I can't see them. Will you tell me where to look?

KH: Underneath Bill's section now. Shall I come down?

DB: No, I have them. Get into formation. Going down. Ken, are you with us?

KH: Just above you.

As 'Dogsbody Section' dived on the enemy, Flight Lieutenant Casson followed with three other aircraft of 'B' Flight.

'Dogsbody 3', Flight Lieutenant Dundas, had 'smelt a rat' in respect of the *Schwarm* of 109s that 'Dogsbody Section' was now rapidly diving towards. Finding no targets to the Section's right, 'Dogsbody 4', Pilot Officer Johnson, skidded under the section and fired at an Me 109 on the left. By this time the whole of 'Dogsbody Section' was firing, although Dundas, still unhappy and suspecting a trap, had a compelling urge to look behind. Suddenly Pilot Officer 'Nip' Hepple shouted over the R/T: 'Blue 2 here. Some buggers coming down behind, astern. Break left!'

The Spitfire pilots hauled their aircraft around in steep turns. The sky behind 'Dogsbody Section' was full of Me 109s, all firing. Without Hepple's warning the Spitfires would have been instantly nailed. As the high 109s crashed into 616 Squadron, Squadron Leader Holden decided that it was time for his section to join the fray and reduce the odds. Informing Flight Lieutenant Denis Crowley-Milling of this decision, Holden led his Spitfires down to assist. Buck Casson, following Bader's Section, was well throttled back to keep his flight together. Also attacking from the rear, Casson managed a squirt at a *Rotte* of 109s. Flying Officer Marples, No. 3 in Casson's section, then shouted a warning of even more 109s diving upon the Wing, while Squadron Leader Billy Burton urged the Spitfires to 'Keep turning', thus preventing the 109s (which could not out-turn a Spitfire) getting in a shot. Suddenly the organised chaos became a totally confused maelstrom of twisting, turning fighters:

'BREAK! FOR CHRIST'S SAKE, BREAK!'

The Spitfires immediately 'broke' – hard. 'Johnnie' Johnson remembers:

There was this scream of '*Break!*' – and we all broke, we didn't wait to hear it twice! '*Round*', then a swirling mass of 109s and Spitfires. When I broke I could see Bader still firing. Dundas was firing at the extreme right 109. There was some cloud nearby and I disappeared into it as quick as possible! I couldn't say how many aircraft were involved, suffice to say a lot. It seemed to me that the greatest danger was a collision rather than being shot down – that's how close we all were. We had got the 109s we were bouncing and then Holden came down with his section, so there were a lot of aeroplanes. We were fighting 109Fs, although there may have been some Es among them. There was an absolute mass of aeroplanes just fifty yards apart. It was awful. I thought to myself, 'You're going to collide with somebody!' I didn't think about shooting at anything after we were bounced ourselves; all you could think about was surviving, getting out of that mass of aircraft. In such a tight turn, of course, you almost black out, you cannot really see where you are going. It was a mess. I had never been so frightened in my life – never!

Chased by three Me 109s, the closest just 100 yards astern, Pilot Officer Johnson maintained his tight turn, spiralling down towards the safety of a nearby cloud which his Spitfire dived into with over 400 mph on the clock. Pulling back the throttle and centralising the controls, the altimeter stabilised, but, speed having dropped to less than 100 mph, the Spitfire stalled. Beneath the cloud, 'Dogsbody 4' recovered control. Having requested and received a homing course for Dover, he headed rapidly for England. Over the R/T, Pilot Officer Johnson could still hear 616 and 610 Squadrons' running battle:

'Get into formation or they'll shoot the bloody lot of you!'
'Spitfire going down in flames, ten o'clock.'
'YQ-C [616 Squadron Spitfire]. Form up on me. I'm at three o'clock to you.'
'Four buggers above us.' [From Hepple]
'All Elfin aircraft [616 Squadron] withdraw. I say again, all Elfin aircraft withdraw.'
'Use the cloud if you're in trouble.' [From Billy Burton]
'Are you going home, Ken?' [From Billy Burton]
'Yes, withdrawing' [From Holden]
'Ken from Crow. Are you still about?'
'I'm right behind you, Crow.'
'Are we all here?'
'Two short.'
'Dogsbody from Beetle. Do you require any assistance?'
'Beetle from Elfin Leader. We are OK and withdrawing.'
'Thank you Billy. Douglas, do you require any assistance? Steer three-four-zero to the coast.'

The silence from 'Dogsbody' was ominous. Flight Lieutenant Casson remembers:

I watched Wing Commander Bader and 'A' Flight attack and break to port as I was coming in. I was well throttled back in the dive, as the other three had started to fall behind and I wanted to keep the flight together. I attacked from the rear, and after having a squirt at two 109s flying together left them for a single one which was flying inland alone. I finished nearly all of my cannon ammunition up on this boy, who finally baled out at 6,000 feet, having lost most of his tail unit. The other three 'B' flight machines were in my rear and probably one of the lads saw this.

I climbed to 13,000 feet and fell in with Billy Burton and three other aircraft, all from 'A' Flight. We chased around in a circle for some time, gaining height all the while, and more 109s were directly above us. Eventually we formed up in line abreast and set off after the Wing.

Billy's section flew in pairs abreast, so I flew abreast but at about 200 yards to starboard. We were repeatedly attacked by two Me 109s which had followed us and were flying above and behind. Each time they started diving I called out and we all turned and re-formed, the 109s giving up their attack and climbing each time.

About fifteen miles from the coastline I saw another Spitfire well below us and about half a mile to starboard. This machine was alone and travelling very slowly. I called up Billy on the R/T and suggested that we cross over to surround him and help the pilot back as he looked like a sitting duck. I broke off to starboard and made for the solitary Spitfire, but then, on looking back for Billy and the others, was amazed to see them diving away hard to the south-west for a low layer of cloud into which they soon disappeared. I realised then that my message had either been misunderstood or not received. Like a greenhorn, I had been so intent upon watching Billy's extraordinary disappearance to the left, and the lone Spitfire to my right, I lost sight of the Me 109s that had been worrying us. I remember looking for them but upon not discovering their position assumed that they had chased Billy instead. I was soon proved wrong, however, when I received three hits in both fuselage and wing. This occurred when I just broke for some cloud at 5,000 feet, which I reached but found too thin for cover and was pursued by the 109s.

I then picked out two more 109s flying above me and so decided to drop to zero feet, fly north, and cross the Channel at a narrow point, as I was unsure of the damage sustained and the engine was not running smoothly. I pressed the teat and tried to run for it, but the two Me 109s behind had more speed and were rapidly within range, while the other two flew 1,500 feet above and dived from port to starboard and back, delivering quick bursts. Needless to say I was not flying straight and level all this time!

In the event, I received a good one from behind, which passed between the stick and my right leg, taking off some of the rudder on its way. It passed into the petrol tank but whether the round continued into the engine I do not know. Petrol began leaking into the cockpit, oil pressure was dropping low, and with the radiator wide open I could smell the glycol overheating.

As the next attack came, I pulled straight up from the deck in a loop and, on my way down, as I was changing direction towards the sea, my engine became extremely rough and seized up as white glycol fumes poured forth. There was no option but to crash-land the aircraft. I tried to send 'Dogsbody' a hurried message, then blew up the wireless and made a belly landing in a field some ten miles south of Calais. The Goons, having seen the glycol, were decent enough not to shoot me up as I was landing, but circled about for a time and gave my position away to a German cavalry unit in a wood in a corner of the field. One of the pilots waved to me as he flew overhead, and I waved back just before setting fire to the aircraft. Owing to the petrol in the cockpit, and because I was carrying a port-fire issued for this purpose, igniting the aircraft was easy. No sooner had I done this than a party of shrieking Goons armed with rifles came chasing over and that was the end of me!

What eventually happened to the lone Spitfire which I went to help out I have no idea. As the 109s followed me, I assume that he got away OK. I certainly hope so.

I will never forget that day, one which I have gone over so often in my daydreams.

93. *Oberleutnant* Gerhard Schöpfel, who shot down Flight Lieutenant Casson on 9 August 1941.

94. Flight Lieutenant Casson's Spitfire, photographed by *Oberleutnant* Schöpfel in a corn field near Calais. The cockpit area has been destroyed by fire because the pilot ignited the Portfire device before he was captured (Don Caldwell).

Flight Lieutenant Casson had been the victim of *Hauptmann* Gerhard Schöpfel, *Gruppenkommandeur* of III/JG26. In 1996, Herr Schöpfel recalled:

My III *Gruppe* attacked a British bomber formation, after which my formation was split up. With the British on their homeward flight, I headed alone for my airfield at Ligescourt, near Crécy. Suddenly I saw a flight of Spitfires flying westwards. I attacked them from above and after a short burst of fire the rear machine nosed over sharply and dived away. While the other aircraft flew on apparently unaware, I pursued the fleeing Spitfire as I could see no sign of damage. The British pilot hugged the ground, dodging trees and houses. I was constantly in his prop wash and so could not aim properly. Because of the warm air near the ground my radiator flaps opened and so my speed decreased. It thus took me a long time to get into a good firing position. Finally I was positioned immediately behind the Spitfire and it filled my gunsight. I pressed the firing button for both cannon and machine-guns, but 'click!' I had obviously exhausted my ammunition in the earlier air battles. Of course, the British pilot had no way of knowing this and I still wanted to strike terror in him for so long as he remained over French soil. I thus remained right behind him, at high speed. Suddenly I was astonished to see a white plume of smoke emit from the Spitfire! The smoke grew denser and the propeller stopped. The pilot made a forced landing in a field east of Marquise. I circled the aircraft and made a note of the markings for my victory report, watched the pilot climb out, and waved to him. Just before being captured by German soldiers, he ignited a built-in explosive charge which destroyed the centre-section of his aircraft.

I returned to my field and sent my engineering officer to the site to determine the reason for the forced landing. He found, to my amazement, that the Spitfire had taken a single machine-gun round in an engine cylinder during my first attack. Had I not pressed on after running out of ammunition, and therefore forcing the pilot to fly at top speed, he would probably have reached England despite the damage. Just a few weeks before, in fact, I myself had made it back across the Channel after two of my engine's connecting rods had been smashed over Dover. On this occasion over France, however, the British pilot, a flight lieutenant, now had to head for prison camp while I recorded my 33rd victory.

While Buck Casson was to spend the rest of the war as a prisoner, Gerhard Schöpfel running out of ammunition had clearly saved his life. With petrol splashing into the cockpit, another hit would no doubt have ignited the Spitfire into a blowtorch. Luck, it would appear, played no mean part in survival.

Returning to the French coast, Pilot Officer Johnson saw a lone Me 109 below. Suspecting it to be one of the three which chased him into the cloud just a few minutes previously, Johnnie anxiously searched the sky for the other two: the sky was clear. From astern, 'Dogsbody 4' dropped below the 109 before attacking from its blind spot: below and behind. One burst of cannon shells sent the enemy fighter diving earthwards emitting a plume of black smoke. Pilot Officer Johnson came 'out of France on the deck, low and fast', his Spitfire roaring over waving civilians, just feet above their fields. At the coast, German soldiers ran to their guns, but in a second the fleeting Spitfire was gone. Climbing over the Channel, 'Dogsbody 4' realised that something might have happened to Wing Commander Bader:

> As I was crossing the Channel, Group Captain Woodhall, who obviously knew that there had been a fight from the radar and R/T, repeated 'Douglas, are you receiving?' This came over the air every five minutes or so. I therefore called up and said, 'It's Johnnie here, Sir. We've had a stiff fight and I last saw the Wing Commander on the tail of a 109.' He said, 'Thank you. I'll meet you at dispersal.'

The silence from 'Dogsbody' over the R/T clearly meant one of two things, either that his radio was unserviceable or he had somehow been brought down. Air Marshal Sir Denis Crowley-Milling, then a flight commander in Ken Holden's 610 Squadron, recalled that:

> The greatest impression I have is the silence on the R/T. Douglas always maintained a running commentary. Had the worst happened? The colourful language and running commentary had suddenly ceased, leaving us all wondering what had happened. Was he alive or dead? Had his radio failed? I know we were above thick cloud on the way home and asked the Tangmere Controller to provide a homing bearing for us to steer. This was way out in accuracy, however, and unbeknown to us we were flying up the North Sea, just scraping in to Martlesham Heath with hardly any fuel remaining – it was indeed a day to remember!

So confused had been the fighting, so numerous the aircraft in this incredible maelstrom over St-Omer, that only Wing Commander Bader himself had the answers to the questions regarding his present state and whereabouts. After the first downwards charge, 'Dogsbody' had found himself alone after flattening out at 24,000 feet. In front of him were six 109s flying in a line-abreast formation of three pairs. Flying alone, Bader knew that he should leave this enemy formation and adhere to the instructions which he had even issued to his pilots as formal instructions: get out and get home. He considered these 109s to be 'sitters', however, and, in a split-second, greed won over discipline and good judgement. Alone over France, Wing Commander Bader stalked the middle *Rotte*. He later reported:

> I saw some more Me 109s. I arrived among these, who were evidently not on the lookout, as I expect they imagined the first formation we attacked to be covering them. I got a very easy shot at one of these which flew quite straight until he went on fire from behind the cockpit – a burst of about three seconds.

As two 109s curved towards him, 'Dogsbody' broke right, violently, although anticipating, with some bravado, that his course would take him between a pair of 109s. Suddenly something hit Spitfire DB. Owing to the close proximity of the enemy aircraft, Bader assumed that he had collided with a 109. The Spitfire went completely out of control, diving earthwards, its control column limp and unresponsive. As he looked behind, Bader's impression was that the entire fuselage aft of the VHF aerial had gone, although he was later to report that it was 'probably just the empennage'.

At 24,000 feet, 'Dogsbody' was unable to consider escape due to the lack of oxygen outside the cockpit at that height. His dilemma, however, was that the doomed fighter was already travelling in excess of 400 mph, so would soon be subjected to forces so great that baling out would become impossible. Yanking the canopy release mechanism, the hood was sucked away, the cockpit immediately being battered by the airflow. Without legs though, would he be able to thrust his body upwards to get out? As he struggled to get his head above the windscreen, he was nearly plucked out of the cockpit, but halfway he became stuck – the rigid foot of his artificial right leg jamming in the cockpit, the grip vice-like. Ever downwards the fighter plunged, the pilot helpless and continuously battered by the rushing wind, half in and half out of his crashing aeroplane. Desperately gripping his parachute's 'D' ring, Douglas Bader struggled furiously to get out. Eventually, at about 6,000 feet, the offending artificial leg's restraining strap broke. Free at last, the pilot was plucked out into mid-air; as the Spitfire continued its dive, he experienced a moment of apparently floating upwards. That terrible buffeting having thankfully ceased, in the silence he was able to think. His hand still gripping the 'D' ring, he pulled. There was a slight delay before the parachute deployed and then he really was floating – gently to earth beneath the life-saving silk umbrella.

At 4,000 feet Wing Commander Bader floated through a layer of cloud, emerging below to see the ground still far below. Alarmed by the roar of an aero-engine, he saw a Me 109 fly directly towards him, but the bullets he must have half-expected never came as the enemy fighter flashed by just fifty yards away. It may surprise many people to know that such a parachute descent, made owing to enemy action or some other mishap while flying actively, was often the first a pilot would actually make, there being no formal parachute training. Consequently, Bader had never before had to consider the practicalities of landing with artificial legs, or indeed one such leg, as he drifted earthwards. Having had some minutes to ponder this matter, suddenly French soil rushed up to meet him and he hit the ground hard, in an orchard near Blaringhem, to the south-east of St-Omer. For Wing Commander Douglas Bader, the air war was over: his personal period of operational service had lasted just eighteen months.

'Johnnie' Johnson recalled the scene back at Westhampnett: 'Group Captain Woodhall was waiting for me on the airfield, and when Dundas, West, Hepple, and the others came back the consensus of opinion was that the Wing

Commander had either been shot down or involved in a collision.' In his flying logbook, 'Johnnie' Johnson wrote that on this penetration over France there had been 'more opposition than ever before'. Squadron Leader Burton's logbook recorded, 'Had a bad time with 109s on way out and had to get into cloud'.

As the clock ticked on, it became clear from fuel considerations that the two Spitfires reported missing during the radio chatter over France were unlikely to return to Westhampnett. Reasoning that if flying damaged machines the pilots might land at one of the coastal airfields, Tangmere telephoned each in turn, receiving negative responses from all.

Douglas Roberts was a R/T (Direction Finding) Operator at the Tangmere 'Fixer' station which was, perhaps oddly, located on West Mailing airfield in Kent:

> We were told that Wing Commander Bader was missing and so listened out for several hours. Our system was basic when compared to modern equipment today, but nevertheless very efficient. The aerial system was a double dipole which, when rotated, would indicate either a true bearing or a reciprocal. Despite our diligence, nothing was heard from 'Dogsbody'.

Had either of the two missing pilots reached mid-Channel, then there was an excellent chance that they would be picked up by air–sea rescue. If their dinghies had drifted closer to the French coast then it was more likely that the Germans would get to them first, unless their positions could be discovered and a protective aerial umbrella established. Consequently Dundas, Johnson, Hepple, and West were soon flying back over the Channel, searching. At Le Touquet, Dundas led the section north, parallel to the coast and towards Cap Griz-Nez. Avoiding flak from various enemy vessels, especially near the port of Calais, a steep turn at zero feet returned the Spitfires to Le Touquet. At one point Hepple broke away to machine-gun a surfacing submarine, but otherwise the only item to report was an empty dinghy sighted by Sergeant West. To 'Johnnie' Johnson, that empty, life-saving, rubber boat was somehow symbolic of their fruitless search. With petrol almost exhausted, the section landed at Hawkinge. No news had yet been received of either missing pilot. Immediately the aircraft were refuelled, the 616 Squadron pilots took off, intending to head back across the Channel to France. Shortly after take-off, however, Group Captain Woodhall cancelled the sortie, fearing that a second trip was too risky as the enemy might now be waiting. Swinging round to the west, Dundas led the Spitfires back to Westhampnett.

For Hugh Dundas, the thought of Bader dead was 'utterly shattering'. Having been shot down himself during the Battle of Britain, and only narrowly escaping with his life, Dundas, then aged twenty, had found Douglas Bader a massive inspiration. In November that year, his own brother, Flight Lieutenant John Dundas DFC of 609 Squadron, was killed in action over the Solent; John's death affected him deeply, so when Douglas Bader arrived at Tangmere he no doubt helped fill a great void in this impressionable young man's life. The two were certainly close, and Dundas was to remain devoted to Douglas Bader until his own death in 1995. Buck Casson's loss was also a serious blow to Dundas's morale: they had joined the squadron together at Doncaster and, until that day, were the last remnants of the old pre-war pilots. When the fact dawned on him that he was now the only member of the old guard left, Dundas found this a 'terrifying thought'. Regarding Bader, as a loyal lieutenant, Dundas felt some degree of responsibility. He drove back to Shopwyke House 'alone and utterly dejected'.

With no news other than the fact that her husband had apparently vanished, Group Captain Woodhall had the unenviable duty of driving over to the Bay House and informing Mrs Thelma Bader. John Hunt, a young Intelligence Officer, was already there, having arrived to give some support only to discover that Thelma had yet to receive the bad news, which 'Woody' tempered by stating that Douglas Bader was 'indestructible and probably a prisoner'. Later, Hugh Dundas arrived and with Jill, her sister, persuaded Thelma to take some sherry, which she only brought up again. As Dundas drove back to Shopwyke House he cried. Back at the mess, he and 'Johnnie' Johnson shared a whole bottle of brandy. Despair had overtaken the inner sanctum.

Just as the Target Support detail had been 'routine' for the Tangmere Wing, so too was 9 August 1941, for JG26, dispersed around various airfields in the Pas-de-Calais. Having urgently responded to the *Alarmstart*, it was 109s from the '*Schlageter*' *Geschwader* that the Tangmere Wing had fought that day high above Bethune. After the action, which developed into a running battle between Bethune and the French coast, the German pilots claimed a total of seven Spitfires destroyed. In reality, the figure was five, three Spitfires of 452 (Australian) Squadron having also failed to return (with one pilot killed), lost somewhere between Bethune and Mardyck. However, although JG26, the only *Luftwaffe* unit to engage Spitfires that day, only lost two 109s (including one pilot killed) during the engagement, the RAF pilots claimed a staggering twenty-two Me 109s destroyed, ten probables, and eight damaged.

Among the successful German pilots was JG26's *Kommodore, Oberstleutnant* Adolf Galland, who had recorded victory number 76, a Spitfire north-west of St-Pol, at 11.32 a.m. Shortly afterwards, *Oberleutnant* 'Pips' Priller, *Staffelkapitän* of 1/JG26, arrived at Audembert to tell Galland about this captured legless '*Adler*', urging Galland, 'You must come and meet him.' While in hospital, at the *Clinique Sterin* in St-Omer, Bader was actually visited several times by two JG26 pilots; he shared a bottle of champagne with them in the doctor's room and concluded that they were 'types' whom he would have liked in the Tangmere Wing. Previous accounts have stated that the Germans recovered Bader's missing leg from his Spitfire's crash site, but in fact French eyewitnesses confirm that the artificial limb in question fluttered down on its own and landed close to Wing Commander Bader's parachute. The villagers handed the article in to the German authorities, after which Galland's engineers made running repairs on the leg to afford the Wing Commander some mobility. A few days later, Galland sent his *Horsch* staff car to fetch Bader for a visit to the *Geschwaderstabschwarm*.

While visiting JG 26, Wing Commander Bader was interested to know what had happened when he was brought down. His explanation was a collision with an Me 109, although he had not actually seen the aeroplane with which he had supposedly collided. Galland was puzzled, however, as none of his aircraft had been involved in such a collision. One 109 pilot had been killed: *Unteroffizier* Alfred Schlager, who crashed at Aire, some ten miles south-east of St-Omer. The Germans therefore conceded it possible that Bader may have collided with Schlager who had not survived to make any report. More likely, though, so far as Galland was concerned, was that Wing Commander Bader had been shot down by one of two pilots, either *Oberfeldwebel* Walter Meyer (6/JG 26) or *Leutnant* Kosse (5/JG 26) who had recorded their eleventh and seventh victories respectively above the area of St-Omer that morning. According to Adolf Galland, for Bader it was an 'intolerable idea' that his master in the air was an NCO pilot. Tactfully, therefore, a 'fair-haired, good-looking flying officer' was selected from the victorious German pilots and introduced to Bader as his champion. Kosse was the only officer of that rank to make a claim that morning, and so it is likely that it was he who Bader met at Audembert. However, neither German pilot's victory report was conclusive. As Galland later wrote, 'it was never confirmed who shot him down'.

Among the officers present at the reception thrown for Bader by JG 26 was *Hauptmann* Gerhard Schöpfel. In 1995, he recalled the occasion:

> My meeting with Wing Commander Bader was memorable and one which I well recall. Our *Oberst* Joachim-Friedrich Huth had lost a leg in the First World War, and when the report about Bader being shot down reached him he was sure that spare artificial legs existed in England. There followed a number of telephone calls, during which Bader's capture was reported to the Red Cross, and it was decided that an RAF aircraft should be offered free passage to deliver the spare legs to our airfield at an appointed time and date. So far as I know, this was initially confirmed by England.

When the Red Cross had announced that Wing Commander Bader was a prisoner, on 14 August 1941, there was absolute euphoria within Fighter Command, and in particular, of course, at Tangmere. Group Captain Woodhall broadcast the news over the station tannoy. Sir Denis Crowley-Milling remembered:

> The loss of Douglas Bader had left us all stunned. A few of us, including Dundas and Johnson, were with Thelma Bader in their married quarters at Tangmere when the telephone rang. After speaking, Thelma came back to join us and very calmly said, 'Douglas is safe and a prisoner.'

When the signal was received from Germany offering free passage for an RAF aircraft to deliver Wing Commander Bader's spare legs, Group Captain Woodhall responded so enthusiastically that he even offered to fly a Lysander to Audembert himself. However, the Air Ministry rejected the proposal out of hand.

Gerhard Schöpfel continues:

On the appointed time and date for an RAF aircraft to arrive with the legs, I was at the *Geschwader-gefechtsstand* in Audembert, having flown in from my base at Ligescourt, home of my III/JG 26. Soon after our meeting, Bader wanted to inspect one of our Me 109s. Galland invited him to climb into a *Geschwader-maschine* and Bader commented that he would like to fly it, but of course this could not be allowed.

Many photographs were taken by the Germans of this visit, which numerous non-flying JG 26 personnel would later recall as the most memorable incident of their entire war. Among the snapshots is a photograph of Bader sitting in the cockpit of a 109, a German officer standing on the adjacent wing. In *Reach for the Sky* and other books the object in this officer's left hand has been described as a 'pistol' – other photographs from the same series show that in fact *Oberst* Huth is holding his gloves! Gerhard Schöpfel:

When told of our arrangement via the Red Cross regarding his spare legs, he was not surprised when no plane arrived, as he felt that high authority in England would take time to sanction such things. He hoped, however, that his own Wing would find a way. One or two days later, our radar announced a Beehive approaching. The Blenheims flew over St-Omer where they dropped a few bombs on our I *Gruppe*. Also dropped, however, was a crate containing Bader's legs which was attached to a parachute.

On 19 August 1941, the 'Leg Operation' took place when, during a Circus to Longuenesse, an 82 Squadron Blenheim dropped the spare legs by parachute. The Tangmere Wing flew close cover, as Ron Rayner recalled:

I flew with 41 Squadron on that particular sortie and I remember it distinctly. The legs were dropped over St-Omer and not without ceremony, it being announced over the R/T that Wing Commander Bader's legs had been delivered. We were weaving around the Blenheims and we were acting as individual aircraft, not a cohesive formation as was usual. Then we continued on to the target before turning round for home.

Woodhall signalled the Germans and so consequently the crate in question was recovered, the legs therein being duly presented to Bader. Galland was most upset that the British had responded so unchivalrously, however; to his mind, 'bombs and charity did not go together'. For Galland, however, his meeting with Wing Commander Bader was to gain an even more bitter aftertaste.

On 17 August 1941, while Wing Commander Bader still occupied Chambre 21 in the *Clinique Sterin*, a local French girl who worked at the hospital in an auxiliary capacity, Lucille de Backer, handed Bader a note. The content was astonishing: a Frenchman was to wait outside the hospital every night from midnight until 2 a.m., poised to guide '*Le Colonel*' to a local 'safe house'. Incredibly, the note was even signed, by a Frenchwoman, Mme Hiecque, in her own name. The Hiecques were a working-class French family who lived at the *Quai du Haut-Pont* in a long row of terraced houses overlooking the St-Omer canal. Gilbert Petit, a young friend of the Hiecque family, was employed at the SNCF railway station in the town. Each night he waited patiently in the shadows of an alleyway across the road from the hospital, risking being caught out after curfew. Within, Bader had received bad news: he was imminently to be taken to Germany. Having been given his new legs, on the night of 20 August, he knotted bed sheets together, lowered the makeshift rope out of a window at the rear of the building, and climbed down. Squeezing through a small gap between the chained gate, Bader met Petit and together they made their way through the cobbled streets, darkness their cloak. Having avoided at least one German patrol, the fugitives eventually reached the sanctuary of the Hiecque household, Bader in great pain from his stumps. '*Le Colonel*' was given a bed upstairs and before drifting off into sleep he thought, 'That's foxed the bloody Huns. I'll be seeing Thelma in a couple of days!'

The following day, Mme Hiecque walked to the hospital and saw many German soldiers searching for the escaped prisoner. Upon her return, she told Bader that '*Les Boches sont très stupides*'. Bader, however, appreciated the consequences for these French patriots if he was found in their house. Mme Hiecque was supremely confident, however, that the Germans would never find him, and awaited word from Gilbert that the Underground had been contacted and an escape plan formulated. That afternoon, '*Le Colonel*' was taken out into the back garden and watched a tangled mass of contrails overhead as yet another drama took place above St-Omer. The Hiecques and their neighbours shouted enthusiastically, '*Vive les Tommies! Vive les Tommies!*', giving Bader another view of the sweeps he had flown so often.

The Hiecque's canal-side house was actually some distance from the *Clinique Sterin*, and the Germans, being convinced that Bader could not walk far, had cordoned off the area of St-Omer around the hospital, which they now searched intently. The hospital staff were questioned, but one female lacked Lucille de Backer's courage and resolve: Hélène Lefèvre betrayed the conspirators. At about 5.30 p.m. there was an urgent bang at the Hiecque's door – '*Les Boches!*' M. Hiecque bundled Bader into the back garden, hiding him in a chicken run. Within a minute the Germans were in the house and seconds later a bayonet was thrust repeatedly into the straw covering the escapee. Realising that the next stab would probably penetrate his neck or back, Bader stood up, raising his hands. As the Germans escorted him out of the front door to a waiting car, he tried to persuade the *Stabsfeldwebel* who had arrested him that the old couple had no knowledge of his presence, his arrival having been during the night and via a back garden gate. It was then that he noticed Hélène Lefèvre leave the German vehicle, and realised that they had all been betrayed.

Bader's escape attempt made life 'very unpleasant' for Adolf Galland. There was an inquiry into the escape and even Bader's visit to Audembert came under scrutiny. Gerhard Schöpfel continues with the German view:

> After Wing Commander Bader received his new legs, we heard that he had escaped by knotting some bed sheets together and climbing out of an upstairs window. For a man with two artificial legs this must have taken incredible guts and willpower. Really, however, in view of the strenuous activity involved, which included hiking over the Pyrenees, he actually had little chance of getting away with it. He was soon found in a house by the canal in St-Omer. Our *Geschwader* was told that on a subsequent train journey into captivity proper, the guards took both his legs away to prevent another audacious escape attempt!

At the end of the month, the 616 Squadron Operations Record Book concluded that August was:

> A disappointing one from the operational point of view owing to the poor weather conditions. Although sixteen offensive sweeps were carried out over France, their effectiveness was in several cases hampered by too much cloud, making it difficult for the squadrons in the Wing to keep together. Wing Commander Bader DSO (and Bar) DFC, and Flight Lieutenant Casson were shot down on 9 August and are now prisoners of war. This was a serious loss to the RAF, the Wing, and the Squadron.

In the overall scheme of things, August 1941 was indeed a disappointing month for Fighter Command: ninety-eight Spitfires and ten Hurricanes were lost. However, JG 2 and JG 26 combined had lost just eighteen pilots, i.e. the loss ratio was exactly a staggering six to one in the *Luftwaffe*'s favour.

Following the loss of its first Wing Leader, the Tangmere Wing itself would never be the same again. 'Johnnie' Johnson:

> When Douglas was shot down it really was his own fault. He was tired, ready for a rest. Leigh-Mallory had asked him to come off Ops, as 'Sailor' Malan, leader of the Hill Wing, had already done, having recognised in himself the signs of strain. Douglas wouldn't go, of course, and so the AOC agreed to let him stay on until the end of what was called the 'season'– the end of September when the weather started failing. Peter Macdonald, our adjutant, a former MP who had served with Douglas in 1940,

also recognised the signs of strain and had insisted that Douglas, Thelma, and he go off on a week's golfing to St Andrews. They were, in fact, booked to go on 11 August. Douglas was tired and irritable; he couldn't see things quickly enough in the air. On the day in question, when Ken Holden sighted the 109s and Bader was unable to see them, he should have let Ken come down and attack as he had suggested. In not allowing this, he lost us six, maybe even seven, seconds, by which time the high 109s were down on us. But of course Douglas was a bit greedy and would not therefore allow this. When I was a Wing Leader later in the war such a situation often arose and it made sense for me, if I couldn't see the enemy, to stay put and cover those who could while they attacked. This is what should have happened.

All of these years later, is it possible, I wonder, to establish from the remaining clues, what or who exactly caused Wing Commander Bader's demise over France that fateful day?

On 9 August 1941, Circus 68 was directed against Gosnay, near Bethune, an oft-visited target lying some twenty miles south-east of St-Omer. The first thing to go wrong for the Tangmere Wing, however, was that as 616 and 610 Squadrons took off and made for the English coast Wing Commander Bader discovered that his Airspeed Indicator was unserviceable. It was accepted practice that any pilot whose aircraft developed a defect should turn back. For example, on 10 July 1941, the 610 Squadron diary records that one of its pilots returned 'after five minutes with a u/s ASI'. For Douglas Bader, however, it was unthinkable that the Wing should go into danger without him. Wing Commander Bader pressed on, therefore, although he handed over the lead to Flight Lieutenant Dundas upon reaching Beachy Head.

By then, Wing Commander Bader's actions had probably contributed to the next problem: 41 Squadron not making the rendezvous. A former 41 Squadron pilot, Ron Rayner, has pointed out that although the squadron had arrived at Merston just two weeks previously, it had already flown many practice sweeps from Catterick and indeed a number over France. The Squadron's CO, Squadron Leader Gaunce DFC, was both an experienced and exceptional fighter pilot and leader. It was also unusual for a squadron not to arrive at its appointed position on time. In this case, however, 616 and 610 Squadrons had taken off from Westhampnett and 41 from Merston, the idea being that the three squadrons would join over Chichester. The likelihood is, however, that as Wing Commander Bader had no ASI, between taking off and handing over to Dundas, he had actually flown too fast for 41 Squadron to catch up. After Wing Commander Bader resumed the lead over France, we have evidence, in fact, that he did indeed fly too fast, as the transcribed radio messages indicate: Squadron Leader Holden asked 'Dogsbody' to 'slow down'. The u/s ASI, coupled with the fact that the Wing Leader did not turn back as he ought, no doubt explains why the Tangmere Wing went into action that day as twenty-four Spitfires instead of thirty-six.

On Circus 68, Fighter Command lost five Spitfires in total: Wing Commander Bader and Flight Lieutenant Casson from the Tangmere Wing, and three from 452 (Australian) Squadron. In addition, 452 Squadron suffered two more aircraft damaged. Two of 452 Squadron's pilots were captured and one was killed. Available information records their attack as having been 'Delivered about 1130 hrs between Mardyck and Bethune, mostly above 20,000 feet but some at 10,000 feet'. Mardyck is virtually part of Dunkirk, Bethune being some thirty miles to the south-east – a lot of sky in which to pinpoint a combat over sixty years later!

Both 315 and 603 Squadrons also suffered one Spitfire damaged each. JG 26 provided the sole German opposition to Circus 68, the *Geschwaderstab* and all three *Gruppen* making contact with the enemy. This represented 100 to 120 Me 109Es and Fs, a substantial force indeed. Consequently, the German pilots made claims for seven Spitfires destroyed, a figure which tallies almost exactly with the actual RAF losses of five Spitfires destroyed and four damaged. The German victory claims were as follows:

Pilot | Victory No. | Unit | Opponent | Time and Location
Oberleutnant J. Schmid | 16 | *Geschwaderstab* | Spitfire | 1125 hrs, 10 km E. of St-Omer
Oberfeldwebel W. Meyer | 11 | 6/JG26 | Spitfire | 1125 hrs, St-Omer
Oberfeldwebel. E. Busch | 6 | 9/JG26 | Spitfire | 1125 hrs, location n/k
Unteroffizier H. Richter | n/k | *Geschwaderstab* | Spitfire | 1130 hrs, N. of Dunkirk
Oberstleutnant A. Galland | 76 | *Geschwaderstab* | Spitfire | 1132 hrs, N.W. of St-Pol
Leutnant. Kosse | 9 | 5/JG26 | Spitfire | 1145 hrs, St-Omer
Hauptmann G. Schöpfel | 31 | *Stab* III/JG26 | Spitfire | 1145 hrs, E. of Marquise

Regarding German losses, it is perhaps worth mentioning that these are sourced from the *Luftwaffe* Quartermaster General's Returns, which were not for propaganda purposes but for internal audit. This original source can therefore be considered to be as complete and accurate as our own records. On the day in question, an Me 109F-2 of III/JG 26 crashed on take-off at Ligescourt, and an FW 190 crash-landed near Le Bourget, the latter incident not believed to be combat-related. The only other losses are as follows:

3/JG 26 | Me 109F-4 (8350) | Crashed near Aire, *Unteroffizier* Albert Schlager killed
II/JG 26 | Me 109E-7 (6494) | Pilot n/k, baled out near Merville

As we have seen, Wing Commander Bader's impression was that he had collided with an enemy aircraft. Certainly, 'Johnnie' Johnson has graphically described the close proximity of the enemy, the maelstrom of fighters being just 'fifty yards apart', but Bader was not lost during these initial seconds of mayhem. Having

95. *Unteroffizier* Walter Meyer of 6/JG 26, who claimed a Spitfire destroyed on 9 August 1941 (Don Caldwell).

96. Wing Commander Bader (with pipe) being entertained by Oberst Galland, Kommodore of JG 26 (seventh left) and his *Geschwaderstab*. Also present are *Oberleutnant* Schöpfel (fourth left, wearing forage cap), and to his left is *Leutnant* Johan Schmid – who shot down and killed the British ace Flight Lieutenant Eric 'Sawn Off' Lock DSO DFC. A topic of conversation was who had shot Bader down, but Galland was unable to confirm this.

levelled out from the diving charge, Bader then went off alone, stalking a section of Me 109s. Again he had broken the rules. Frank Twitchett of 145 Squadron once explained to me: 'If separated over France, the only sensible thing to do was get down on the deck and get home fast.'

When repatriated in 1945, Wing Commander Bader reported that after his subsequent attack, during which he set a 109 alight rear of the cockpit: 'In turning away right-handed from this, I collided with an Me 109 which took my tail off. It appeared as far up as the radio mast but was actually only the empennage.' However, in a letter dated 5 August 1981, Group Captain Sir Douglas Bader wrote: 'My impression was that I turned across a 109 and that it collided with the back of my Spitfire, removing the tail. On the other hand, if the pilot of the Me 109 had fired his guns at that moment he could have blown my tail off. The result would have been the same.' The crucial question that must therefore be asked is did Wing Commander Bader collide with an Me 109 or was he actually shot down? None of Galland's pilots had been involved in a collision, however, so the only candidate for such an occurrence was JG 26's single fatality *Unteroffizier* Albert Schlager whose aircraft crashed near Aire-sur-la-Lys. The evidence, however, suggests that *Unteroffizier* Schlager was not involved in a collision, but actually shot down by Pilot Officer 'Nip' Hepple, whose combat report states:

I was Yellow 3 when 616 Squadron took off from Westhampnett at 1040 hrs. Shortly after crossing the French coast south of Boulogne the Squadron went into a left-hand orbit. After a few minutes, about twenty Me 109Fs were seen to the east of us and several thousand feet below, climbing up over white cloud. Wing Commander Bader into attack in a steep dive, when I got down to their level the E/A had split up.

I climbed up to the right and saw an Me 109F come up in front of me. He appeared to be on the top of a stall turn and so I gave him a long burst, closing to point-blank range. I saw on the side of his a/c, as he turned to the left, a large '6' just behind the cross on the fuselage. He then went into a very slow gliding turn to the left and I had a vivid view of his hood flying off and the pilot jumping out of his machine. I watched him falling and turning over and over until he had dropped down to some low white cloud; his parachute had still not opened so I assume he was killed. This a/c is claimed as destroyed.

The camouflage was a dirty grey and black, in addition to the usual cross there was a '6' behind it. The tail was painted orange and the spinner black and white. I was flying an aircraft with 'Watford' and its coat of arms marked on it.

To assist recognition in the air, German fighters were specifically marked on the fuselage with either a thick horizontal or wavy line adjacent to the black cross. In the case of I *Gruppe*, however, no such marking was carried, and Schlager's 109F was of I/JG 26's 3rd *Staffel*. Hepple remarks on the number six painted on the fuselage, but makes no mention of any line marking, which would have been highly visible. Hepple's reference to an 'orange' tail was more likely red, and specifically the vertical rudder. Unfortunately, we do not know what identifying colour 3/JG 26 used at this time, which could assist with identifying Hepple's victim, and nor are we aware of what individual number Schlager's aircraft was. The German pilot, however, baled out, and Hepple makes no reference to seeing a parachute open: Schlager's parachute failed to open and he died as a result. It is reasonable, I believe, to credit Schlager's demise to Hepple's guns, and not a collision with Wing Commander Bader. Moreover, and conclusively, in recent times, enthusiasts excavated the crash site of Schlager's 109, recovering the tail wheel assembly. This proves that Schlager's aircraft did not lose its tail unit, as did Wing Commander Bader's Spitfire.

The only other 109 down that day was at Merville, some fourteen miles south-east of Blaringhem, a distance in itself not altogether ruling out this aircraft as a collision contender. However, the pilot baled out safely and must have subsequently reported on the incident, details of which presumably did not include a collision. The 452 Squadron's pilots also claimed two Me 109Es destroyed in their fight, so the enemy fighter of that type down at Merville was most likely one of them – Flight Lieutenant Brendan 'Paddy' Finucane DFC claimed an Me 109E in the 'Gosnay-Bethune area', and Flight Lieutenant 'Bluey' Truscott a 'E', his first-ever combat claim, between 'Mardyck [and] Bethune'.

Bader himself conceded that he did not see the Me 109 which he thought he had struck, a collision being just his 'impression' of the destructive forces acting upon his Spitfire at that time. The same effect could have been achieved had the Spitfire been hit by 20 mm cannon shells. If Wing Commander Bader was actually shot down, though, who was responsible?

Looking at the table of German combat claims, and bearing in mind that 'Dogsbody', although not lost in the initial charge, was nevertheless hacked down within the opening few minutes of the engagement, only one claim stands out: that of *Oberfeldwebel* Walter Meyer of 6/JG 26, who claimed his eleventh victory over St-Omer at 1125 hrs. However, that Meyer was Bader's victor is a theory slightly diluted by the claim for a Spitfire destroyed at the same time but at an unknown location by 9/JG 26's *Oberfeldwebel* Busch. Aircraft 9/JG 26 was a part of *Hauptmann* Schöpfel's III *Gruppe* which, according to the *Kommandeur*'s account, had actually intercepted the 'beehive' proper and therefore some minutes after the initial skirmish in question. It appears unlikely, however, that Busch's claim relates to the same engagement in which Wing Commander Bader was lost.

When researching Douglas Bader's biography, his brother-in-law, Wing Commander 'Laddie' Lucas, working with Henry Probert, the then head of the MOD's Air Historical Branch (AHB), examined the German claims and was sufficiently satisfied with the timing of Mayer's claim to conclude that he was responsible. Although making a connection between Bader and Mayer, Lucas wrongly referred in print, in his *Flying Colours: The Epic Story of Douglas Bader*, to 'Max Mayer'. Lucas and Probert also wrongly assumed that Flight Lieutenant Casson had been shot down in the same area as Wing Commander Bader. Thus they decided that *Leutnant* Kosse, who claimed a Spitfire over St-Omer at 1145 hrs, had shot down Buck Casson. In reality, again as we have already seen, Flight Lieutenant Casson was shot down by *Hauptmann* Schöpfel, who even had a photograph taken of the downed Spitfire. Those who have previously attributed Casson's loss to Kosse, however, have not approached Squadron Leader Casson for his account, but have merely assumed that he was shot down in the action over St-Omer. Buck was actually shot down some minutes *after* the Tangmere Wing's original skirmish over St-Omer and while heading back towards the French coast. This connects Casson's loss with Schöpfel's claim timed at 1145 hrs over Marquise, near the French coast.

Regarding *Leutnant* Kosse's claim, it is unlikely, in fact, that this pilot even fought the Tangmere Wing. The Tangmere Spitfires, as the Target Support Wing, were first to arrive over the target area. Kosse recorded that his combat had occurred at 1145 hrs, some twenty minutes after the initial 'bounce' during which *Oberfeldwebel* Meyer destroyed a Spitfire at 1125 hrs. A time lapse of twenty minutes therefore represents a long interval considering the speed at which these fighter aircraft flew. By 1145 hrs, the Tangmere Wing was re-crossing the French coast, this being confirmed by the fact that Buck Casson was shot down near Marquise, just three miles from the coast at exactly that time. As *Hauptmann* Schöpfel went to some trouble to obtain evidence for his victory report, such as even flying low over the crashed Spitfire to record its code letters, we can, I think, accept his timing as accurate. In view of these times, and the fact that the Tangmere Wing was heading home at 1145 hrs, I believe that *Leutnant* Kosse actually engaged Spitfires of 452 Squadron.

While *Oberfeldwebel* Walter Meyer's claim *might* fit, the fact that a claim has been made is inconclusive in any case. As we have seen, the Germans only lost two Me 109s that day, Schlager who was killed at Aire, and an unidentified pilot who baled out near Merville. The Spitfire squadrons engaged, however, claimed a staggering twenty-two Me 109s destroyed, ten probables, and a further eight damaged! In *Flying Colours*, Lucas concluded that the German losses tallied fairly closely to the Tangmere Wing's claims of five Me 109s destroyed, and two probables, but he did not take into account that JG 26 was the only *Jagdgeschwader* to suffer losses, and then offset these statistics against all of Fighter Command's claims that day. Clearly, a rigorous analysis puts a totally different complexion on the matter: the Spitfire pilots over claimed by at least ten to one!

In respect of German combat claims, today we have for each reference only the most basic of details, such as the pilot's name, type of enemy aircraft claimed, location, date, and time. Unfortunately, the majority of German pilots' personal combat reports have not survived. Therefore, with merely 'Spitfire destroyed, 1125 hrs, St-Omer', it is impossible to conclude with certainty that *Oberfeldwebel*

Mayer shot down Wing Commander Bader. Whatever the accuracy of Meyer's claim, however, I would again refer to Adolf Galland's statement 'it was never confirmed who shot down Douglas Bader'. Shooting the tail, or much of it, off a Spitfire is fairly significant damage to observe; if Bader was shot down by a JG 26 pilot, why were their reports inconclusive? In a letter to me dated 19 February 1996, Lucas summed up the situation perfectly:

> When having dinner at Douglas Bader's house in the country, Adolf Galland told me categorically that DB had been shot down over the Pas-de-Calais in 1941. Galland stated that there had not been a collision. I can say in fact that, in my own humble experience, receiving a volley or two of cannon shells from an Me 109 could certainly sound like a collision with a London bus! I put this view to Douglas, who responded: 'In that case, old cock, because it was *me*, why didn't they have the bugger responsible goose-stepping down the *Under-den-Linden?*'

Having fully researched and considered all of the available evidence from both sides, I can now offer another suggestion.

On 9 August 1941, Flight Lieutenant Buck Casson was also captured. He therefore did not return to Tangmere to report on the incident. However, in 1945, at Douglas Bader's request, Buck wrote to his former Wing Leader regarding his own experiences of that fateful day. The account in question has already been reproduced in full earlier in this chapter, but I would particularly draw to the reader's attention the following extract: '[A]fter having a squirt at two 109s flying together [I] left them for a single one which was flying inland alone. I finished nearly all of my cannon ammunition up on this boy, who finally baled out at 6,000 feet, having lost most of his tail unit.' Who did Buck Casson shoot down?

We know that JG 26 lost but one Me 109 in this engagement, and that Schlager crashed at Aire was confirmed by the discovery of an identification plate when that crash site was excavated in 2003. A tail wheel was also recovered, proving that the tail section of that aircraft was still very much attached upon impact. Buck could not, therefore, have shot Schlager down. Neither do I believe that Buck shot down the Me 109E lost by II/JG 26, the pilot of which is known to have baled out, as Merville is just too far away to be relevant.

What cannot be discounted, however, is that the circumstances described by Buck Casson are exactly those which are known to have befallen Wing Commander Bader, i.e. that his tail unit was badly damaged and he baled out at about 6,000 feet. One might ask why Douglas Bader himself did not question this when Buck wrote to him in 1945, but at that time the pilots concerned no doubt considered that they had been involved in a hectic dogfight with the aircraft of both sides being shot down all around; certainly this is reflected by the RAF's gross over-claiming on the day in question. Had Buck ever submitted an official report, which would have been made available to the general public

97. A Spitfire Mk V under fire from *Oberleutnant* Schöpfel on 27 June 1941.

98. An Me 109F taking fire – its curvaceous lines and similarity to the Spitfire are obvious.

during the 1970s, perhaps another aviation detective would have suggested that these events be linked, or maybe the connection would have been made on the actual day in question? That Wing Commander Bader was the victim of 'friendly fire' would certainly explain why the German combat reports were so inconclusive. Furthermore, as the pilot possibly responsible had absolutely no idea himself of what had happened, and indeed was also captured that day, these two factors could also help explain the mystery.

In recent years, the public has become accustomed to 'friendly fire', such tragedies now being known to have occurred on countless occasions. In fact, such situations were far more prevalent during the Second World War than most people are aware. The so-called 'Battle of Barking Creek' of 6 September 1939, when Hurricanes and Spitfires fought each other over the Thames Estuary, is an oft-quoted example, but of course just three days into the war pilots lacked experience so such unfortunate mishaps were inevitable. By the end of the Battle of Britain, however, no fewer than twenty front-line British fighters, bombers, and transports (but mainly Spitfires, Hurricanes, and Blenheims) had been mistakenly shot down by 'friendly' anti-aircraft fire and a further nine had been accidentally shot down by RAF fighter pilots. At the time, such information was suppressed, but the loss of what statistically amounted to nearly two squadrons of aircraft to 'friendly fire' could not be ignored.

While gathering material for a Spitfire-related day of lectures, I obtained several reels of hitherto unpublished and random cine-gun film from the Imperial War Museum. Surprisingly, several incidents of 'friendly fire' were discovered. For example, on 7 July 1940 Sergeant Franklin of 65 Squadron reported having attacked an 'Me 109', but the camera footage clearly shows that his target was another Spitfire. On 26 September 1940, 609 Squadron's Sergeant Alan Feary engaged an He 111, but also had a determined squirt at a Hurricane, which took evasive action. On 27 September 1941, Sergeant Wright of 611 Squadron the Hornchurch Wing flying in support of Circus 103b, subsequently reported that:

> I was flying as Red 4 in Ground Control Broadhurst's Section of 611 Squadron at 16,000 feet, and after crossing the French coast I saw two Me 109s at 500 yards to port, about 400–500 feet below. I turned and dived to attack, giving him a quick burst of about two sec., after which he turned on his back and went down in a steep dive. I followed and gave him another 3–4-second burst, seeing him hit and apparently out of control. While I was still diving I looked to my rear and saw another aircraft diving on me. I pulled out of the dive and turned, but in doing so I lost sight of the plane I was attacking, and also the plane that was diving on me. My height was 4,000–5,000 feet, so I dived to 100 feet and returned home.

The camera-gun footage proves conclusively that Wright determinedly attacked at least one other Spitfire, not the 'Me 109E' claimed probably destroyed.

Veteran wartime fighter pilots agree that in the heat and confusion of fighter-to-fighter combat such mistakes did happen, as indeed are confirmed by the several foregoing examples and statistics. Aircraft recognition in combat was sometimes demonstrably questionable. During 1940, for example, RAF fighter pilots frequently reported combat with 'He 113s': on 5 November 1940, Flight Sergeant George 'Grumpy' Unwin DFM being credited with the 'first of this type shot down by Duxford'. We now know, however, that the He 113 was merely a propaganda ruse by the Germans, as the type never actually entered service – Unwin's adversary was in fact more likely a JG 26 Me 109. With even more frequency, the identities of German bombers engaged by Spitfire and Hurricane pilots were incorrectly reported. On 30 September 1940, the last great daylight battle of the Battle of Britain took place when a large force of KG 55 He IIIs, escorted by both Me 109s and 110s, were briefed to attack Westland Aircraft at Yeovil (see *Angriff Westland: Three Battle of Britain Air Raids 'Through the Looking Glass'*, by this author (Ramrod Publications, 1994)). However, a number of intercepting RAF fighter pilots that day incorrectly identified the German bombers in their combat reports, among them such experienced men as Squadron Leader Herbert Pinfold, 56 Squadron's CO, who reported, 'God knows how many Do 215s' and Flight Lieutenant Ian 'Widge' Gleed DFC, a flight commander in 87 Squadron, who wrote of '70 Ju 88s'.

We know that on 9 August 1941, the Tangmere Wing fought Me 109Fs. The '*Franz*' entered service in early 1941 and, unlike its angular '*Emil*' predecessor, with its square wing-tips, had rounded, smooth lines and no tail struts. In a split 'd', as an image jockeyed into the reflector ring, it would have been easy to mistake. On 17 May 1941, 616 Squadron's Sergeant Morton mistook Me 109Fs for Spitfires, an error which could have cost him his life. Furthermore, the difficulty making split-second decisions in combat is emphasised by the following entry in Squadron Leader Burton's logbook, written on 21 July 1941: 'Should have shot an Me 109, but failed to open fire until too late owing to uncertainty of identification.'

So, back in 1995, I put the evidence, such as it is, to key survivors of the Tangmere Wing's engagement fought over St-Omer on 9 August 1941. Air Vice-Marshal 'Johnnie' Johnson: 'I would be very surprised if an experienced and *careful* fighter pilot such as Buck Casson would make such a mistake, but do agree from his description of events that he has almost certainly seen DB come down.' Group Captain Sir Hugh Dundas: 'Nothing is certain, nor ever will be.' Air Marshal Sir Denis Crowley-Milling: 'Absolute rubbish!' At 'Johnnie' Johnson's insistence, I did put the matter to Buck Casson, whose view was clear: 'I was an experienced fighter pilot and well knew what a 109 looked like. I shot down a 109 that day.'

Having flown throughout the Battle of Britain and during that long summer of offensive operations in 1941, Buck most certainly would have seen many Me 109s. Indeed, he had shared one destroyed on 22 June 1941 and probably

99. Pilot Officer Hugh 'Cocky' Dundas at Tangmere in 1941, who, as Sir Hugh Dundas, in 1995 'urged' Dilip Sarkar not to make public his discovery that Wing Commander Bader had been the victim of 'friendly fire'.

destroyed another on 19 July. But if his trigger finger did make a mistake in the great confusion and heat of the moment, it was perfectly understandable, not least given the prevalent chaos and similarities in appearance between the Spitfire and Me 109F.

In 1996, my *Bader's Tangmere Spitfires* was published but I decided against including any reference to my belief that Buck accidentally shot down Douglas Bader. At the time our search for Bader's Spitfire was causing immense media interest and there was no doubt that if this story was released then a host of journalists would descend upon the elderly and infirm Cassons. Moreover, it was unethical, I felt, to publish the story and cause Buck any upset given that it had only come out due to his kindness in providing me a copy of his private correspondence with Douglas Bader. At the time this story would undoubtedly have whipped the press into a frenzy, and I could probably have named my price, but integrity and the feelings of two dear friends, Buck and 'Dorfy' Casson, meant far more to me than fame and fortune. Indeed, I took respected author and former fast-jet pilot Air Commodore Graham Pitchfork into my confidence at that time, so he at least is aware of the timing of my discovery and how tortuous the whole thing became.

No matter how hard you try, however, it is impossible to keep a story like this secure indefinitely. Sadly, Squadron Leader Casson died in 2003, and it was not long before the vultures were out to publish the story. Early in 2004, I was contacted by a magazine publisher who asked for my co-operation with regard to releasing the story. Apparently another researcher, whom I knew and had discussed the matter with on several occasions, was claiming the story as his own and intending to publish in both the historical journal in question and a British national newspaper. As poor old Buck was barely cold and Dorfy still alive to be harassed by the media, I was appalled and refused the offer of involvement. Unfortunately, those concerned took no heed of my arguments against publishing the story at that time, and so an uninformed version appeared in both the magazine in question and a Sunday newspaper. For some reason, however, the 'revelation' failed to excite the popular press, as had so clearly been intended. The matter largely passed unnoticed, much to our relief in considering the potentially adverse effect such a trial could have had upon Mrs Casson's health.

In trying to achieve sensationalism, the published story suggested that Douglas Bader and Buck Casson were aware of what had happened, and that the latter had been virtually excommunicated as a result. This, I can assure the reader, is complete nonsense. The 'evidence' put forward to support this theory is that Buck was not mentioned in either the book *Reach for the Sky* or the feature film of the same name, and nor was he a guest in Douglas Bader's appearance in the television series 'This is Your Life'. First, very few pilots are actually mentioned by name in *Reach for the Sky*, so that is no argument whatsoever. Secondly, with regard to the television programme, the guest list was limited, and there were many other people more pivotal to Douglas Bader's story than Buck Casson. The fact is that after the war Bader and Casson regularly played golf together, and Group Captain Bader even opened the Sheffield ATC Wing HQ, of which Buck was commodore. So, the unremarkable reality is that Bader and Casson were not, in fact, estranged in any way.

I would also add that I had known Buck Casson, Sir Hugh Dundas, Sir Denis Crowley-Milling, and 'Johnnie' Johnson for over ten years before discussing with them my 'friendly fire' theory. I was an experienced and professional investigative police officer, so have no doubt that had any of these men been hiding something then I would have known – instinctively and immediately. Moreover, if Buck Casson had had something to hide he would hardly have furnished me with a copy of the letter in question and permission to publish it, for all to see, and which I did in *The Invisible Thread* (1992), *A Few of the Many* (1995), and *Bader's Tangmere Spitfires* (1996). To suggest that there was some kind of cover-up or conspiracy is absolute fantasy.

It is also worth reporting how, back in 1981, the tale took on yet another twist. In *Flying Colours*, Lucas wrote that in March 1981, Sir Douglas Bader opened the Schofield Air Show, Sydney, where, by chance, he was introduced to former *Luftwaffe* fighter pilot, 'Max Mayer'. The pair exchanged pleasantries, but no more. The following day Bader was apparently astonished to read in the press an article based upon an interview which Mayer had given a journalist after his meeting with Sir Douglas in which he claimed to have shot down the Tangmere Wing Leader. Lucas, having researched to some extent the German records, assumed that this was actually *Oberfeldwebel* Walter Meyer (note the difference in spelling of the surname), who claimed the destruction of a Spitfire over St-Omer at 1125 hrs on the day in question. What Lucas did not know was what had happened to *Oberfeldwebel* Meyer: he died in 1943! On 11 October 1942, Meyer collided with his *Rottenflieger*, crashed, and ended up in hospital. He did not recover, dying of tuberculosis in January 1943.

Another Bader book, using Lucas's biography as a principal source, accepted the information that *Mayer* had shot down Bader. This account also claimed that the 'Australian Fighter Mafia' had unsuccessfully attempted to trace Mayer. Why there should have been any difficulty, I cannot understand.

So who was 'Max Mayer'? Having contacted the Sydney *Daily Telegraph–Mirror* in 1995, I received a copy of the article in question, written by a C. J. McKenzie. Mayer claimed to have shot Bader down with 'one cannon burst, which ripped away the tail of Bader's Spitfire'. Mayer continued, 'I saw him spiralling down, I saw his face. I followed him down because I had to confirm the kill. When I saw his parachute coming up I turned away. I reported where he had crashed.' McKenzie was advised, by one of Bader's entourage, not to 'bring that up or you'll get an argument'. Mayer claimed that it was the second time he and Bader had shaken hands, the first having been in the *Clinique Sterin* in St-Omer: 'He was surprised when he found out it was me. He was a Wing

Commander. I was a mere *Leutnant*. He was very warm towards me and we shook hands strongly.'

Already it was possible to identify major inaccuracies in Max Mayer's story, not withstanding of course that Walter Meyer had died in 1943! First, it would be *impossible*, of course, to identify a pilot's face in the circumstances discussed. Secondly, Mayer gives the impression that at the time, so far as the Germans were concerned, his claim was accepted. Refer again to Adolf Galland: 'It was never confirmed who shot down Douglas Bader.' Furthermore, whereas Mayer claims to have been a *Leutnant*, Walter Meyer was an NCO. Incidentally, *Leutnant* Kosse, the JG 26 pilot *possibly* introduced to Bader, did not survive, having been killed late in the war with an RVT unit.

In C. J. McKenzie's article, Martin Maxwell Mayer also claimed to have destroyed thirty-four enemy aircraft, a tally including victories not only on the *Kanalfront*, but also over Russia and North Africa. Such a score had, he stated, won him the coveted Knight's Cross. Anyone checking the list of fighter pilots who were *Ritterkreuztrager* would discover no reference to a Martin Max Mayer. *Oberstleutnant* Egon Mayer received both the Knight's Cross and Oak Leaves, but was killed in action on 2 March 1944. *Hauptmann* Hans-Karl Mayer received his Knight's Cross on 3 September 1940, but was lost over the Channel on 17 October 1940. *Leutnant* Wilhelm Mayer's Knight's Cross was awarded in March 1945, by which time he was already dead, having been killed by Spitfires on 4 January 1945. *Leutnant* Eduard Meyer's 'throat ache' was cured in 1941, but the following year he collided with a comrade over Russia and was also killed. No *Ritterkreuztrager* of spelling 'Mayer' or 'Meyer' therefore survived the war.

After the Second World War, Martin Maxwell Mayer claimed to have flown with the French Air Force in Algiers, but my friend and colleague Professor Bernard-Marie Dupont, himself a former French army officer, confirms that there is no record of such a pilot, a non-French national, having flown with the French Air Force.

Kerry Taylor of the Sydney *Daily Telegraph–Mirror* was able to put me in contact with C. J. McKenzie himself, now retired. In a letter to myself dated 31 August 1995, 'C. J.' enclosed a copy of a letter from Sir Douglas Bader, then aged 71, to Max Mayer dated 5 August 1981:

Dear Max Mayer
You will recall that we met on Saturday, 28 March at the Schofield Air Show near Sydney. We were both pleased to meet each other because we were ex-fighter pilots (on opposite sides) and we had an agreeable conversation for some minutes.

The next morning, 29 March, I read an article in one of the newspapers quoting an interview with you, during the course of which you said that you had shot me down over France on 9 August 1941 and had followed me down until you saw me bale out. Having read that, I was hoping to see you that day so that we could discuss it. None of us could find you on Sunday. We tried on the Monday to contact you, but were unsuccessful. Then I left to go elsewhere in Australia. Dolfo Galland, who commanded JG 26, has become a great friend of mine since the war. He cannot tell me about the incident on 9 August 1941.

My impression was that I turned across an Me 109 and that it collided with the back of my Spitfire, removing the tail. On the other hand, if the pilot of the Me 109 had fired his guns at that moment, he could have blown my tail off. The result would have been the same.

Please write and tell me your account of this incident, if you can remember it. You told the Australian press that you followed my Spitfire down until you saw me bale out. I imagine you knew it was me because you saw, when I baled out, that one leg was missing. I know that you had lived in Australia for twenty-five years but cannot think why you did not tell me all this when we talked to each other on 28 March. We could have had a tremendous laugh about it and really enjoyed it.

I shall greatly look forward to hearing from you.

Best wishes

Yours sincerely

DOUGLAS BADER

My letter from C. J. McKenzie was also interesting:

Dear Dilip

I enclose a copy of a letter Bader wrote to Max Mayer, dated 5 August 1981, which you might find interesting. I must say that he has put more 'spin' on his meeting with Mayer than Shane Warne puts on a 'leggie'! Bader met Mayer at Mascot Airport (our Sydney Kingsford Smith International) not at the Schofields Air Show. It had taken me sometime to tee-up the meeting and Bader knew precisely who he was meeting and why. I introduced Mayer in those terms. He knew also why I was there, why the photographer was there, yet he seems to express surprise at the story of 29 March.

He says, after reading the story, 'I was hoping to see you that day so we could discuss it.' What day does he mean? And discuss what? He says further that he tried to find Mayer on the Sunday and Monday. He had only to phone the *Sunday Telegraph* to have been put in contact with Mayer.

The meeting between the two was brief, not as Bader says 'an agreeable conversation for some minutes'. Indeed, I was embarrassed by Bader's attitude. It is not always easy in words to give the right tone to something said. Bader's use of the word 'Kraut', instead of German, surprised me. The way he said it was, in my view, intended to be insulting or at least denigrating. Max Mayer died some years ago.

I hope that some of this might be of interest to you and wish you well with your project.

I remain. etc.

C. J. McKENZIE

As Kerry Taylor said, 'the weaving of the web becomes even more intriguing! There is no doubt, however, that Martin Maxwell Mayer was certainly not the man he claimed to be, nor indeed the man who shot down Douglas Bader. Lady Bader (Sir Douglas's second wife whom he married in 1973 following Thelma's death two years previously) had no knowledge of any response from Mayer to her late husband's letter. Had Sir Douglas been aware that he had been shot down by another Spitfire pilot why would he have written in such terms to 'Max Mayer'?

On 9 August 1941, Wing Commander Bader was flying a presentation Spitfire, 'Lord Lloyd I', W3185, a Mk VA armed with eight Browning machine-guns (not 20 mm cannon). The crash site of that aircraft might just provide clues to complete this jigsaw, and this we set out to discover back in 1996. Bernard-Marie Dupont made enquiries in the St-Omer area and talked to a local historian of the wartime generation, Georges Goblet, who claimed to know where W3185 crashed. His friend, Arthur Dubreu, had even seen the legless pilot land by parachute, he claimed. I lost no time in getting across the Channel and met the two Frenchman. Arthur told me that:

I was thirteen years old at the time, living in Steenbecque, and remember the incident vividly. I saw a lot of planes; it was mid-morning on a sunny day. There was a big dogfight and many contrails in the sky. I saw an aircraft coming down very fast and then a parachute opened. The aircraft crashed in a field and a cloud of black smoke and debris rose over the site. Due to the wind the parachute drifted slightly. It was the first parachute I had ever seen, in fact, so I remember it very well. I wanted to see the pilot, so I ran after the rapidly descending canopy. The parachute seemed to land very fast, but the pilot hit some trees in an orchard which took the shock. The pilot was just sitting there, silk billowing around him. I was horrified to see that he only had one leg, which was twisted at an unnatural angle. There was no blood and, although he seemed to be stunned from the landing, he did not appear otherwise concerned about his legs. I could not understand it at all. I was the first on the scene but before I could help a German officer ran into the field, took charge, and told me to clear off, which I did as I was very frightened of the soldiers. The Germans then carried the pilot to their waiting car and I went straight away to see the aircraft's crash site, a crater in a field. It was only after the war, when *Reach for the Sky* was published in French, that I realised who I had seen.

Georges Goblet:

I was eleven years old, living in Blaringhem, and with other boys from my village I went to the Spitfire crash site that afternoon. There was a large crater, smoke still rose through the soil, and the ground remained warm. The wings had been detached and lay in another field. It was about twenty years after the war, while conducting my own research into local matters, that I too realised whose Spitfire this was.

100. Dr Bernard-Marie Dupont (right) at the crash site of what both Arthur Dubreu (left) and Georges Goblet believed was that of Wing Commander Bader's W3185.

101. Arthur Dubreu points out where he saw the legless pilot land by parachute all those years ago.

The Spitfire, Georges said, crashed at Blaringhem, some 10 km south-east of St-Omer, Steenbecque being nearby. Circus 68 was a raid against the power station at Gosnay, 25 km south-east of St-Omer. Circumstantially, the area seemed a good start. The Frenchmen took us to both the orchard where Arthur saw the parachutist and to the field where the Spitfire crashed. At the latter location we found various pieces of mangled aircraft, including an oval bracket bearing a long number prefixed by '300': this was a Spitfire! Moreover, the bracket was stamped '6S', meaning that the part was built at Woolston and not Castle Bromwich, which also appeared significant: W3185 was a Mk VA built at Woolston, whereas the Tangmere Wing's other Spitfires were Mk VBs, the majority of which were built at Castle Bromwich.

Circumstantially, we had certainly found a promising site, but unfortunately the news accidentally got out before our excavation. Needless to say the media grossly exaggerated the story, it being declared to all and sundry that we had actually found Bader's Spitfire when we had said no such thing! One British newspaper, the *Independent*, did quote me accurately when I said that aviation archaeology was like going fishing: until you had been you didn't know what you would catch. On that basis, I made it clear that we could not confirm the aircraft's identity before the recovery and that even then it may prove impossible.

For some reason the world's media leapt on the story, continually harassing and misquoting me. *The Times* agreed to sponsor our excavation, the deal being struck hinging not on this being Bader's Spitfire but on our sponsors having

102. The excavation underway.

103. The excavation was a great success given that a substantial amount of Spitfire was recovered, including its Merlin engine – but this proved not to be W3185 but a Mk IX.

104. Items recovered from the site included the pilot's head, seat, and fuel tank armour plate, both compressed air bottles and the pilot's oxygen supply bottle.

exclusive rights to the recovery. So it was that our team went to France and excavated the site on 4 May 1996.

The afternoon before the recovery, however, in pouring rain and appalling Flemish mud, we pinpointed the bulk of wreckage using a proton magnetometer. During this survey we found the remains of an exploded 20 mm ball round. Examination confirmed this to be British ammunition: Bader's aircraft was not armed with cannons, and so we knew that this was not W3185, even before turning a spade. Soon after the excavation started a metal propeller blade was found together with an airscrew hub engineered to accommodate four such blades. We knew then that it was definitely not W3185, which had a three-bladed airscrew, and suspected our find to be a Mk IX that had crashed some time after 1941. Our concern increased when a wristwatch was found, but fortunately no human remains came to light, not that we were contravening any continental legislation, but such a discovery would have provided the media with a sensation. A massive amount of Spitfire was recovered, including the Merlin engine, but very few cockpit items. Naturally, we were all extremely disappointed that the aircraft recovered was not W3185, the question now being which Spitfire was it?

Team-member and author John Foreman, our expert on losses and claims, worked out a shortlist of sixty-seven possible Spitfire casualties that could be our Spitfire. Eventually it was ascertained that we had found LZ996, a Mk IX of the Canadian 421 Squadron, shot down on 17 June 1943. The pilot, Squadron Leader Phil Archer DFC, had only been promoted to command the Squadron that very day. During the afternoon, 421 Squadron had participated in a Kenley Wing sweep, coincidentally led by Wing Commander 'Johnnie' Johnson, over southern Belgium. Over Ypres the Spitfires engaged FW 190s of III/JG 26, chasing them south to St-Omer. During the running battle, *Oberleutnant* Horst Sternberg, *Staffelkapitän* of 5/JG 26, shot down Flying Officer J. E. McNamara of 421 Squadron, but was shot down himself by Squadron Leader Archer. This success was short lived: seconds later 421's new CO was shot down by *Unteroffizier* Paul Schwarz of 6/JG 26, 10 km south-east of St-Omer. We found Phil Archer's grave in the war cemetery at Longuenesse, his headstone being incorrectly inscribed 'Air Gunner/Instructor'. We immediately contacted the CWGC which corrected the error by engraving the word 'Pilot'. At that time we also found an eyewitness, Monsieur Queurleu, who told us that the victorious German pilot had visited the LZ996 crash site, from which the pilot's body was removed together with a quantity of wreckage, thus explaining why we found no human remains or many cockpit parts. This was, however, Paul Schwarz's only aerial victory: he was killed in a flying accident in 1944.

So, we had the answer regarding which Spitfire we had found, but, as is always the case with historical research, even more questions arose! First, we remained convinced that Arthur Dubreu really had seen Douglas Bader's parachute descent, but over the years, possibly fuelled by wishful thinking, their memories

105. *Oberleutnant* Horst Sternberg of 5/JG 26, who shot down Spitfire LZ996 on 17 June 1943 (Don Caldwell).

Above: 106. The pilot of LZ996 was Squadron Leader Phil Archer DFC, who had only been promoted to command 421 Squadron on the day he was killed in action.

Right: 107. Squadron Leader Phil Archer's grave was found in nearby Longueness cemetery at St-Omer. The headstone, however, incorrectly recorded him as an 'Air Gunner/Instructor'. Dilip Sarkar alerted the CWGC, providing documentary evidence confirming that Archer was, in fact, a pilot and the error was rapidly corrected.

108. The Spitfire recovered was identified by John Foreman as LZ996 – a photograph of which was coincidentally found in the album of Air Vice-Marshal 'Johnnie' Johnson. The Spitfire is seen here with Canadian pilots of the Kenley Wing in 1943.

had become confused, incorrectly linking the LZ996 crash, which happened nearly two years later, with the same incident. As a former police detective I know only too well how notoriously unreliable eyewitness evidence can be, and we must bear in mind that we are dealing here with the memories of over half a century ago.

The oval plate stamped 'AB6S170782' transpired to be a 'red herring'. LZ996 was built at Castle Bromwich but that particular part, a flap mechanism component, was built at Woolston; how unlucky can you get? Well, unluckier than even that, it later transpired: another expedition to recover the 'Bader Spitfire', like us, found a Spitfire, this one containing a flying helmet inscribed with the initials 'DB'. The trouble was that it stood not for 'Douglas Bader' but 'Don Bostock'!

The big question for us, of course, back in 1996, was still 'where is Bader's Spitfire'? The discovery of LZ996 stimulated widespread media coverage in France and Belgium, and both Bernard and I agreed that if anyone knew where the site was they would come forward. Sure enough, two French aviation archaeologists soon contacted me, claiming to have found the W3185 crash site at the Mont Dupil Farm at Basse-Rue, near Racquinghem, just three miles away from Blaringhem and, according to my former SAS police colleague, within the required radius of where Bader landed by parachute at Boesinghem. The Frenchmen told us that the farmer dated the Mont Dupil crash as 1941, and a newspaper article in January 1945 referred to the crash, confirming that the pilot had landed by parachute at Boesinghem. On 3 August 1996, I examined the site but could find absolutely no trace of a crashed aircraft whatsoever, and our investigation was thorough. At the time I was working as a consultant for Twenty Twenty Television on their Channel 4 'Secret Life' documentary about Sir Douglas Bader, and the director provided a mechanical digger and other resources to assist us. We were soon agreed, however, that nothing remained at the site and we returned to England.

Given the circumstances of W3185's demise, and our experience in recovering the remains of crashed Spitfires, I remain of the opinion that this Spitfire would have either gone in or at least made a reasonable impression in the French sod. Without a tail it would certainly not have fluttered down and gently alighted in France, leaving no trace. The farmer at Mont Dupil told us that the aircraft there was tail-less but otherwise intact. I do not, therefore, believe this to be Bader's crash site, and never have.

Another interesting thing is that the RAF Museum has on display at Hendon a clock, allegedly from the instrument panel of W3185 and removed as a souvenir by a *Hauptmann* Rudolf Ortmann. The Director, Dr Michael Fopp, had been presented with the artefact by the late Rudlof Ortmann's son in 1984. The clock, however, is intact, even the glass! We have recovered clocks from several Spitfires, none of which crashed from as high an altitude as W3185 but all of which were badly mangled. Given the circumstances of Bader's crash, I just cannot accept that this pristine item, therefore, is from W3185. More likely it is from a Spitfire that made a controlled forced landing in enemy territory and represents, therefore, more wishful thinking so far as W3185 is concerned.

In 2005, Wildfire Television commissioned me as a programme consultant for 'The Search for Bader's Spitfire', a documentary to be broadcast by Channel 4 in September 2006. As the 'friendly fire' theory had already been publicised by someone else, and was now in the public domain, I agreed to co-operate so that the full and accurate story of the whole issue could at last be told. Bernie Moss, a former test pilot and air crash investigator, was also commissioned to work on the programme, and we were agreed that the Mont Dupil site was not a contender for W3185, for reasons previously explained. Bernard-Marie Dupont and I, however, remained of the opinion that if the site was discoverable then, given the massive interest generated by the media following our expedition in 1996, we or someone else would have found it years ago.

The fact must also not be overlooked that any remaining wreckage may already have been disturbed, by accident, during agricultural work by someone unfamiliar with either the origin or significance of their find. Also, conclusive proof, especially in the absence of documentary evidence, can only be ascertained from the aircraft's maker's plate, which is not always discovered. We very much doubted that another search would be any more successful than our previous operation, and so this proved to be. Although we had been shown the Schlager crash site in 1996, we had decided against excavating it, and so this 109 was recovered for the programme. The discovery of a maker's plate confirmed the identity beyond doubt and, as previously mentioned, the presence of a tail wheel indicated that the tail was still attached upon impact. Two other Spitfire sites in the area were excavated and confirmed not to be W3185: BM303, a 611 Squadron Mk VB, shot down on 8 June 1942, the pilot of which, Sergeant Jack Misseldine, successfully evaded, and Mk IX, MA764, brought down on 25 November 1943; coincidentally, the pilot, Flight Sergeant Don Bostock, also evaded.

It seems to me that the 'Search for Bader's Spitfire' is far from over, although I repeat what I wrote in *Bader's Tangmere Spitfires*, published in October 1996: 'it is as if the mystery intends to remain patently unsolved – forever!' The reason for that could be, I have concluded, that the Spitfire broke up in mid-air, scattering wreckage far and wide, which was subsequently recovered from the surface by the enemy and hence why the crash site persistently defies discovery.

Perhaps our final thoughts, however, should be of Squadron Leader L. H. 'Buck' Casson DFC AFC, a courageous and experienced fighter pilot, one of the Few, who fought bravely in Britain's hour of greatest need. Whatever happened that fateful day high over St-Omer, I am sure we all agree that Buck's memory should always be revered.

12

FLIGHT LIEUTENANT BOB POULTON DFC

I was born on 19 September 1918, in Dorking, Surrey. My father was killed in France a month later and in 1927 I was sent to the London Orphan School in Watford. I left there in 1934, aged sixteen, to work as an assistant to an antiques buyer in London, but in 1938 I joined the RAFVR and started flying at Woking. I was called up in September 1939 and went to 1 ITW at St John's College, Cambridge; on that course was none other than 'Johnnie' Johnson, who would became the official RAF top-scoring fighter pilot in the Second World War.

I flew a Spitfire for the first time at 7 OTU, Hawarden, and was commissioned in August 1940. After brief spells with 616 and 64 Squadrons in 12 Group, after the Battle of Britain I was first posted to 611 Squadron for a few days and then to 74 Squadron at Biggin Hill. The 74 was, of course, a famous squadron commanded by the legendary 'Sailor' Malan; he was good, very good indeed.

In January 1941, we moved from Biggin Hill to Manston. On 4 March, I was flying No. 2 to my Flight Commander, Flight Lieutenant John Freeborn DFC, and we shared a Do 215 probable that we attacked over the Channel. Then, on 7 May, I encountered Me 109s for the first time; my combat report reads as follows: 'I was White Leader patrolling Canterbury below cloud at 2,000 feet, with one section of 'B' Flight, when we were ordered to Mansion. There four Me 109s were sighted, flying low down over the sea just off Westgate. I went down to attack. As I was getting into position to attack one of these four, another 109 went past me, heading east, out to sea. I opened fire on this E/A and gave it a three- to four-second burst from about 150 yards, dead astern. The E/A climbed up into the clouds, still heading east. I climbed up behind him and upon coming out of the clouds found myself about 400 yards behind him. I closed to about 200 yards and opened fire, from dead astern. The E/A turned to the left and I closed to approximately fifty yards, finishing off with a quarter attack. Black smoke and glycol poured from the E/A, which turned on its back and plunged down through clouds, bursting into flames before it hit the sea and disappeared. It took me about ten minutes to reach the coast again and upon reaching Margate I sighted three 109s circling over the town. I opened fire at one

Left: 109. Flight Lieutenant Bob Poulton DFC – note the top button undone, the sign of a fighter pilot.

Below: 110. Pilots of 74 Squadron at Gravesend in 1941. From left: Pilot Officer Poulton, Flight Lieutenant Freeborn DFC, Squadron Leader Baker (supernumerary), Flying Officer Woods, and Pilot Officer Tony Mould. The Spitfire, P8388, was presented under the auspices of Lord Beaverbrook's Spitfire Fund by the Black family, of London Palladium fame, and was named 'Black Vanities'.

111. Pilot Officer Poulton at Manston with Spitfire P8047, 'The Malverns'.

112. Another snapshot of 'The Malverns', flown many times by Pilot Officer Poulton.

of them, delivering a four-second burst from astern. I saw no effect from this burst and had to break off the engagement as my ammunition was expended.' During the summer of 1941, we were continually flying sweeps over France, and on 24 June, I claimed a 109 probable over Gravelines. On 3 July, 74 Squadron flew as part of the Target Support Wing for six Blenheims on a Circus to Hazebrouck. Over the target my Section was bounced from above by six Me 109s; my combat report refers: 'I pulled sharply to port and saw one of the E/A diving in a gentle left-hand turn, straightening out into a dive back in the direction from which the E/As first appeared. I followed, but at first made no impression in respect of the distance between us. At about 2,000–3,000 feet I got within range and fired a three-second burst of cannon and machine-gun fire from 100 yards astern. The port wing of the E/A broke away at the root and the aircraft spun down into a small wood. I then came down to ground level and flew at that height back to the coast. I claim one Me 109E destroyed.

At around this time I got into big trouble for taking my ground crew for a flip in a Magister and got reported for low flying. We beat up a golf course but unbeknown to me there were some senior RAF officers on the course! Anyway, I was chucked off the Squadron and sent to 1 Delivery Flight at Hendon. The following August, I was tried for the offence but found not guilty! That led to me being posted again, to 53 OTU at Llandow. That was a bit hairy as the aircraft were all old ones. The Station Commander was none other than Group Captain Ira Jones, who served with distinction in 74 Squadron during the Great War, and for which reason I always felt that he looked after me.

113. Flight Lieutenant Poulton while an instructor, having got into trouble for unauthorised low flying!

On 15 February 1942, I was involved in a fatal mid-air collision. It was an exercise with the local Home Guard, which was 'attacking' the airfield. The briefing was not good, and most pilots went off alone to find the 'enemy'. Unfortunately, Flight Lieutenant Pickering and I attacked a Home Guard convoy simultaneously. He made a run along the column and I 'attacked' from 90 degrees. We hadn't seen each other and I hit him just behind the cockpit. His Spitfire was cut in two and went straight in, killed outright. My aircraft was badly damaged but I managed to control it sufficiently to land straight ahead in a field, suffering just a couple of bruises. Pickering was a Battle of Britain veteran too and it was such a waste for him to die in this accident.

In March 1942, I was promoted to Flight Lieutenant and joined 611 Squadron at Drem. In May, we moved south, to Kenley, and the following month to Redhill. In June, however, I was injured in a car accident and admitted to the RAF hospital at Ely. By September, I was fit and well and posted to 64 Squadron at Fairlop. We led a nomadic lifestyle, as ever, moving to Harrowbeer, then Predannack, arriving at Hornchurch in January 1943, where we remained until April. That month I was awarded the DFC for having flown on operations over such a protracted period. We had an interesting excursion around that time, making deck landings in Seafires on HMS Argus, although I never found out why they made us do this. It was quite an experience: an aircraft carrier's deck is actually pretty small against an awful lot of sea!

In July 1943, we returned to Kenley and began long-range bomber-escort sorties. These were made possible due to the new auxiliary 'slipper' tanks, which contained an extra forty-five gallons of fuel and were fitted under the fuselage. We used to use the fuel from these first, then jettison them and switch over to the main tank so that we didn't lose any manoeuvrability in combat. The slipper tanks were a clever idea and made of papier mâché.

On 14 January 1944, we of 64 Squadron flew on Ramrod 453, providing close escort, alongside 611 Squadron, to 54 Marauders attacking flying bomb sites near Fruges. I was leading a section of four Spitfires when my aircraft suddenly started leaking glycol near Abbeville. Accompanied by Flight Sergeant Thorne, I had to turn around, my intention being to bale out over the sea and get picked up. It soon became obvious that I was not going to make it and so I had no choice but to bale out over land, not an attractive proposition because the likely end result was being captured by the Germans. Somehow I managed to get my leg trapped between the seat and cockpit side, only managing to get out very low, the parachute only just breaking my fall. I came to in a field surrounded by German troops who gave me first aid and sent me off to a village called Gamaches. There I was taken to a German military hospital where they patched me up and set my broken right leg. Two months later I was moved to a Luftwaffe hospital in Amiens where I had two operations on my leg, but the break would not join. The treatment I received was good, although limited because supplies were short. The hospital was actually adjacent to Amiens prison, which was bombed by our Mosquitoes to release the French Resistance prisoners

114. Flight Lieutenant Bob Poulton DFC with his 64 Squadron Spitfire Mk IX, shortly before baling out over France.

held there by the Gestapo under sentence of death. The hospital was also hit and many German patients were killed – me very frightened and not very popular! The Squadron actually thought that I had been killed, as Flight Sergeant Thorne reported that although he saw something leave the aircraft at 2,000 feet this appeared not to be me but the cockpit canopy. On 14 January 1944, my wife, a WAAF, received a telegram to the effect that I was 'missing'; it was some weeks before news of my survival reached home.

In March 1944, I was moved to *Dulag Luft*, an interrogation centre, at Frankfurt. While en route a daylight raid by American bombers came in so I sheltered with my guards beneath Frankfurt railway station. There were many civilians down there too and again me not very popular! They then sent me to *Stalag Luft* 1, a four-day journey with a plastered leg in the back of a cattle truck – not nice. By September, my leg had still yet to mend and so a Swiss Red Cross Commission approved me for a repatriation exchange. In January 1945, I started the journey home, but while at Berlin railway station there was another raid by Mosquitoes and yet again me not very popular!

Back home I had a major operation on my leg and after a long period of recuperation and rehabilitation I was granted a 20 per cent disability pension and released from the RAF: we no longer want you, goodbye.

After a period working in radio and television I re-joined the RAF in May 1951, being granted a Short Service Commission as a Flying Officer in the Air Traffic

Control Branch. I eventually left the RAF in 1968, and before retiring in 1983 worked as an air traffic controller for Airwork Services at the Army Air Corps base at Middle Wallop, Hampshire. Naturally it was my time flying Spitfires, however, that was the most exciting, and something I have always remained very proud of.

13

FLIGHT LIEUTENANT RON RAYNER DFC

I joined 41 Squadron at Catterick in 1941, with some fifty hours' flying time in Spitfires recorded in my logbook. The Squadron was re-forming after the Battle of Britain and the fighter combats of late 1940 and early 1941. The Squadron was still using the Battle of Britain period formation, which was virtually four aircraft in line astern. No. 4, or 'Arse-end Charlie' as he was called, was supposed to protect the rear of the formation by weaving frantically behind; as I am sure you can imagine, this slowed the whole formation down as he was travelling a much greater distance with his weaving than the rest of the formation. This continued until we got down to Tangmere. The line-astern formation was one of attack, and very useful if you were attacking hordes of bombers, but of course our role on the south coast was to change completely, so the formation also had to change, as we were going to be both attacking and being attacked over France. Therefore the virtual line-abreast formation was evolved.

This was not a close formation but had sufficient distance between each aircraft so that each pilot could look over and inwards towards the leader of the formation and thereby protect that sector of the formation. In other words, he is looking behind to the far side of the formation, so that if you were on the port side you would look out to starboard and protect that sector from 90 degrees right round to 180 degrees. The pilot on the starboard side would be doing exactly the same for the port section. This provided a large degree of protection because directly behind in a Spitfire you could not really see anything – there was a rear-view mirror but it was not really that efficient. In line astern it is very easy to turn, as a formation, to either port or starboard, but in line abreast that is when the difficulty arises. Of course, a method had to be evolved which allowed us to turn relatively quickly but still maintain formation, so the leader would give instructions: 'Turning port' or 'Turning starboard', whatever, and on the former those Spitfires on the port side would go over the top of the leader, and the other two on the starboard side would go below him. You ended up at 90 degrees and in virtually the same formation. Those from the starboard side then transferred to the port side and port to the starboard side. You were therefore still able to protect each other immediately the turn was complete. The leader himself had to ensure that his rate of turn was correct so that the rest

115. Flight Lieutenant Ron 'Cloudy' Rayner DFC.

116. Sergeant Rayner pictured at Merston while flying Spitfires with the Tangmere Wing in 1941.

of his little formation would maintain their positions throughout the turn. I say all this because over France during the sweeps of 1941 we were going to be the targets and therefore the attack would obviously come from above; by the time we got over France the German controllers would have been made aware of our approach and deployed their aircraft accordingly at 30,000 feet or even higher. The foregoing introduction to the sweeps will probably help the reader understand what happened to me on one day in August 1941.

At 11.30 am on 31 August 1941, 41 Squadron, led by Squadron Leader Gaunce, provided twelve Spitfires for a sweep over France. The 616 Squadron added a further eleven Spitfires to the offensive formation from Westhampnett. We usually rendezvoused over Dungeness or Beachy Head, depending on what your particular squadron was briefed to do, and we then went out across the Channel in layers to protect each other. Our objective on this particular sortie was not to either bomb or strafe, but to entice the German fighters to come up and attack us. We would set our course to sweep the area as previously instructed by the ops room, and of course by then we were on the alert for German fighters, each protecting the other's tail, so in the squadron there would be three sections of four. We would progress along these lines looking out for ourselves and also, perhaps, for those squadrons below us. On the day in question, we were between 25,000 feet and 30,000 feet and progressed towards France.

Suddenly there was a shout of 'BREAK!', which meant that we were about to be attacked. When that shout went up you did a steep turn, as hard as possible, either port or starboard, to get away from whoever was diving at you from above. No use going into a dive to get away – that was hopeless as if you stuck your nose down then the engine would cut. The only other possible action was to half roll and get away that way. But that took a long time, so the best evasive action was to break hard and do a very, very tight turn – when I say tight I mean tight, so that you were virtually blacked out with the g-force as you executed the turn. By the time that I came out of my turn, I discovered that my canopy had been shot away and dust from the Perspex had got into my oxygen mask. The engine temperature was rising rapidly, and after a very short time it exceeded the maximum for safety. Now here was my dilemma: I could see the English coast and I must have had about 25,000 feet to play with, so I tentatively fiddled about to see how much engine power I actually had left. Then I had to decide what shall I do: shall I make for the English coast and hope to get that far with my advantage? Or should I bale out over France, over land, or get to the Channel and bale out over the sea? Without having made any decision, I experimented to see how far I could get. Gradually descending, and hoping that I would not be attacked again, I managed to get over the Channel and over the coast. There in front of me was Mansion which, despite being in a frantic state by now really, I decided to try and reach. As I got closer and lower, I realised that I would make it with a certain degree of comfort, and decided that perhaps a wheels-down landing was possible, so I managed to get my undercarriage down. I was streaming coolant, clouds of glycol coming out of the aircraft, and by the time

I got over the airfield both the ambulance and fire tender were on the perimeter. As I made my approach and put down they were dashing out after me. I got down without any engine at all, got out of the aircraft which was hardly damaged, in fact, and was greeted by the Station Commander who said 'By jingo, that was a bloody awful landing you made!' So that was all the greeting I got! I also remember the ground crews swarming over the Spitfire and collecting the Perspex – out of which they made brooches and the like.

I abandoned the aircraft and reported what had happened to the Intelligence Officer. He said that arrangements would be made to return me to Merston, the Tangmere satellite where 41 Squadron was based. I went into the headquarters and the clerk there gave me a railway warrant, but it was routed through London. All I had with me was my flying kit, Mae West, flying boots, long stockings, and a parachute to carry, so I decided that that was the end: no way was I going to travel like that through London! Eventually I persuaded them to give me a warrant to travel by Southern Rail along the south coast to Chichester, near Tangmere, from where I was picked up by the Squadron Transport.

The postscript to this episode is that the next occasion I climbed into a Spitfire cockpit and prepared for another sortie, I noticed that some comedian had crayoned an Me 109 in a head-on attitude on my rear-view mirror!

The Tangmere Wing at this time was of course commanded by the legendary Wing Commander Douglas Bader. As I previously explained, we were not actually flying from Tangmere itself but from the little grass satellite airfield at Merston. Should Tangmere be bombed again, our chances of saving the Wing's Spitfires were obviously greater if they were dispersed in this way – there was also another Tangmere satellite airfield at Westhampnett, which later became Goodwood motor racing circuit. At Merston I remember the dispersal hut there with a stove in the centre. Bader would come along and give us a pep talk, standing in the centre of the dispersal hut by this stove, rocking on his artificial limbs – I do not think it was possible for him to stand still with tin legs – he would make little movements to maintain his balance. I remember him saying on one occasion, 'If you follow my instructions in this new formation that we are now flying nobody will get shot down.' That was very encouraging, but shortly afterwards Bader himself had to bale out over France. We then learnt that he had left his legs behind in the cockpit and was therefore not in a very comfortable state. The Germans offered to allow an RAF aircraft safe conduct over France to drop some replacement artificial limbs by parachute. Of course, we could not make such an exception for any pilot, so to get round it a Circus was organised involving six Blenheims which were to go out on a normal raid and drop the legs before hitting the target. That way it was not a special trip but Douglas Bader could have his legs back. The Tangmere Wing had the privilege of providing close escort to the Blenheims, and I was personally privileged to be among those members of 41 Squadron who flew on that sortie. All I can recall now, though, was hearing over the R/T that the legs had been released from the Blenheim.

Of course, the Blenheims were very vulnerable in any case as they were obsolete. On one occasion we provided close escort to these Blenheims attacking shipping on the Dutch coast. We were attacked and I understood at the time that not one of the Blenheims returned; but years later I discovered that just one had survived.

After a brief spell as an instructor, I joined 43 Squadron in mid-1942 and began a nomadic existence. The squadron was based at Wittering and had completely packed for a move overseas. We aircrew were taken to Padgate in Warrington and then, late one evening, we were put on a train and went to the Clyde, from where we embarked on the *Loynster*. For a fortnight we sailed a zigzag course through the Atlantic, and back again, but one night we found ourselves in the Straits of Gibraltar. We were disembarked from the ship immediately and taken in covered three-tonners to the top of the Rock. There was there an abandoned barracks where we were bedded down for the night. The next day we were taken to the garrison theatre and told that the invasion of North Africa was to commence the following day, and that one squadron would fly into Maison Blanc, the airport in Algiers, and that squadron would be us. We were equipped with Hurricanes with long-range tanks to enable us to make the 500-mile sea crossing to Algiers. If the reception we received there was bad, then there would be no chance of getting back and we would have to fend for ourselves.

We were allowed to go down to the runway that afternoon, in pairs, and run up our Hurricanes to ensure they were to our satisfaction. Of course, these Hurricanes had never been flown before. They had been shipped to Gibraltar in crates and assembled on the Rock. Before dawn the next day we took off, circled the Rock, and set course for Algiers. About half an hour out into the Med I discovered that my generator had packed up so I had no radio, no fuel gauge, no gunsight, but fortunately I was No. 2 to the Wing Commander, out in front of the formation of eighteen aircraft, so I managed to stick close to him and signal that I had no communication. Eventually the Wing Commander and I landed in formation on the runway at Maison Blanc before the rest of the squadron – fortunately, there was not a hostile reception so the Wing Commander signalled for the rest of the squadron to land. A little while later we were greeted by the commander of the RAF's Commando Servicing Group who were there to re-fuel and rearm us.

From Maison Blanc we patrolled the Mediterranean and often escorted the *Aurora*, a cruiser, on raids against German shipping bringing supplies to the Tunis area. We would take the cruiser out from Algiers just before dusk, but return at nightfall, landing in the dark on the flare path. Of course, the Germans soon realised what was going on so they waited for us and bombed as we were landing. We had to disperse our aircraft as quickly as possible and dive into the nearest irrigation ditch for cover. This went on for several days until we were leapfrogged by Spitfires as landing strips had by then been prepared further inland. We then joined in the leapfrogging until we eventually made Tunis after the army had gone through some extremely bitter fighting, as did the Merchant Navy who were bringing supplies in along the coast. The Eighth Army, however, met up with the First Army, and thousands and thousands of German prisoners were taken and massed on the plains at Tunis.

From North Africa we flew to Malta, which was then relieved. When we landed on the island our aircraft were put into dispersals and we then went to live in buildings surrounding the bay. This was quite a treat for us having lived for so long under canvas. It was May 1943, and the Allied forces were amassing for the invasion of Sicily as a prelude to landing in Italy. From Malta we flew on bomber escorts to Comiso in southern Sicily.

On 10 July 1943, the invasion of Sicily commenced, Operation HUSKY, and on that day we actually landed at Comiso. I remember it well as I parked my aircraft in a dispersal area adjacent to a runway, which was an established airfield – my Spitfire was dispersed next to a *Stuka* with Italian markings which had tipped over on its back with the two dead crew members still hanging in their straps, right next to my aircraft!

In Sicily we started the slog up the western coast, and flew patrols of Augusta and Catania, eventually landing at the latter. From there we began escorting American daylight bombers attacking targets in Italy itself. We were escorting Mitchells and Bostons, and I must say that the American pilots were extremely brave – they would be flying along in formation (we would be weaving above them) and although the anti-aircraft fire would be bursting among them they would still maintain tight formation. Very brave. In addition to our escort work, we ourselves were attacking the retreating Germans who were escaping up the coast to Messina, so we were strafing the equivalent of our tank landing craft as they tried to make the mainland. We were then transferred to an airstrip which had been made for us on the northern side of Sicily, and we continued the patrols of Messina and Augusta. Eventually we arrived at Falcone, again a strip prepared for us by the army engineers.

It was in Sicily that we received our Spitfire Mk IXs. They were marvellous – absolutely incredible. I remember that on my first flight in a Mk IX, an air test, I went up to 35,000 feet, just for the joy of experiencing what it was like to operate a Spit IX at high altitude. It was definitely a different aircraft altogether at high altitude from the Mk V: it was really something. We had only received a certain number of IXs, so we actually flew a mixture of Vs and IXs, so much so that the IXs were not even painted with an individual aircraft letter, they were just given a number. My personal aircraft was still a Mk V, and I always flew FT-J.

On 8 September 1943, we were assembled and told that the invasion of Italy was to commence the next day. Our role was to support the army who were going to land on a beach in the bay of Salerno. On 9 September, therefore, Salerno was our patrol area, about 170 miles across the sea from our base at Falcone. We patrolled the beaches, milling about with German aircraft attacking the ground forces, and while the navy shelled the German positions. In addition, the FAA also supported the army, their Seafires patrolling from their aircraft carriers. This went on until 15 September, by which time the army had secured the bridgehead, and a landing strip, called 'Roger', had been pushed up parallel to the beach at Salerno. We were then able to land at Salerno itself, but that was fraught with danger as not only were the Germans still shelling us but the trajectory of our own artillery also went across the airfield.

117. 43 Squadron Spitfire Mk IXs at Catania, Sicily. Flight Lieutenant Rayner's aircraft is 'J'.

The Allied invasion of Italy, at Salerno, is very much an unsung D-Day of the Second World War. In contrast to the landings in Normandy on 6 June 1944, the *Luftwaffe* did get up in force over the bay of Salerno. Although the British troops involved had fought in North Africa, their American comrades were untested. The Italian coastline at Salerno was defended by combat-experienced German soldiers, including many tough and feared paratroopers. For several days, the success of 'Operation Avalanche' really did lie in the balance.

At 1310 hrs on 16 September 1943, six of our Spitfires, led by our Polish CO, Squadron Leader Horbaczewski, patrolled the Salerno beaches. Upon returning to Roger we spotted twelve FW 190s approaching from the south at 2,000 feet. My combat report: 'Closing on one of the enemy aircraft he turned to the left and I carried out a deflection attack on him, firing two bursts of about two seconds each. Strikes were seen on top of the engine but I then broke off the attack because of another FW 190 which was attacking me. Squadron Leader Horbaczewski saw the enemy aircraft I attacked crash near Eboli.' Squadron Leader Horbaczewski claimed two of the 190s destroyed in the fight, and, in addition to my 190 destroyed, Flying

Officer 'Dizzy' Deuntzer claimed one as damaged. Years later, Dilip Sarkar researched this and commented that: 'German records indicate that II/JG77 lost two Me 109s and an FW 190 on the day in question, but details are vague. However, II/SKG 10, a fighter–bomber unit, suffered the loss of their *Kommodore, Hauptmann* Wiglev von Wedal, who was killed near Salerno. While 'Horby' also submitted claims for destroyed FW 190s, the fate of Flight Lieutenant Rayner's victim was conclusive and seen by Squadron Leader Horbaczewski himself to 'crash near Eboli'. It is possible, therefore, that it was von Wedal whom 'Cloudy' Rayner shot down that day.' If I did get von Wedal, and it looks like I did, I just think it was a pity he was killed.

Because the Americans were completely new to battle conditions, they shot at every aircraft in the sky regardless of whether it was German or Allied. Unfortunately, on one occasion when we came in to land at Roger, one of our Spitfires was shot down by these trigger-happy people. Very easy to be critical, but they were absolutely scared stiff of course, as everybody is in battle. We continuously patrolled the battle front, making sure that the army was not troubled by the *Luftwaffe* too much.

Eventually the Germans got the message that we were not going to be pushed out of Salerno and so the pressure started to ease off as the army pushed inland and north towards the town of Salerno and then on to Naples. I notice in my logbook that on 19 September 1943 we made our first offensive sweep over the airfield at Foggia, which was really a gesture just to show the enemy that we were in command.

My stay in Salerno came to an abrupt end on 22 September 1943. I had been on patrol and when I landed began to shiver. On our way back to our dispersal encampment, I sat on top of the 15 cwt truck's engine to try and get warm, shivering quite violently in what was a scorching hot September. When darkness fell I was beginning to feel really ill. Then we had an alert that the Germans had launched a counterattack with paratroopers, so we all had to dive into slit-trenches. That is the last I remember. I passed out completely, only to discover two days later, when I came round being sponged with ice-cold water at a field dressing station, that I had malaria. I was then evacuated in a hospital Dakota to Tripoli.

I returned to continue flying Spitfires during the remainder of the Italian campaign, and later became a flight commander on 72 Squadron. The fighting in Italy for what were just small hills was intense. I once walked over one with the squadron padre and found it littered with bodies. Truckloads of bodies were also driven past our landing strips as the battlefields were cleared. For us it was a time of living in tents, often in deep mud – very uncomfortable to say the least. We were largely engaged in ground attack against the German army, and strafed convoys of their motor transport and armour. This entailed flying very low, and once I returned to our base trailing a length of telegraph wire from my wing tip – the airfield cleared rapidly!

By March 1945, we were still attacking German army positions in support of our advancing soldiers. One day that month we were ordered off to drop what were described to us as 'fire bombs' on some German positions. These bombs had been made up in drop tank shells. Off we went and dropped them accordingly and watched rivulets of fire running into the enemy positions. On reflection I believe that

118. Flight Lieutenant Rayner's 72 Squadron Spitfire at Ravena, 1945. A round came through his wing during a strafing attack.

this was napalm, and possibly the first use of it. During a strafing sortie I also had a narrow escape when a shell came up through my Spitfire's wing root – just three feet from my seat; there was no armour plate beneath the pilot!

Two months later, by which time 72 Squadron was based at Klagenfurt in Austria, the war in Europe was over. I went home and married 'Midge', whom I had met while based at Tangmere and who was the dancing partner of a friend of mine who went missing. After the war we lived in Wales, where I worked as a jeweller, raised a family and eventually retired to Malvern. A day has not gone by, however, since the war that I have not thought about my time flying Spitfires and what we had to do in the war, strafing and dive-bombing, for example. The Spitfire was wonderful and I wouldn't have missed the experience, but war really is an absolutely terrible thing – the memories of which also haunt many other survivors to this day.

14

FLIGHT LIEUTENANT JOHN SLADE

I was born in Bristol on 6 June 1922, into a nice but ordinary working-class family. My father was a Master French Polisher and his business went through rough times during the depression. Mother always ensured that we were somehow well fed. I had two brothers, both younger. We got through. Then war came. We lived near Bristol airport and the Germans did come over and there was quite a bit of damage around us. We even had our garden shed destroyed by an incendiary. That illuminated the landscape!

I went to a decent boys' school until I was aged fourteen and was top of the class. I left school and got a job, apprenticed as an aircraft technician at Filton, the other side of Bristol and about a seven-mile bike ride away. A friend of my mother's, who was a Civil Servant, advised her to get me into the Civil Service as it was a guaranteed job for life. I went in as a Boy Messenger, taking telegrams around, and at the age of sixteen passed top in the exam to go inside the Telegraph Room. I worked there various hours and long nights, especially during the Blitz. I joined the Home Guard which, I can assure you, was just like 'Dad's Army' – people doing such silly things! Then my friend Norman came up to me in the office one day to tell me that there was a notice saying that we could be released from the Civil Service if we volunteered for aircrew training. My Mum wasn't very keen but Norman and I decided that we would.

First of all we went to an RN recruiting office where we didn't get a very good reception as they were only looking for regulars. So we went down to the Joint Services Recruitment Office and put our names down. They gave us a medical and put us on the list. A couple of months later I had a letter telling me to go to Weston-super-Mare, which was the Aircrew Recruiting Centre, and we had three days there doing interviews, tests, and medicals. I was accepted for pilot training but Norman, who was exceptionally good at maths, was offered a navigator's job and finished up on Pathfinder Force.

Then I had to wait until October 1941, when I was called up and sent to the Aircrew Reception Centre at Lord's Cricket Ground, Regent's Park, and there we were given

119. John Slade pictured when a Flight Sergeant.

120. John Slade in Italy, June 1944.

uniforms and did a bit of drill. Fifty of us were told that we were being posted to Leuchars in Scotland. We didn't even know where it was! Most of the initial training was done in quite big wings of hundreds, but this was just fifty. Travelling overnight, I can remember crossing the Forth Bridge for the first time, looking down from the train and seeing the river. Eventually we pulled into Leuchars station, which was on the main London to Inverness line. There we were offloaded and taken to RAF Leuchars, which was an operational base where they flew Bostons and Beauforts. While we were there they actually lost quite a few. We had all our ground training there: navigation, meteorology, armament, theory of flight, etc. We took our exams after about three months and I passed. I was promoted to LAC, although I was still getting paid more by the Post Office, which was making up my money!

We then had some leave and were sent to Brighton, where we stayed at the Metropole Hotel – quite posh – and we had a great social life there. Then we were sent to Manchester, which was an embarkation centre, and told that we were going to America. They didn't waste any time – just put us on this ship, which wasn't all that big and not exactly designed with passenger comfort in mind! There were just two ships and two destroyers, but plenty of valuable lives, and we crossed the Atlantic in six days. The rolling of the ship was awful. If we had been torpedoed I don't think I could have cared less! Eventually the waters calmed and we spent the last couple of days talking about the food we were going to have when we landed! Canada and America, you see – plenty of food, no problem. We got to Halifax, Nova Scotia in Canada where they put us on a train that took us to Monkton in New Brunswick, which was a transit area. Then we embarked upon this long and memorable train journey, all the way down through Canada, into the United States, through Chattanooga, Tennessee. We didn't have sleepers and it took about three days. We eventually arrived at a place called Albany in Georgia.

Some of us went to a twin-engined flying school but I was sent to learn on single-engined Stearmans. I had a lovely instructor, Mr Diamond, and passed the course. Then we went to Macon in Georgia to fly intermediate aircraft: metal monoplanes. There we did quite a lot of night flying, although night flying in America was a lot different from night flying over here because they had the Airways Lights on! If you went on a night cross country you just followed the lights, although a surprising number of people took wrong turnings! It is amazing really when you think that this was only 1941, yet the Americans were already so well geared up. We were then sent to Napier Field, Alabama, a very modern school, with good accommodation but a tough Commandant! We had to get up at six o'clock in the morning, shave, make our beds, with sheets folded into 'Hospital Corners', 45 degrees. Then we went across to breakfast. If anyone was late they missed the meal.

Ultimately we won our 'wings' being presented both RAF and American flying badges, which I still have. We then came back home and first did a series of courses to gain experience of flying in English weather. Then we went on to fly things like Masters. Eventually I was posted to 58 OTU, which is where I came into contact with my first Spitfire. I fell in love with it straight away. You could fly along straight and level easily, do slow rolls, whatever you wanted. I don't think we actually completed that course, however, as the unit was moved away into Lincolnshire. So we went down there to finish off. We were then kept hanging around until sent on advanced flying courses, flying Spitfires. Then in June 1944 I met my wife Betty and married her, and we were then told that we were being posted overseas. Let me tell you we were dreading being sent to Burma. I remember creeping into the CO's office and seeing a signal indicating that we were going to the Mediterranean.

We went by sea, heavily escorted and with other troop ships, landing in Algiers. We were put ashore there and it was so hot, with masses of flies and so on. I caught dysentery and I was up seventeen times one night. But I must have been fit and healthy back then to have survived it. We were there for a while, not doing very much – no flying – then we got pushed into a DC3 and taken to Italy. I can remember approaching Naples and seeing Vesuvius smoking. We landed at Naples and were taken to some transit quarters there, which weren't in exactly the best part of town. Our rations were not very good, but we existed. Then a crowd of us were gathered together and told that we were going to Sardinia, ready for the invasion of Southern France. They put us on an Italian cruiser and took us to Corsica, but the ship couldn't dock. So they rowed us all ashore, put us in a field, and said 'Get on with it'! I remember going to sleep and being woken in the morning by a cow licking my face! Then we had a most eventful run across Corsica, which is a very mountainous country with no flat roads. We had this Black American driver and he had just one idea: keep right-foot down regardless. We were doing it in our pants, we really were! He would approach these sharp bends, pull up at the last minute, and there were definitely one or two passengers who needed changes of underwear! It was not the kind of thing you volunteer for!

We eventually arrived at the southern tip of Corsica – just a small harbour with no proper facilities of any kind. We had been given travel rations: tinned food and biscuits, and we stayed there the whole weekend. Fortunately it was warm, and I remember sleeping on a plank of wood by the harbour and cooking up some food for everybody. Anyway, we enjoyed that and then they put us on a ferry, a short journey across to Sardinia. We were near the northern end of Sardinia and our base was at the southern end, which is where we kicked our heels for a while. I flew a Spitfire Mk VIII there for the first time. You couldn't really go out into the local town. We may have done once or twice, but we were just biding our time, playing cards. We weren't very happy as we hadn't joined the RAF to do that. They hadn't lost Spitfire pilots on operations to the extent anticipated and so the reserve was too big.

Eventually we were taken back to Italy where my friend and I went to the CO and asked if we could be posted to a squadron, saying that we would even go back to England to get in one. We were called in later and posted to 'Rhodesia' Squadron. We were in Naples and they were at Falconara. Somehow we got a lift on an army truck with an army officer driving. We drove up through mountainous country and stopped in Rome for a night. We stopped at Assisi and saw St Francis's birthplace. I was a Christian then. We went on from there and finished up at the aerodrome, a proper

Italian air base that had been knocked about. Initially we had to stay in tents, and it was starting to get cold. The CO went down to the local town and commandeered this big house to live in. We heated it by using 100 octane fuel, the gravity feed being a home-manufactured nozzle, and hoping it would take. Sometimes it did, but sometimes it took too much. I remember the two cooks coming out of the cook house once: the heater had exploded! Of course it was getting well into winter now – November 1944 – so we didn't do much flying in Sardinia. I went up with the CO, just local flying and went on practice battle formation. My first operational trip was on 23 November, when we escorted Beaufighters rocketing an armed reconnaissance ship. I think they hit it.

On the way back I was told to divert to the nearest aerodrome, on my own. When I landed there I discovered that my No. 1 had landed and collided with an American airman, killing him. Mind you, you just accepted these things. I flew back and went on various patrols, escorting MTBs. A lot of our jobs though were protecting Beaufighters. The first experience of death I had was when there were two of us detailed to escort these two Beaufighters on a shipping strike. The visibility over the airfield was very low, so we were told to climb up through and meet them above the cloud. So far as cruising control is concerned, the difference between a Beaufighter and a Spitfire is very wide. Anyway, we got up there and the Beaufighter leader said that we would descend. I just couldn't hold on to my No. 1. It was so slow I had no control. I shut my eyes, pulled away, and concentrated on blind flying by instruments, which we had practised a lot on the Link Trainer. I was lucky: I got down. The other Spitfire pilot was never seen again.

We went on these various recces: an island off the Adriatic coast where they thought there were armed German ships – quite a flight across the Adriatic. We used to fly at zero level for as far as we could to keep under the radar. We hit this island, had a good look around, but couldn't see anything. Went back and reported that all was quiet. Then we were called together that evening and told that the Navy was making an attack, early dawn, and that they wanted air cover, meaning that we had to get up and do some night flying. For some reason they changed their minds and the mission never went ahead. Then we got involved with various other things – looking for aircraft which had gone into the sea, armed recces, armed weather recces. We used to get up early, fly off to the north and report back the weather for today. Escorting more Beaufighters, more ASR, at the same time we were always looking for anything that moved on the ground, but anything seldom did.

By February 1944, our Spitfire Mk IXs had been fitted with bomb racks and I remember practising dive-bombing, getting back to be told that one of our friends had been killed. He had been shot down, baled out, but somehow hit the tail. You couldn't allow these things to consume you but of course it was still upsetting. Then we started dive-bombing road bridges. But a Spitfire was a fighter: all it had was two 50 lb bomb racks, or you could carry a single 500 pounder and a gunsight. The theory was: fly over to your target, No. 1 would pick it out, do a double turn, and dive. When you were doing about 450 mph let your bombs go. All a bit haphazard, really.

121. 'Beating up billets!' – Spitfire Mk IX snapped low and fast!

122. John's original caption: 'Roy doing a beat up in "J", taken from top of billets, Cecina, Italy, June 1945'.

We also got scrambled sometimes, looking for enemy aircraft. On one occasion two of us took off, started climbing and climbing, but there was no sign that the Germans had started using jets then. Eventually, instead of climbing to 26,000 feet my leader had climbed to 36,000 feet, where the atmosphere is not very stable! Anyway, we got back down and went on various fighter sweeps, dive-bombing ammunition dumps, etc., shooting up trucks. The Germans moved by day, but very cautiously, so we were mostly dive-bombing bridges and rail yards, doing armed recces around Milan. Sometimes we even got direct hits. We patrolled a couple of destroyers, shelling German positions up north. They were afraid that they might be attacked from the air so we had to circle the destroyers and be sure the naval people were all right. We also bombed barracks and were busy – up three times a day.

We lost quite a few pilots. One, Max, spun in. In three days we lost another three: Tim Ward, John Carlisle – he was a flight commander – and Sam Elwood, a Rhodesian. I used to fly No. 2 to him – he was a lovely chap. On 29 March 1945, I wrote in my logbook: 'Direct hit in area, plenty of smoke. Sam blew up. Badly shaken.' We were flying along, Sam in front. I can remember pulling over and the next thing I was flying through debris – Sam and his Spitfire just disappeared. His bomb must have exploded for some reason. I don't think he had been hit. It was terrible.

I then became a Section Leader, carrying on with all of this dive-bombing and armed recces. I remember looking for a particular target once when suddenly we were over loads of great railway engines – we were right over Milan marshalling yards, a very heavily defended target! My friend said, 'I will never forget you suddenly weaving like hell!' Fortunately, I was only hit by flak once, at high level, never low down when it could have been much more dangerous.

Then, on 8 May 1945, that was it – war over. In the last ten days we lost six pilots. What a tragedy at such a stage. I just happened to be one of the lucky ones. During my service I flew Spitfire Mk Is, IIAs, IIBs, VCs, VIIIs, and IXs. The IXs were super – the performance, the speed – a vast improvement on the Vs. The big jump was from the V to the IX, no doubt about that – gave you so much more confidence. And it was the IX that we operated in Italy.

Once the war finished, though, we had to reduce our flying, as the Americans immediately cut off aid. We kicked around for a while in a village right on a beach – and I mean, right on the beach. I actually stepped out of my room onto the beach! Then in September the Squadron was posted back to Rhodesia, so I had to find another job: of all things an accounts job down near Naples. I had my full Warrant Officer's pay and everything but it was just so boring. Christmas came and just afterwards the Staff Sergeant in charge of discipline came up to me, grinning, and said 'I bet you thought you were going home on leave, didn't you?' I said that I was indeed. But he then told me that I wasn't and that I had been posted to the Middle East. I had so been looking forward to getting back home to my wife and, having been overseas for quite a while, I went to the CO and said, 'Look, I've done my flying, I don't want to go.' So I saw my service out in Italy; and did we count the days until

123. 'A kite: June 1945'.

124. Falconera: February 1945.

125. 'My kite: June 1945'.

126. 'Flak hole in Pat's kite. Pat injured in arms. Rosignano, April 1945'.

127. John Slade (second left) and fellow pilots sightseeing at Monte Cassino, September 1945.

128. Flight Lieutenant John Slade, Italy, April 1945.

our demob! I was fortunate, I suppose, because aircrew were being demobbed earlier than the others, so we really did just count off the days.

Am I proud of flying Spitfires? I think so. There are two facets: the good and the bad. The good: flying the Spitfire and surviving. And we did have a wonderful social life while training in the United States, so you have to consider both angles. Looking back, I was fortunate. I had some nasty experiences, some of which have stayed with me forever – such as Sam blowing up like that in front of me. The bad: things like that; the killing – terrible – all of it. Of course, there was nothing like the Spitfire, and never will be again. So, yes, I suppose I am proud.

Sadly John Slade died shortly after this interview was recorded.

15

FLIGHT LIEUTENANT RODNEY SCRASE DFC

My first flight was in a Tiger Moth flying from Marshall's airfield outside Cambridge. That was in early 1941 and I was enrolled in the Cambridge UAS. I loved every minute of it. Shortly thereafter I visited the airship sheds at Cardington and took the King's shilling. The next stage was flying training. Together with a group of fifty UAS undergraduates we were to travel across the Atlantic, first to Toronto and then by rail down to Florida. We were among the first chaps to doff our uniforms and to wear Burton suits as the USA had not yet come into the war. In March 1942 and with 180 hours' training on the PT17 Stearman, the BT13a Vultee, and finally the AT6a Harvard. I became the proud wearer of a pilot's wings and I was to sail back to the United Kingdom.

In November 1942, with 345 hours' flying experience I came to the end of my training and was assessed as 'Fighter Pilot – Good average'. And that was probably why I was sent on attachment to 611 Squadron at Biggin Hill, there to gain some 'experience on type'. During a one-week stay I made two trips on a Spitfire Mk IX – total flying time one hour and twenty-five minutes – just enough to have those responsible for postings to mark my records as 'send him off to North Africa', there to join one of the two squadrons which it was planned were to be equipped with a more effective Spitfire fighter than the Mk V.

A two-week trip on a transport HMT *Salacia* brought us to Gibraltar where we arrived in early January 1943. During our last night on board we had the constant boom of depth charges going off to protect the many ships anchored in Gibraltar Bay. The trip was an opportunity for me to establish a warm friendship with Tom Hughes – something we continue to enjoy to this day.

Our time in Gib was spent testing Spit VCs that were being assembled as replacements for the Tunisian Front. And it was at the end of the month that Tom and I were ferried by USAAC Dakota to Maison Blanche – the airfield for Algiers – and then on 28 January 1943 to Souk-el-Arba. So commenced my fifteen-month stay with 72 Squadron.

129. Flight Lieutenant
Rodney Scrase DFC.

A short drive in a 15 cwt Bedford and we arrived at the new airfields at Souk-el
Khemis, where 72 were flying from one of the several strips named after London
main line termini – ours being Euston. The Squadron was taking off as one of a
formation in Wing strength. Our first sight was to see a mid-air collision at less
than 1,000 feet. The recently appointed Flight Commander to 111 Squadron, Flight
Lieutenant Mortimer Rose, had hit the Wingco's plane. Mortimer Rose lost a wing
and went crashing into the ground. The Wingco – 'Sheep' Gilroy – baled out and
landed safely. On 30 January, I did my first flight with 72. A forty-minute sector
reconnaissance ably shepherded by Warrant Officer 'Sexton' Gear. I never did
discover how he got that name – probably a symbol of his extraordinary moustache.
And then came confirmation of the news that we were to go back to Gibraltar to
collect our Mk IXs.

So, on 3 February, a long drive by three-tonner and 15 cwt over the mountains
to Constantine. There, another few days waiting for USAAC Dakotas to fly us back
first to Maison Blanche and then on to Gib. In our week back in Gibraltar there
was some flying the Mk IX to gain experience on type, but most interestingly the
chance to make a round-the-Rock cruise in a submarine. We had got to know some
of the Navy types and their CO invited us to take to the underwater on board HMS
Thames, a large River class boat in which half a dozen of us watched a different kind

of handling and peered through the periscope. Sad to think the sub was to be lost in action soon after our trip.

Our return from Gib was full of incident. First, a three-hour-and-forty-five-minute trip to Maison Blanche, and the next day another of two hours and twenty-five minutes to continue with the rest of the journey. But we made a late take-off and were gradually facing worsening weather conditions. On arrival at Souk-el-Khemis we faced a thunder-charged rain storm. Several of our new planes were damaged on landing, others diverted to Paddington – which had a longer landing strip – while one poor chap didn't make it. Sadly, Sergeant Passmore spun in on landing and was killed. The last day of the month – 28 February – and I flew on my first operational trip as Yellow 2. We were giving High Cover to Hurribombers in the Beja/Mateur front: lots of activity both on the ground and in the air. I managed a short squirt at an Me 109 as we passed each other head-to-head!

In the month of March, I was to do just nine operational flights. Why so little? Our camp site had suffered from the theft of parachutes by some village baddies. When the local police came on camp they were able to converse only in French. Silly Scrase started talking to these guys in their own language. Well, that fixed things, as from then on I was designated as the Squadron Interpreter. Not only that, but some days later and greatly daring I chased some young lads who were wandering around our camp site. They were carrying stolen goods so I pulled out my .38 revolver and fired, admittedly in the air but to good effect, as the boys stopped sharply and I was able to hand them over to the burly expat *Gendarmes* for appropriate attention.

Another diversion was our wine collection run. Some twelve miles away was the village of Thibar. During the latter part of the nineteenth century the White Fathers had come out from France, originally with the intention of proselytising the local population. But the Fathers soon realised that the best way to achieve their object was by example, so they set about cultivating the land in that area which benefits from the waters of the ever-flowing Medjerda River. The rich red soil was cultivated to produce wheat, fruit, vegetables, and vines. And as well as the Church, a seminary, a hospital, and a school were set up in the village. Houses were built for the local population. To find more work for the locals they also began the production of fine carpets. But for us there was the opportunity to buy wine and also the thick and sticky liqueur Thibarene. Soon, at the end of most days there was a queue of Army and RAF vehicles waiting to purchase wine and also to collect supplies of beer. On many occasions I was called on to deal with the purchases for 72 Squadron. Perhaps that's how I got the nickname Joe!

March was a month when we continued to receive unwelcome visits from the Hun FW 190s – including our airfield as a regular spot for dropping bombs. One such occasion happened as I came back from a sortie. Bombs dropped around us. An old school friend had driven up to see me. He was serving with an LAA Essex Regiment stationed nearby. I had written to Lawrie at his home address in South London. My letter was forwarded back to him in North Africa and, surprise surprise, we found that we were only three miles from each other. Lawrie and his driver were astonished to find that we showed such little concern!

April was a much better month for me operationally. I was called on to do twenty-six flights – thirty-four hours' flying. In a sweep of the Kairouan area I fired at an Me 109G which I claimed as damaged. It was my first. A few days later, flying as Red 2, I got another Me 109G damaged. Really a fantastic dogger-ho. And was the perspiration flowing within me!

On 19 April, we were one of five squadrons providing freelance cover to 48 Bostons and Mitchells. A further three squadrons flew as close escort. We ran into some 109s and 72 Squadron claimed two E/A destroyed and one damaged. This was the biggest show in which I had taken part. There was a similar operation the following day but then we met much less enemy opposition. Close on 100 Spits in the air on one operation! The drier weather, the better flying conditions, and improved serviceability of our aircraft. We were really getting on better terms against the enemy. One could see that in North Africa the end was in sight.

In May, my involvement was nineteen operational flights, totalling twenty-five hours. A lot of strafing, little opposition. I claimed an SM79 destroyed on the ground and a 109 damaged. There was always a price to pay for low-level attacks, as when attacking some barges off the port of Tunis I was hit in the port wing by part of one of the barges on which I had been firing. With the end of the campaign, we were called on to cover sundry duties such as escorting convoys bringing supplies in to Bizerta and Tunis. On 12 May, we moved away from our base at Souk-el-Khemis. Remaining flights that month were few. Bringing repaired kites back to our new location at La Sebala just north of Tunis was one such task.

The Axis Forces surrendered on 13 May. Next day I was one of a group of chaps who drove out in our 15 cwt truck to the Cape Bon Peninsula, where the enemy troops, now disarmed, were marching back towards their POW camps. Revolvers and binoculars were being thrown into the bushes – available for one to pick up. I got a pair of super binoculars. Unfortunately, they were to be lost many years later when I visited Epsom Downs for the Derby!

What can I say about my progress? I had learnt something about operational flying but I was still a new boy and I felt my shooting had to improve. At the same time, I had fitted into the team and could be relied on to carry out the instructions I was given.

Malta was our next base. We flew to Hal Far on 10 June, one of the five squadrons in 324 Wing led by 'Sheep' Gilroy. Just a few days later, on 18 June, we flew at 27,000 feet as top cover in a Wing sweep over Comiso, the major Italian Air Force base in south-east Sicily. We saw some twenty Me 109s in three groups but did not engage. Meanwhile, one of our team, Flight Lieutenant Prytherch, reported engine failure and that he would have to bale out. This was ten miles south of Ragusa. Two of our Squadron went down to observe and fix the spot. His parachute was seen to be dragging him along in the sea. Sadly, he was drowned.

In a separate incident, George Keith, a Canadian, was returning to base himself and saw and engaged a 109G. The E/A was hit and the pilot, none other than the

Kommandeur of II/JG 53, Major Michalski, baled out with a wounded leg and broken ankle. He was picked up quickly and taken to hospital. George's own operational career ended sadly just six weeks later when he was hit by flak while ground-strafing near Catania. He baled out over the sea and was picked up by an ASR Walrus and taken to hospital. But, in baling out he hit the tail plane of his aircraft and badly injured his leg. Despite all the efforts made in hospital he was to succumb to his injuries the next day.

We had been one of the first squadrons in Tunisia to be equipped with the Spitfire Mk IX. Now, in what we saw to be a retrograde step, we were to give up our exclusive use of that fine model to share the planes we had with other squadrons in the Wing. It was to be six Mk IXs for each, and we co-opted clapped-out Mk Vs to make up our establishment. My own record in June was six operational flights totalling seven hours. During the six weeks we spent on Malta our non-flying activity was limited to looking at historic buildings, drinking plenty of beer, joining the evening throng in Main Street, swimming, and sailing. One challenging swim was out to Kalafrana Bay, where lay the remains of one of our merchant ships. She had been hit in the summer of 1942 and was so badly damaged that she had been beached there. It was a good half-mile swim out to reach the rusting sides of the ship, and then after resting and sunbathing we could race back to shore.

July brought us back into a full operational state. There were now six wings of Spitfire aircraft in Malta, a total of twenty-three fighter squadrons of which three were USAAC. Numerically this force of over 400 aircraft was substantially in excess of the *Luftwaffe* and the *Regia Aeronautica,* but in terms of individual performance the Me 109G remained superior to the Spit V.

On 9 July, I wrote: 'A truly wonderful sight. The invasion starts tonight.' For the next few days we were patrolling 'Acid Beaches'. On 12 July, occurred one of those extraordinary clashes. The 72, in full squadron strength, encountered what we took to be Macchi 200s. The Squadron claimed a total of seven destroyed, one probable, and seven damaged. My personal bag was one destroyed and one damaged. I chased two aircraft from the Italian formation. They kept on flying in echelon, a spick-and-span Air Show formation. My two guys just kept on straight and level. I lined up behind the No. 2 and fired. He fell away, smoke billowing from his fuselage. His leader continued and in my excitement I kept my finger on the gun button for much longer than necessary. The plane was damaged with bits flying off the wing. All I could do was watch and hope he would have to bale out. No such luck. He went on back to base. I returned to our base to be greeted by my ground crew and to have to confess ammunition for twelve or thirteen seconds was nowhere long enough for me! It was only later that we learnt our opponents were Fiat G50 fighter–bombers and very likely on a non-operational move out of the immediate combat area.

At the end of the week, in company with other pilots and ground crew, we were taken by Dakota first to Paehino and then to nearby Comiso, a regular air force base with a 2,000 metre runway. Imagine our surprise: not only were there a number of u/s aircraft lying about but also cases of wine and Asti Spumante, which presumably the *Luftwaffe* had been unable to load onto their last departing transport plane. These supplies were very welcome to us!

Other great finds at Comiso were a number of Me 109s. One of these our Engineer Officer, 'Spanner' Parish, ably assisted by Tom Hughes, was able make serviceable. It did have problems with one undercarriage oleo, and some days later when coming in to land after a test flight 'Sexton' Gear had no option but to land on one wheel, ground loop, and make her completely u/s. But we found another plane nearby. She was a Caproni Saiman. We called her the 'Pisser'. After some weeks were able to make her airworthy. A two-seat bi-plane and faster than a Tiger Moth, we found the Pisser very useful as a communications aircraft: shifting mail, messages, and passengers too. And of equal benefit, we could offer familiarisation trips to any of our ground crew who wanted to get airborne. But our stay at Comiso was all too short. We were soon moved back to Paehino, at the south-east tip of Sicily. Hot and dusty and set among olives and vines it was not a very good base. Flies in the daytime and mosquitoes at night; plus a very boring diet – the corned beef almost melted off your plate!

For the month of August, I show twenty-five operational flights totalling fourteen hours. An unusual entry in my logbook reads: 'Squadron practice, 1 hr 20 mins flying versus 43 Sqn.' The comment 'bags of steepers ho!' will describe our activity. It was during this month that I was first to lead a sub-section flying as Yellow 3.

One extraordinary thing about the campaign in Sicily is that the Germans and Italians were left to get back across the Straits of Messina without any concerted effort being made to prevent their escape to the toe of Italy. So different from what had happened in Tunisia.

'Sunshine' was the Gift of War name of a brand new Spit IX, MA520, which, on 6 September, I was asked to fly on a thirty-five-minute ferry trip from Cassala to Falcone. She was still fitted with her ninety-gallon long-range tank. Coming in to land I hit some trees at the threshold to the runway. On landing, the undercarriage collapsed and the propeller blades were broken off: no damage to me personally, except hurt pride!

Now we were to prepare for the invasion of Italy. But in the meantime I had a very brief stay in Taormina. And that was why I yearned to return there for a holiday. We used Palcone on the north coast of Sicily as our base from which to fly for the invasion of Italy. 'Peaches Beaches' was the name given to the strip of coast south of Salerno which we were to patrol. That was 180 miles away and about as far as we could go using slipper tanks and still carry out an effective patrol. My logbook records flying times of two hours thirty minutes – two hours forty-five minutes for these missions. About one-third of the way to our patrol point was the Aeolian Island of Stromboli – a live volcano. Our heading point showed puffs of smoke and occasional bursts of red flame day and night. This served as a marker, as from there all one had to do was to head due north.

My task was one sortie a day for the four days between 9 and 12 September. Then, on the 13th, it was time to fly over to our newly constructed landing strip at Tusciano, close to the river of that name. British artillery units were almost in the field next door. Our first full day at the base and German infantry came down to within two miles of the airfield. It was only much later that we came to know that General Clark had considered whether the 6th Corps should be withdrawn from the beachhead! Reinforcements by sea and the effects of shelling by heavy guns of the fleet helped to restore the situation. But this was at some cost, as the Germans then used Do 217Ks of *Kampfgeschwader* 100 to bomb, hit, and sink or seriously damage a number of our British and American warships, including HMS *Warspite*.

On 17 September, flying with Roy Hussey on a 'catch the bombers' two-man patrol, we engaged two *Dorniers*. We were at 20,000 feet and to my chagrin I had trouble with my supercharger cutting in and out. I descended 1,000 feet or so to put the matter right. Roy continued with his attack and engaged first one and then the second Dornier, destroying both. As I came up to join in the melee I flew past the second aircraft from which one after another of the seven crew members were baling out. Sadly, the last one to emerge got his parachute entangled with the tail assembly; no safe landing for him.

September was a busy month. I record sixteen sorties, twenty-eight hours' operational flying. On the ground it was hard going. Mosquitoes and high temperatures; poor, tented accommodation; and basic rations. We thought this would be somewhat livened up when our cooks slaughtered one of the cows in the nearby field. The Squadron's Coles Crane was used to hang the beast, but no one was prepared to wait and let it hang properly. So it was a tough old beast to eat!

October was the big surprise for me. No one had explained properly, but a request from HQ for a Flight Commander for 74 Squadron, then in Cyprus, led to my being posted away. Ferry flights by Dakota, via Malta, Libya, and Cairo and I was on my way to Nicosia, Cyprus. There I did two reconnaissance flights. Next I met Squadron Leader Hayter, the boss, and five of his pilots just returned from Cos. The invasion of the Dodecannese Islands had gone quite badly wrong. Four of his pilots had been captured and remained there as POWs. There was no place for a chap like me, so within a week I was back in Cairo at HQ ADEM. And from there it was Dakota flights back to good old 72. I was just in time to make one trip that month, but from our new base, Capodichino, the airfield for Naples.

In Naples we were billeted in very splendid flats in the streets adjoining the main railway station. The contrast between our life in the field in Tunisia or in Sicily was beyond belief. Now restaurants and bars offered a very real social life where you met people of all kinds. You were juggling the demands of military service with the reality of the world around you. Our quarters were cleaned and tidied by local folk – very probably they had been so employed by the previous residents. The price of goods and services increased day by day as the locals realised we knew little about the cost of life in Naples. They had lived through the years when Mussolini got the trains to run on schedule but even he had not been able to get the Neapolitans to behave in an honest manner!

As squadron pilots our favourite dinner spot was the Giardini degli Arand (Orange Garden), high up on the hillside and with lovely views across the Bay of Naples. But cars 'commandeered' by some of our pilots meant there were drives along the road network to this or that restaurant. A visit to the opera house, the San Carlo, which I made many years later reminded me of a leap I had made in an effort to catch a chandelier. By great good fortune I landed on a table some ten feet below me and did myself no physical injury! Another incident concerned the friendly swap we did with soldiers on an American Army truck. They were gesticulating as we drove slowly up the hill to Capodichino. We stopped. They wanted to know whether we had any victuals to swap. The net result was we got some coffee for our surplus tea.

A quite different contact we had was that with two Italian air force officers who wanted us to support them at a meeting where they, Royalists, were hoping we would speak up in support of their King and play down the Republican feelings that many local people were displaying. Needless to say we steered clear of things like that.

The army was advancing beyond Naples towards Capua. Much of our time was spent in giving escort cover to destroyers shelling coast towns such as Mintumo. We did have one major engagement with Me 109s described in my logbook as a 'freelance de-lousing sweep'. The lice were shot down, five of them. And then our Group Captain, 'Sheep' Gilroy, was about to leave, end of his tour. He wanted one last flight north over the Appenines. As his No. 2 we did a flight in clear blue skies high up at 21,000 feet looking down the snow-capped mountains to the sea far away beneath us. Yes, the memory is still clear on that. Equally clear was my task in bringing home a 'Finger Four' group in very dirty weather conditions with low cloud dogging our return. A total of fifteen operational sorties and twenty hours' 'ops' flying.

In December, we had a busier spell. For the first time for months we flew twelve aircraft in a three fours formation, but were recalled due to 10/10ths cloud. On 15 December, and while escorting A-20 bombers to Frosinone, we met formations of 109s and 190s. They attacked the bombers. I got an M 109G destroyed, others claimed a number of E/A damaged. Then it was a shaky dogfight with another 109, the perspiration pouring off me as I turned and fought before we both flew off home. The fight left me and some of my colleagues very short of fuel. I report one gallon left!

On 18 December, we lost Tom Hughes. He was hit by ground fire and landed, made a POW, and required considerable hospital treatment. Later he was to be one of the last POWs exchanged through the Red Cross in Switzerland. Another crash involved Red Weller. This was on Christmas Day. Hit by flak he baled out, happily landing in our lines. Driven back to Naples he joined us for Christmas dinner when officers and aircrew served the ground crew in a show of our appreciation. A busy month: twenty-two 'ops' with a total of thirty-two hours. It was also a month when we had 'Danny' Daniel posted tour expired. He was our Boss and the last person to have served through the campaigns right from the beginning in North Africa. His replacement, Major Bosman, was to be with us only a short time as within a month he took command of an SAAF Wing. In his place, in January, came 'Chips' Carpenter, a Battle of Britain veteran who had spent time as a flight commander during the siege years in Malta.

In January, we became an all Spitfire Mk IX Squadron again. My plane, MH669, RN-N, was my pride and joy. Most of the sorties we made during January were at four- or six-aircraft strength. For a number of these I was leader. But on the non-flying side January was a month when, in company with Roy Hussey, and ably conducted by an Italian guide, we climbed Mount Vesuvius. At 4,200 feet it was not a great height, but one needed a guide to be able to get there and back safely, this at a time when the volcano was not quiescent. The trick for the guide was to get us to give him a coin which he then pressed into the next flow of molten lava to land nearby. Hard to believe, but I still have my souvenir, a 1942 Italian coin with its black-lava surround. Vesuvius was showing danger signs, and some months later there was a major eruption which altered the shape of the crater.

On 16 January, we said goodbye to Naples and went off to Lago, an airfield by the sea and just north of Castel Voltumo. So, although this was a canvas encampment, at least we had the pleasure of sea bathing. And in the small village twenty miles from Capua there was an atmosphere more closely resembling that of the Medjerda Valley.

Just a few days later came the Army landings at Anzio and Nettuno. We had some activity, but limited in scale and encounters with the enemy were by chance. On 27 January, flying as Black 1, I found and destroyed an FW 190. This was ten miles south-west of Rome. Following the early days after the 'Shingles Beach' landing we did get some enemy reaction but it was very much in and out flights by E/A bombing or striking at our ships off the beach. Forty hours' 'ops' flying, seventeen missions, made this a very busy month. I was now serving as Deputy Flight Commander. There were several changes in the man in charge of 'B' Flight so it gave me the opportunity to put myself down.

February 1944 was to be my last month with 72 Squadron. On the 14th and while leading six aircraft we met a gaggle of eight FW 190s escorted by eight Me 109Gs. We were ten miles north of Anzio. There followed an encounter. We claimed several E/A as damaged. I got a good burst in on a 109G, claimed as destroyed. On the 16th, I led a team of six 72 Squadron pilots escorting the second group of bombers attacking Monastery Hill at Monte Cassino. These were Marauders. Their bombing was good and on target but sadly it did not do a lot of good in the land battle to breach the German lines.

Next I had a seven-day period of leave at a five-star hotel near Sorrento, the Coccumella at Sant'Agnello. It really was a splendid place, provided for RAF Officers. We were feted and treated as very special people. Only 2 km from Sorrento Town Centre with its wonderful Club for Visitors and its long-time links with British people, I had a really super time. In 2003, I was there again as a guest. This time they showed me their record books from the period and I was asked to write about my stay and sign the VIP visitors' book! Made even more pleasant during the visit was the friendship I enjoyed with an RAF nursing sister whose uncle had been appointed British Government Port Manager for Naples. He gave us the use of his chauffeur-driven limousine and in that vehicle we spent some days travelling along the Amalfi coast – Positano, Amalfi, and Ravello. I suppose as young men do I boastfully told her of our role in the Salerno Landings and the occasion when in the Squadron 15 cwt we had driven from Tusciano for a day out, travelling beyond Salerno to Vietri-sul-Mare.

The Germans still controlled the road north to Cava dei Tirreni. You had to have road traffic control going along the coast road and every minute or so an 88 mm shell would land. When you had the signal to go you went like hell and the number of burnt-out vehicles showed this was no idle threat. Well, we made it safely. She listened politely and I thought of the number of much more serious medical cases with which she would have had to deal. Back at Lago I made what was to be my last trip for No. 72 Squadron. That was a one-hour forty-minute flight patrolling Shingle Beaches. It was my 200th operational flight with the squadron and I had logged 275 hours, with a further fifty hours non-operational flying. This included seven hours forty minutes 'sliding round the skies' in the Caproni Saiman.

My combat record was four enemy aircraft destroyed, one probable, and two damaged. In March 1944, I went to Ismailia and the Central Gunnery School at El Ballah as an instructor. There I learnt of the award of the DFC. I stayed on in Egypt until September 1944. My last posting was back in the United Kingdom where I joined 1 Squadron at Detling and Manston engaged on bomber-escort duties, called 'Ramrods'. A further thirty-five hours of operational flying followed. We also engaged in various non-operational activities, including escorting Winston Churchill on a return visit from Paris. On 17 September, after our Battle of Britain Day celebrations at Church Fenton, my Class B release came through. I had 1,018 hours' flying time and now I was to return to university to find a very different and difficult life learning how to study for my B.Com. degree! Now aged twenty-four and ready to enter the commercial world!

It was a very happy period in my life and to this day I remain proud to have flown Spitfires and served with 72 'Basutoland' Squadron.

16

FLYING OFFICER GEOFF BATES

I volunteered for aircrew duties in 1941 when aged eighteen. After my flying course (No. 47) in Rhodesia, the majority of us were posted to the Middle East where we expected to convert onto fighters and join operational squadrons. Alas, however, we were told that we were to be posted to Transport Command in Egypt where we would convert to fighters and become ferry pilots. We were all most disappointed at the news.

Some half a dozen of us were granted an interview with the CO to request that we be posted to a fighter squadron. The CO, having heard each of us out, leant back in his chair and quietly said: 'A ferry pilot's job is as vital to the war effort as any squadron pilot, as squadrons rely on deliveries made by ferry crews to ensure that their strength is maintained and that aircraft requiring major overhauls can be flown to maintenance units. You will probably have the opportunity, which normally is unavailable to many squadron pilots, of flying many different types of aircraft. That experience will, no doubt, make you very proficient pilots. You will find that the world of ferrying produces its own excitement, pleasures, and satisfactions. Finally, you have all been in the Royal Air Force long enough to know that you obey orders, so off you go and be proud of the fact that you are doing a worthwhile job.' I came to realise that he had a point, because I did enjoy my flying experience as a ferry pilot, on twenty-two different aircraft types as first pilot and seven as second pilot (including to four-engined aircraft). My travels took me to both some very interesting places and others which were hell-holes where one was glad to get away with the minimum of delay!

After converting to Spitfires, Hurricanes, and Kittyhawks, I was posted to No. 1 ADU based at Heliopolis, just outside Cairo. At that time the Unit was ferrying Hurricanes from West Africa to Cairo where another ADU ferried them to squadrons fighting the Japanese. The overall journey – Cairo to Takoradi or Cairo to India and back to Cairo – was some 13,000 miles. Perhaps being a modest person I shouldn't be saying this, but flying this route was not for the faint-hearted, especially for a single-engine pilot flying over dense forest with little hope of pulling off a successful

130. Flying Officer Geoff Bates.

forced landing. The course was also across scrub, marsh, and desert where sandstorms reaching up to 10,000 feet could spring up without warning.

Then I got a posting to North Africa to ferry mostly Spitfires to Cairo, Sicily, Italy, and Corsica before a home posting in 1945 when I spent more time abroad than in the United Kingdom, ferrying Spitfires, Mustangs, Tempests, Corsairs, Hellcats, and others to such places as India, Egypt, Malta, Italy, France, Czechoslovakia, and Norway. During this period I survived a forced landing in neutral Sweden. My travels took me to thirty-two different countries, and, among others, I flew eighteen different single-engined aircraft which included 244.45 hours on Spitfires.

Once I was flying in a convoy of six Spitfires en route to Fayid, near Cairo. We were escorted by a Beaufighter, flown by a rather cocky pilot who knew it all and had done it all and was our Convoy Leader. At Elmas, near Cagliore in Sardinia, I had trouble starting my Spitfire Mk XVIII. The rest of the convoy had started theirs and were taxying out for take-off, so as not to overheat. The Beaufighter pilot suddenly jumped up on to my wing, sticking his head in the cockpit, saying that the engine needed priming. Before I could stop him he grabbed the throttle and pushed it back and forth to prime the engine. Despite him outranking me, I got really cross and told him to stop and that I was well aware of how to start a Spit – something *he* had never done. 'All engines are the same,' he replied. But I told him that he could easily have over-primed the engine. I pressed the start button again; there was a loud explosion, the propeller turned slowly, and flames shot out of the engine! I was already strapped in; I had the harness undone in record time, was out of the cockpit in a flash, and did fifty yards in a Mae West, with a parachute and dinghy strapped on, in about five seconds! Fortunately, the ground crew got the fire out with an extinguisher quite quickly, although the aircraft nevertheless sustained category 'C' damage and was struck off charge. I duly submitted a report and handed it to the Convoy Leader; I was not surprised to hear no more about the incident!

All these years later it amazes me that people are interested in which particular Spitfires we flew, so here is a list of those in my logbook:

Mk V
EE779, EE865, EF649, EF686, EF718, ER476, ER557, ER938, ES239, ES246, SM177, JG798, JK173, JK360, JK391, JK392, JK399, JK402, JK544, JK649, JK968, MA293, MH581.

Mk VIII
JF414, JF416, JF745, JG337, MT768.

Mark IX
EN261, EN334, EN500, EN581, EP891, ES213, MA301, MA765, MA809, MH482, MH559, MH568, MH655, MH672, MH772, MH932, MJ197, MJ520, MJ588, MJ665, MJ989, MK154, MK313, MK464, MK483, MK625, MK690, NH262, MH305, NH518, PE400, PT377, PT482, PT603, PT715, PV120, RR189, SM177.

Mk XVIII
TP229, TP369, TP373, TZ214, TZ228, TZ238.

17

SUB-LIEUTENANT JACK LLEWELLYN

I first came into touching range of a Spitfire – or more accurately a Seafire – in the spring of 1943. I had joined the FAA in January as a trainee pilot, spending the first three months in ground studies. Our base was Lee-on-Solent, but in either April or May we were despatched to HMS *Argus*, a training carrier based in the Clyde, for two weeks 'sea experience'.

Monday morning, first thing was to manhandle a Swordfish into position for take-off. Then we started with deck landings. That morning we had Spitfires. First, they made dummy approaches, being waved off before landing by the batsman, but then one by one they landed. We had three accidents that morning. One Spit missed all the arrester wires and crashed into the crash barrier; another came down heavily on one wheel, the undercarriage leg collapsed, and the plane skidded into the side nets (these being a gangway each side of the deck, about four feet below deck level, for the deck party to retreat to while aircraft were taking off or landing).

The third accident, however, was the worst. The batsman waved off the pilot, he tried to climb away, stalled, and slid into the sea. Only the pilot's headrest came to the surface. Operations were suspended for the rest of the day. We all went to dinner rather quiet. Most of us were nineteen to twenty years old. I had just had my nineteenth birthday, and until that moment it had all been rather exciting. We were going to learn to fly, but now it was suddenly no longer a game. The rest of the two weeks were uneventful.

So, eventually, after getting my wings in Canada I was selected for fighter-pilot training and posted to Yeovilton, still the FAA base. That was in late June 1944 – just after D-Day. After cockpit drill and briefings about swing on take-off, the tendency to overheat the engine if you did not get a move on taxying out, etc., I had my first flight in a Spitfire. Yes, it was wonderful to a twenty-year-old. I was flying this iconic machine, which by this time in the war was so famous. It felt great.

I won't bore you with details, but after finishing training only a few were picked for operational squadrons. They had trained more pilots than required. So I went to 770 Squadron, based at Drem near Edinburgh. This was a Fleet Requirement Squadron. We had Martin Martinets for target towing – both for ships working up at Rosyth and

131. Jack Llewellyn pictured during training.

132. A Seafire picketed on HMS *Argus*.

133 and 134. A Seafire lands on HMS *Battler*.

135. Seafires taking off from HMS *Battler*, a merchantman converted to an aircraft carrier by the Americans.

for an FAA base at Crail, training torpedo-bomber crews. Also, we had Hurricanes which were used for dive-bombing exercises on ships, mainly, and also for radar calibration runs. Then we heard that the Hurricanes would be replaced by Spitfires! The fleet needed the extra speed to make things a little more authentic.

Then someone had the idea that we could tow sixteen-feet wingspan gliders with a Spitfire to give gunnery practice. They devised a way of using the arrester-hook mechanism to attach the towing rope, so when one returned after an operation you could release the glider before landing. For take-off, the glider was put at the far end of the take-off strip with the cable being taken back to the start and attached to the Seafire. (By this time we had a mixture of Spitfires and Seafires – which incidentally gave another problem: the airspeed indicator on a Spitfire was in mph, of course, but on a Seafire it was in knots. You had to remember which you were in when landing.) Got a bit expensive on gliders, though, so it didn't last!

And that was the end of flying Spitfires for me. In July 1945, I was posted to a squadron in Australia to fly Corsairs, but the war with Japan ended before my transport sailed, so I never had that experience.

I flew both Hurricanes and Spitfires and also other aircraft, because we also ferried planes for the RN. We all preferred flying the Spitfire, but it wasn't perfect: the undercarriage was narrow and it really was not sturdy enough for deck landings. Moreover, you had to *fly* it; other planes you could get the trim right and they were stable, but the Spit always needed a watchful hand on the stick. Nevertheless – and above all, however – you felt a bond with a Spitfire. The cockpit was so small that you were part of it. Someone coined the phrase that it was as though you 'put the Spitfire on' – like a coat – while you just 'got in' other aircraft.

18

FLIGHT LIEUTENANT KAZEK BUDZIK

Kazimierz Budzik had joined the Polish Air Force as an officer cadet before the war. Military service was in his blood, as both his father and brother were regular career officers in the Polish army. Upon the outbreak of war he was undergoing training at the Fighter School at Ulez, from where he was evacuated with his unit. Via Romania and Syria he arrived in France where he received further training in the French Air Force. Before he could fly to battle in a Dewoitine, France collapsed and 'Kazek' was on the run again. In June 1940, he arrived in England and joined the RAF.

Initially serving with the ATA at Maidenhead, Pilot Officer Budzik began training to be an RAF fighter pilot and flew a Spitfire for the first time at 61 OTU, Rednal. In August 1941, over a year after arriving in the United Kingdom, he reported for flying duties with 303 Squadron at Speke. A month later he joined 308 'City of Krakow' Squadron at Northolt. The 308 comprised a part of the Northolt all-Polish Fighter Wing, and the Squadron was constantly participating in the Fighter Command Offensive, flying daylight bomber escorts and sweeps. Kazek Budzik flew on numerous such sorties, and makes an interesting observation concerning fighter tactics:

I have no doubt that during the early part of the war the Polish formations were superior to those used by the British squadrons who flew in tight vics of three where each pilot has to be constantly aware of his neighbour's position to avoid collision. In that kind of formation you just cannot concentrate on searching for the enemy. They also flew in line astern, watching each other's tails. I have seen Me 109s latch onto the end of one of these formations and shoot a couple of aircraft down before disappearing, the rest of the formation oblivious to what has happened. Our formation was loose, stepped up, and in line abreast, just like the Germans. You were far enough away from your neighbour not to have to worry about collisions and so could search for the enemy. Each Spitfire was also stepped up, according to the sun's position, each aircraft therefore covering the other. Again, just like the Germans, in

136. Flight Lieutenant Kazek Budzik VM.

combat our four aircraft broke into pairs. It was adopted by the RAF who called it the 'Finger Four'; the Germans of course called it the 'Schwarm'. It was certainly the safest formation to be in.

Kazek continues regarding his feelings on being a new pilot:

When I first commenced flying operationally I could fly a Spitfire – but flying *and* fighting in one is a very different matter. On my first trip with 308 Squadron I was detailed to fly as No. 2 to the CO, Squadron Leader Marian Pisarek. Someone said to me, 'Pisarek is the best there is. Go where he goes, do what he does, watch him like a hawk and you will be all right. You will come home.' I took that advice and on my first few trips I stuck to Pisarek's tail like glue, all the way to the target and back again. I was so intent on following him, though, that I saw virtually nothing of what was going on around me. The more experienced pilots could fly, fight, and search the sky all at the same time, which is why they were so successful. The most successful pilots were those who would hold their fire until they were so close to the enemy that they could not miss. My problem was always that I opened fire too early. I was just unable to keep calm enough for all this sneaking up behind people – I just wanted to let them have it immediately I saw them!

The Polish squadrons were sometimes criticised by the British for using Polish over the R/T in a dogfight. I think that this was a little unfair as we could not speak English all that well anyway. When you have a split second to warn a comrade of danger then instincts take over and you just do not have time to convert your thoughts from Polish to English.

It was strange going off to war for an hour or so, then coming back to clean and comfortable living conditions with good food in the Mess. It was strange being shot at one minute but being back in London the next, possibly having a drink in a pub just a short while after escorting bombers to a target in France. People have got the impression that we fighter pilots had it easy, but what they fail to consider is that we flew long tours of operational duty. That type of flying in those circumstances caused great stress but I do not think people generally appreciate that.

After his first tour of operational duty, Budzik flew briefly with the AFDU at Wittering during May 1943. The following month, however, he resumed operations with 306 'Torun' Squadron, another Polish Spitfire unit. From September 1943 onwards the squadron flew an increasing number of sweeps over enemy-occupied Europe, and Flying Officer Budzik flew on most of these. In May 1944, he was posted to 317 'Wilno' Squadron with which he flew numerous offensive sorties in the build-up to D-Day. On the great day, 6 June 1944, 317 Squadron flew four separate patrols over the invasion beaches. Kazek recalls:

We must have been among the first fighter aircraft over the beachhead as dawn was just breaking upon our arrival. The invasion armada was enormous. Most of the landing craft were still in the sea, heading towards the beaches, it really was quite a spectacle. There was flak everywhere though, mostly from the fleet, and that was quite frightening. Watching the start of Europe's liberation was a fantastic experience, particularly the naval bombardment. You could see the guns fire and the shells landing on the coastline, getting further inland the more our troops advanced. It was amazing.

As the Allied ground troops advanced they required support from the air to neutralize German strongpoints and other stubborn pockets of resistance. The air over Normandy became full of Allied fighter–bombers: Spitfires, Mustangs, and rocket-firing Typhoons, all ruthlessly seeking out German military transport, armour, and troops as the enemy was pushed towards the Seine and out of France. With bridges blown and under constant attack, the German army was eventually forced to retreat via the Falaise Gap, and there, in that beautiful French countryside, the carnage really began. Formerly quiet country lanes reverberated as aero engines howled overhead as the Allied fighters strafed, dive-bombed, and rocketed the retreating German columns. Kazek flew many sorties during this period, his logbook noting the destruction of numerous enemy military vehicles and armour.

On 17 August 1944, 317 Squadron was strafing enemy transport in the Lisieux area. So low did the Spitfires fly in fact that one aircraft was damaged by steel cables! However, the squadron was bounced by five FW 190s which came down out of the sun; despite aerial superiority being overwhelmingly Allied, the *Jagdwaffe* had continued to fly in support of the German army from bases around Paris. The Germans failed to score in this instance, and the Poles damaged five of their assailants, one by Flight Lieutenant Budzik:

After the attack I climbed up to 4,000–5,000 feet to look for more Huns. While making a turn I saw a lone 190 flying very low and to the east. I put my aircraft into a steep dive and went after it, closing range to 700 yards. Our height was virtually zero. Flying in the enemy aircraft's slipstream I fired one burst but saw no result. I closed to 500 yards but fired repeatedly without result. I then fired again from 300 yards and saw strikes on both wings. That burst exhausted my ammunition, so I turned back and re-joined the squadron.

In October 1944, Kazek was posted back to 308 Squadron, this time as Commander of 'A' Flight. On 29 October, the Squadron flew an 'armed recce', during which Flight Lieutenant Budzik was shot down by light flak near the Breda–Dordrecht bridge in Holland:

It was a low-level attack, strafing, and I was leading four aircraft. I cannot remember the exact target but it was probably a flak position or something like that. Anyway, I went in first so got hit first, turned back, and crash-landed safely.

137. Flight Lieutenant Budzik with his 308 Squadron Spitfire Mk IX on the continent, 29 October 1944. Minutes later he took off on a strafing sortie, destroying a staff car, but was shot down by flak and crash-landed near the Breda-Dortrecht bridge in Holland. He was back in action shortly afterwards.

There were another four Polish Spitfires not far away doing a similar job, but their leader, Flight Lieutenant Krzemanski, was also shot down by flak as he went in first. He was sadly killed while I came out in one piece. I actually force-landed in 'no man's land' and was told this by a Dutch woman that the Germans had gone but the Allies had not yet arrived! When the latter eventually did, I was a guest of the 49th British Division. I remember that the soldiers had a bear motif on their sleeves. I spent a pleasant evening in their Officers' Mess before returning to the Squadron.

Just two days later, Kazek was back in action. On 6 November, however, he was again shot down by flak, while leading the Squadron on an attack against a train on the Zwolle–Mardewijk line. Having located their target the Poles dive-bombed the train and caused many direct hits. The Spitfires then proceeded to strafe the train and set several cars on fire. The flak was both intense and accurate, and again Flight Lieutenant Budzik, the leader, was hit. Fortunately, Kazek controlled his Spitfire Mk IX sufficiently to make another safe wheels-up forced landing, this time near Gorinchem. Just a few days later he was up again, flying an 'armed recce' over the Arnhem area.

Left and below: 138 and 139: Flight Lieutenant Budzik receives his award of the highest Polish gallantry decoration, the Virtuti Militari (Vth class).

In April 1945, one month before the war in Europe finally ended, Flight Lieutenant Budzik was posted from 308 Squadron to learn how to instruct. In May, he became an instructor at 61 OTU, now based at Heston, the very unit with which he had himself flown a Spitfire for the first time way back in 1941. The wheel of fortune had turned full circle. Kazek Budzik had survived the Second World War.

Kazek's flying days were not quite over. But he was less than impressed, having survived for so long as a combat pilot, with the prospect of life as an instructor. He was relieved, therefore, to be posted back to an operational squadron in September 1945, this time as a Flight Commander with 309 'Ziema Czerwienska' Squadron flying Mustang IIIs. In February 1946, he moved to command a flight in 303 Squadron, equipped with Mustang IVs. His final flight was a 'formation' practice in a Mustang IV on 4 November 1946. Kazek Budzik had hung up his flying helmet and parachute for the last time.

But what after flying for a man like Kazek Budzik who had experienced all the highs and lows of an operational fighter pilot for over six years? While instructing, Kazek had met a young administrator in the Polish Women's Air Force, and upon demob he and Helen were married. From his mother in Poland,

140. Flight Lieutenant Budzik at the end of the Second World War with his Polish wife, Helen, an administrator at RAF Hucknall.

however, he was warned not to come home with Stalin and Soviet Russia now in control but instead urged to make a new life in England. He discovered too that both his father and brother had been among those Polish officer POWs massacred by the Russians during the Katyn Wood atrocity. The Budziks settled in Nottingham, near Helen's wartime station at Hucknall. Kazek became a British citizen and found employment – as a bus driver. Appreciating that his family in Poland were virtually minor aristocracy, and that driving a bus is in no way comparable with flying Spitfires, one wonders how a man like Kazek Budzik coped: 'Yes, I suppose it was a bit degrading, and it was not exactly either what I wanted to do or was used to doing. But I had a wife and soon two children to support. Times were hard and I was grateful to have a job.' Kazek retired as a bus driver in 1984, and exchanged his Spitfire for a Skoda motor car!

For many years Kazek did not discuss his wartime experiences, believing that he was 'just one of hundreds of thousands of Allied airmen just doing my job'. Living in the Midlands, and with a growing family to support, he and Helen were unable to travel to London and attend the Polish Air Force Association's reunions. He therefore closed the door on this important chapter of his life. In early 1988, however, I traced Kazek in connection with my interest in the life of another Polish airman, Flying Officer Franek Surma. The Budziks' kindness and warm welcomes during my research trips became legendary. Unlocking Kazek's memory after all those years was like a dam bursting, as the memories came gushing forth. As we sat for hours in his sitting room talking of past times, he was back in his Spitfire, left hand pushing open the throttle and right hand controlling the stick as he related so many stories, all so very nearly unrecorded and forgotten. Although aged seventy-five, his bright eyes flashed and sparkled as he remembered bygone heady days: 'Yes, they were exciting,' he said, 'no doubt about it. The Spitfire was wonderful.'

19

SQUADRON LEADER 'TOMMY' DRINKWATER DFC

Thomas Henry Desmond Drinkwater was born on 26 September 1914, at Truro in Cornwall. 'Tommy' was to travel an interesting road towards achieving his ultimate ambition of becoming a fighter pilot.

Formerly a butcher, on 25 February 1936, Drinkwater enlisted in the air force as No. 529527 Aircraftman 2nd Class/Aircrafthand under training and joined the Training Depot Squadron. On 15 May, he reported for duty at 3 School of Technical Training. That course successfully completed, he became a 'mate' on 26 June, commencing training as a Flight Rigger on 3 July at 2 Wing, Henlow in Bedfordshire. As a fully fledged Rigger, on 10 September, 'Drink' joined the ground staff of 9 FTS, Hullavington. Two years later, he became an Aircraftman 1st Class, and on 1 August 1939, a Leading Aircraftman. A month later, the day that Germany invaded Poland, Tommy became a Flight Rigger under Pilot Training. At this time many squadrons either formed or re-formed, one of the latter being 219 which had initially served as a fighter squadron during the Great War. On 4 October, 219 Squadron reformed at Catterick, equipped with Bristol Blenheim Mk IF night-fighters. Two weeks later, LAC Drinkwater joined the Squadron, remaining with 219 until 19 August 1940, when he then joined 4 ITW, beginning at last the procedure leading to becoming a fighter pilot. He later returned to Hullavington, as a trainee pilot, on 4 December 1940, and thereafter attended 57 OTU at Hawarden on 23 April 1941. Now a 'Temporary Sergeant', upon completion of operational training he joined 234 Squadron on 9 June 1941.

The 234 'Madras Presidency' Squadron had also been a Great War combatant, disbanding in 1919 but reforming at Leconfield on 30 October 1939. Having flown Fairey Battles and Gloster Gauntlets, the Squadron received Spitfires in March 1940. During the Battle of Britain, 234 operated initially from St Eval in Cornwall, undertaking convoy protection duties, moving to Middle Wallop, inland of Southampton, during August. A month later, having lost five pilots, the Squadron returned to St Eval. On 24 February 1941, 234 moved to

Warmwell, in Dorset, where Sergeant Drinkwater joined the unit four months later.

The Squadron was providing protection for convoys in coastal waters, an often monotonous task. It was on such a sortie that Sergeant Drinkwater made his first flight with 234, in Spitfire P8194, between 0620 and 0650 hrs on 18 June 1941. On 5 July 1941, 234 re-equipped with the so-called 'Long Range' Spitfire with a seventy-gallon-capacity external fuel tank attached to the port wing. This was to increase the range of squadrons operating over the Cherbourg peninsular. On 10 July, flying P7984, Drinkwater flew his first offensive operation when the Squadron undertook a sweep of Cherbourg. Squadron Leader Blake destroyed two Me 109s, and Sergeant Jacka probably destroyed another. Blake was actually shot up himself, however, alighting on the sea with a damaged radiator and was later rescued by an MTB. Other sorties were made on 14 July, when 234 provided high escort cover for bombers on a Circus to Cherbourg, and on the 17th when more Me 109s were claimed during a search over the sea for a missing Blenheim crew.

On 6 August 1941, Squadron Leader H. M. Stephen DFC, who had flown with 74 Squadron during the Battle of Britain, was appointed to command 234. On that day, Drinkwater flew Long Range Spitfire P7907 on a bomber-escort sortie. Other participating pilots were Flying Officer Wootten, also a Battle of Britain veteran, Flying Officer Baynham, and Sergeants Fox and Jacka. On 18 August, the Squadron flew from Coltishall, led by Wing Commander Boyd, providing low escort to eighteen Blenheims attacking shipping off the Dutch coast. A ship was sunk but one bomber crashed into the sea. On 21 August, the Long Range Spitfires, which were unpopular with pilots due to the loss of manoeuvrability caused by the bulbous external fuel tank, were replaced by Spitfire Mk IIAs. Among these was P8046, 'City of Worcester II', which was flown for the first time by Sergeant Jacka on 26 August, when 234 Squadron undertook a 'beat up of Maupertus aerodrome', on the Cherbourg peninsular, between 1130 and 1225 hrs. During the attack, P8046 was hit by flak. Twenty-six-year-old Cliff Jacka, a motor racing enthusiast from Bournemouth, headed out to ditch off the French coast. His body was later washed up on the peninsular and buried in the town's cemetery.

September continued in similar vein, convoy protection patrols punctuated by offensive operations over Cherbourg. Sergeant Drinkwater flew P7543 on an uneventful sweep of Cherbourg on 4 September. On that day the Squadron operated from Ibsley in Hampshire with 118 and 501 Squadrons, providing medium escort to six Blenheims on Operation GUDGEON VII ('GUDGEON' and 'BLOT' operations were attacks on fringe targets). The sortie was 'uneventful'. He next flew P7668 during a Channel sweep two days later and P8366 on a similar sortie on 20 September. On that day, 234 again operated from Ibsley with 118 and 501, providing escort to six Blenheims attacking a whale oil ship in Cherbourg Harbour. Light flak was experienced over the target, but no German

141. Tommy 'Drink' Drinkwater pictured at Warmwell while flying Spitfires with 234 Squadron in 1941.

fighters were engaged. Ten days later, 'Drink' flew Spitfire Mk VB AB186 during an attack by twelve Spitfires on nine ships off Cap-de-la-Hague. Black smoke was seen to issue from the largest vessel, and one had already been sunk by a previous attack. Return fire was experienced but only one aircraft was damaged when a single bullet passed through its port aileron.

By 1 October 1941, 234 Squadron was fully equipped with the Spitfire VB and, with 118 and 501 Squadrons, operated with the Ibsley Wing. On that day, Sergeant Drinkwater flew AB816 over Cherbourg seeking enemy shipping, but without success. Two Me 109Fs were sighted at 20,000 feet but were too high to intercept. On 13 October, the Squadron flew from Redhill in Surrey, providing medium escort for six Blenheims with the Middle Wallop, Kenley, Tangmere, and Biggin Hill Wings. The target was the airfield at St-Omer. Light flak was experienced over Gravelines, and heavy anti-aircraft fire over Boulogne. Thirty Me 109Fs were intercepted in the St-Omer area, but one of the enemy fighters destroyed a Blenheim. Two Me 109Fs were engaged by Flight Lieutenant Rose DFC and Sergeant Fox, the latter claiming a probable. On 15 October, 234 flew Ramrod 69 out of Westhampnett, the Tangmere satellite; the Ibsley Wing providing high cover, the Portreath Wing flying close escort. The twelve Blenheims attacked the Le Havre docks, battle was joined and a number of Me 109Fs were claimed by the RAF pilots. Sergeant Drinkwater was a participant, flying AB816. On 17 October, he flew the same machine when the Squadron escorted twelve Blenheims on Roadstead 6, sweeping from Pas-de-Querqueville to Pas-de-Barfleur, unsuccessfully seeking enemy shipping.

The first sortie of November 1941 was on the 8th, when Drinkwater flew AA728 in Flying Officer Glaser's section. The Ibsley Wing swept the Cherbourg peninsular covering eight Whirlwind fighter–bombers of 263 Squadron. On 11 November, Sergeant Drinkwater flew W3937 on a sweep of St-Saens. The target was not located, however, so, instead, high-tension cables were attacked and destroyed. On 15 November, the Ibsley Wing attacked various alcohol distilleries, 234 Squadron destroying the plant at Bricquebec, 'Drink' flying W3937 again. The weather, however, was patchy – Sergeant Drinkwater having to turn back when the visibility closed in over France on the 17th. The weather was equally poor throughout December, although on 30 December, 234 Squadron closely escorted Halifax bombers attacking Brest. Likewise, January was quiet from a flying perspective, though on the 5th Tommy Drinkwater was finally commissioned and became a 'Pilot Officer on Probation'.

On 12 February 1942, Pilot Officer Drinkwater flew Spitfire W3936 on an escort sortie with a difference: Operation FULLER, more commonly called the 'Channel Dash'. The Joint Chiefs of Staff were aware that the Germans intended to break out the battleships *Scharnhorst*, *Gneisenau*, and *Prinz Eugen* from their base at Brest to a less vulnerable port. Contingency plans were drawn up to oppose any course that the ships might take when they reached the open sea. With any such break-out under way, the RN and RAF were to execute immediate counteraction. The classified codeword to initiate these operations was FULLER. Unfortunately, this information failed to filter through to 11 Group's fighter squadrons.

On that morning, Squadron Leader Bobby Oxspring, CO of 91 Squadron, received a telephone call from Squadron Leader Bill Igoe, the Senior Controller at Biggin Hill, informing him of considerable German fighter activity over the Somme estuary. Igoe was puzzled as to the Germans' intentions as they appeared to be staying roughly in the same area. He suspected that they were providing aerial cover to some sort of shipping, and asked Oxspring to have a look, adding 'but be damned careful as there are an awful lot of Huns about'. Squadron Leader Oxspring and Sergeant Beaumont subsequently took off and flew just under the cloud base between 1,200 and 1,800 feet. Following the coast past Le Touquet towards the Somme estuary, the two Spitfires suddenly flew into a heavy barrage of flak. Banking into a turn, Oxspring and Beaumont saw a large formation of destroyers and E-boats protecting three much larger ships, all of which appeared to be travelling at speed. They then saw two Spitfires below them attacking E-boats on the periphery of the convoy. Being unaware of Operation FULLER, Squadron Leader Oxspring broke radio silence and reported to Igoe what he had seen. Returning immediately to Biggin Hill, Beaumont suggested that the larger of the three battleships was the *Scharnhorst*. Telephoning in his report to Bill Igoe, Oxspring was immediately put through to the incredulous 11 Group controller. Unfortunately, the AOC, Sir Trafford Leigh-Mallory, was away at Northolt and Squadron Leader Oxspring got nowhere in conveying the gravity of what he and Beaumont had seen. Thirty minutes later, the other two Spitfires, flown by Group Captain Victor Beamish and Wing Commander Finlay Boyd, landed at Kenley. They had maintained R/T silence, but their report both corroborated Oxspring's and, due to their senior rank, carried more weight. According to the late Group Captain Oxspring, when I interviewed him at Duxford in 1988, the delay in alerting the various commands was both 'interminable and inexcusable'.

Indeed, that delay permitted the *Scharnhorst*, *Gneisenau*, and *Prinz Eugen* to steam safely through the Dover Straits and escape into the North Sea.

Shortly after the Channel Dash, his first operational tour complete, Pilot Officer Drinkwater was posted away to No. 2 School of Air Navigation, with which he remained until 24 April 1942, when he rejoined 234 Squadron as a Flight Commander. On that date he was also promoted to Acting Flight Lieutenant. Enthusiastically undertaking his new appointment, Flight Lieutenant Drinkwater led his Flight on an escort mission to Hurri-bombers attacking enemy shipping off the September Isles. By the end of that operation, one German destroyer was at the bottom of the sea.

During this period the other 234 Squadron Flight Commander was Flight Lieutenant David Glaser, who recalled the following amusing story:

When we were at Ibsley for some reason we won a pig, but when we went to collect it the animal was still alive. We sent the Flight Van over to collect it and back at the airfield Tommy was in charge as he had been a butcher before the war. Combat was joined, the pig leaping all over the place, jumping in and out of the van pursued by 'Drink' brandishing his service revolver. Then a shot was fired from within, and the pig came charging out – no sign of 'Drink'. We all peered inside to find him flat on his back, having been knocked over by the pig's charge, the round having fortunately caused neither injury nor damage. We then spent two hours trying to catch the pig!

During May 1942, 234 Squadron moved to Portreath in Cornwall. Throughout that entire month the squadron's pilots flew a seemingly endless rota of convoy patrols. June, however, was to see a return to offensive operations against the enemy. On 2 June, Flight Lieutenant Drinkwater flew Spitfire Mk VB AR383, between 1745 and 1845 hrs, on a 'shipping beat up, NNE of Ushant'. On that occasion, 234 Squadron had escorted Hurri-bombers of 175 Squadron. Later that evening the Squadron flew an ASR sortie and another 'shipping beat up'. The following day, 234 flew down to Middle Wallop and provided rear cover escort to 10 Group's Circus No. 6. The next day, 234 operated from Warmwell, flying a sweep over Maupertus airfield. Jannion airfield was the target on 5 June, when the Squadron escorted Whirlwind fighter–bombers. An uneventful sweep of Le Treport occurred on 8 June, the Squadron pursuing its nomadic existence and operating from Redhill in Surrey. On 23 June, 234 Squadron flew low cover escort for six Bostons bombing Morlaix aerodrome, Flight Lieutenant Drinkwater flying AA383 between 1825 and 2045 hrs. The conclusion of that sortie was to have an important future effect on the air war over France.

German aircraft designer Kurt Tank had produced a lethal single-engined fighter, the Focke Wulf 190, which made its operational debut on the Channel coast in the hands of II/JG 26 in July 1941. Tank had absorbed a BMW radial engine into the airframe of his new fighter which remained well proportioned and aesthetically appealing. The advent of *Die Würger* (the Butcher Bird) caused great consternation among Fighter Command's pilots. Previously, their Spitfires had at least maintained a status quo with the Me 109, but the FW 190 was to prove an entirely different matter. This new fighter could out-perform the Spitfire Mk V in every respect excepting turning circle. The first descriptions of the new fighter's appearance and performance were treated with disbelief. Fighter Command felt it inconceivable that the Germans could have secretly produced such a machine and suggested that the pilots had encountered captured Curtis Hawks. The RAF pilots, however, who knew that the American Hawk was in no way comparable with their Spitfires, immediately rejected such a proposal. Although the first FW 190 was shot down on 18 September 1941, the new fighter was only correctly identified by the RAF on 13 October, when clear cine-gun camera evidence was examined. Between 14 June and 31 December, the RAF had lost 411 fighters over the Channel coast and the Continent, while the Germans had only lost 103, including forty-seven pilots killed in action, seventeen in flying accidents, and three captured. Such losses, although serious, were tolerable for the *Kanalgeschwader*. Understandably, therefore, they were confident that during 1942 the FW 190 would further increase their margin of superiority. By April 1942, as a direct result of the FW 190, RAF losses on the Channel Front reached prohibitive levels. During the course of that month alone over 100 Spitfires were lost in action. Inevitably, the morale of the Spitfire squadrons suffered enormously. This desperate situation saw the hatching of various schemes to obtain an FW 190 for evaluation, one such plan being a commando raid, to be led by Captain Philip Pinkney of E Troop, 12 Commando, on a *Luftwaffe* fighter base to steal a 190 which would be flown back to England by that great airman and Supermarine Chief Test Pilot, Jeffrey Quill. Fortunately, as an indirect result of the sortie to bomb Morlaix airfield on 23 June, such a hazardous undertaking was not required.

Both the Portreath and Exeter Spitfire Wings, returning from France, had been shadowed by FW 190s of the *Gruppenstab* of III *Gruppe* and 7 *Staffel* of JG2. David Glaser recalls that 'the Spitfires returned in battle formation. As we approached Start Point on the Devonshire coast, the FW 190s attacked. As the Spitfires roared low over the town, someone shouted "For Chrissake Break!" as the 190s hurtled down'. In the ensuing melee, *Unteroffizier* Willi Reuschling collided with Wing Commander Alois Vasatko's Spitfire. The German safely took to his parachute and was later rescued from the sea, but the Czech Wing Leader remains missing. With both sides low on fuel the combat was short. Four Spitfires were scrambled by the Exeter Wing to intercept the escaping Germans, but in the process 312 Squadron's Flight Sergeant Mares collided with 310's Pilot Officer Strihavka. Only one Spitfire became airborne, BL517, flown by Sergeant Frantisek Trejtnar. As the combat broke up over Start Point, Egon Mayer's fighters returned to France – all, that is, except one flown by *Oberleutnant* Arnim Faber, who headed north instead of south. Subsequently engaged by Trejtnar, Faber demonstrated the 190's superiority by despatching the Czech after a protracted dogfight. Then the German continued northwards, crossing the Bristol Channel. RAF Fairwood Common's Operations Record Book takes up the story:

2028 hrs: One of Germany's latest fighters, a Focke Wulf 190, landed undamaged at Pembrey. The pilot's story is that after shooting down two Spitfires he was forced north, and, running short of petrol, landed at the first available aerodrome which happened to be Pembrey. He was escorted to Fairwood Common and was guest of the Officers' Mess for two days until he was sent to London for interrogation.

As the 190 landed off a steep turn, the quick-thinking Duty Pilot, Sergeant Jeffreys, promptly jumped on the intruder's wing, thrusting a Verey pistol into Arnim Faber's rapidly colouring face – thus capturing FW 190A-3, Werk-Nr 5313, in a fully serviceable condition. The following day, several 234 Squadron

142. Flight Lieutenant Drinkwater with *Oberleutnant* Arnim Faber's FW 190 at Pembrey, 23 June 1942.

143. Faber mistook the Bristol for the English Channel and landed by mistake at Pembrey – thus delivering an intact FW 190 to the RAF, the first intelligence officers had seen. The cockerel's head emblem is that of III/JG 2, the *Kommandeur* of which was *Hauptmann* Hans 'Assi' Hhan and whose name in German means cockerel.

144. The hapless *Oberleutnant* Faber of Stab III/JG 2 *Richthofen* at Pembrey.

pilots, including Flight Lieutenants Drinkwater and Glaser, flew to Pembrey and examined the captured 'Butcher Bird'. David Glaser recalls that he met *Oberleutnant* Faber himself on that occasion, and expressed his admiration for his *Gruppenkommandeur*, Hans 'Assi' Hahn. JG 2's badge was a cockerel's head, Hahn also translating to 'cock'. The British pilots, however, thought that their German adversary's name was Cock, so, not understanding the problem in translating his *Kommandeur*'s name, Faber appeared evasive. Glaser, who survived the war and retired as a Squadron Leader, stressed how much he and the other British pilots admired Hahn, whom he considered a brilliant aerial tactician and leader. Glaser also recalled Faber offering to 'take on a squadron of Spitfires. We all knew what his game was, of course, he would have just baled out to destroy his 190.'

The RAF rapidly took advantage of Faber's gift. The FW 190 was promptly transported by road to the RAE at Farnborough where it was dismantled and analysed. Allocated the RAF number MP499, on 3 July, the captured machine was test flown by Wing Commander Hugh Wilson. Ten days later, the AFDU took delivery of the invaluable prize and commenced intensive performance trials. The information arising was absorbed by the Spitfire development programme and taken into account in the production of later marques. In the meantime the stop-gap Mk IX had been produced to combat the 190 menace. This new Spitfire was basically a Mk V airframe combined with the Merlin 61 engine. The first Spitfire Mk IXBs were delivered to 64 Squadron at Hornchurch in June 1942. On 30 July, the new Spitfires destroyed four FW 190s over France. The latter type, however, performed best between 14,000 and 22,000 feet, at which heights the Mk IX did not. The Merlin 66 engine was consequently developed which performed best between 10,000 and 20,000 feet. None the less, the Spitfire Mk IX undoubtedly met the FW 190 on equal terms, restoring confidence and morale. The deliverance of Faber's machine, therefore, saved the lives of countless RAF fighter pilots.

For 234 Squadron, July 1942 continued much as the previous month: monotonous convoy patrols punctuated by the occasional offensive sortie. August and September, however, were completely taken up by convoy protection duties. On 25 October, Squadron Leader Banning-Lover AFC arrived to command the Squadron, on which date the squadron Operations Record Book also recorded that 'only five more Huns are needed for our century'. An interesting sortie took place on 27 October, as described in the Squadron diary:

The Squadron joined 19 for an offensive sweep. Twelve Spitfire Mk VBs of 234, including Wing Commander O'Brien, up at 1540 hrs, down, at Perranporth and Portreath, at 1700. The rendezvous was at 1545 hrs, 10,000 feet above the Lizard. When climbing through layers of cloud the squadrons became separated. The 234 flew to 23,000 feet and patrolled for three minutes, fifteen miles north of Ile de Batz, which was five miles north of the intended patrol line. The 19 Squadron then received a warning from the Controller that the bombers were climbing above the Spitfire squadrons. The 234 Squadron turned right into the sun at the end of the patrol when three or four FW 190s dived on them from behind. Squadron Leader Palmer (supernumerary) was seen by Flight Lieutenant Drinkwater to go down in flames and bale out fifteen miles north of Ile de Batz. At the same time Flight Sergeant Drayton was seen in a spin. The formation broke up and three had a crack at the Huns but no claims were made.

On 7 November, another interesting sortie is reported in the squadron diary:

At 1313 hrs six aircraft of 'A' Flight patrolled the Lizard at 5,000 feet as additional rear support to Ramrod 36. The flight was then directed to search for a pilot (Teacher 41) from the Exeter Wing who had called Mayday while returning from the operation. They found a patch of oil and a pilot in the sea. Flight Lieutenant Drinkwater and Red Section orbited at zero feet with two other sections at 1,000 and 2,000 feet. One Defiant of 276 Squadron was also sent out to search for Teacher 41, but its pilot called Mayday at a position twenty miles from the Lizard at 120 degrees. A second Defiant and a 406 Squadron Beaufighter were then sent to search, so when Flight Lieutenant Drinkwater saw these in the vicinity he left Teacher 41 to search for the Defiant crew. He instructed the rest of the flight to remain over Teacher 41 but, owing to a faulty radio, the other pilots failed to receive the message and followed

145. Flight Lieutenant Drinkwater at Gravesend with a 19 Squadron Spitfire Mk IX in 1943. He had by now been awarded the DFC.

him. A second patch of oil was then seen in the sea some six to eight miles west of Teacher 41, but no dinghy or pilot was seen.

Flight Lieutenant Drinkwater's second tour was completed that month, during which he also received the DFC in recognition of having flown fifty operations over France. On 26 November, the Squadron diary recorded that: 'The popular Flight Commander of 'A' Flight, Flight Lieutenant Drinkwater DFC, posted away to 57 OTU. He has been with the Squadron for eighteen months and rose from Sergeant to Flight Commander. We are all very sorry to see him go and wish him the best of luck at OTU.'

Drinkwater then flew as an instructor until 6 July 1943, when he joined the staff of 52 OTU at Aston Down. Six days later he reported for Flight Commander duties with 19 Squadron, who were still equipped with Spitfire Mk VBs, at 122 Airfield, Gravesend.

In January 1943, 19 Squadron exchanged Spitfire Mk Vs for Mk IXs. Throughout this time the Squadron was heavily engaged upon offensive operations over France. These sorties invariably found the Spitfires escorting Hawker Typhoon fighter bombers, or American heavy bombers. On 11 November, the Squadron diary relates the following events – a red letter day for 19 Squadron and 'Drink's' finest hour:

Clear fine morning. Briefed at 1115 hrs. Role was a fighter sweep in the St-Pol area as diversion for Marauders bombing construction work on Cherbourg Peninsular. Squadron up at 1155. The Squadron had been over France for thirty minutes when 122 Squadron, on port side, was jumped by fourteen to sixteen Huns. The 19 Squadron turned towards them and as we approached an FW 190 turned away and dived down. Flight Lieutenant Drinkwater followed from 18,000 to 1,000 feet. He fired a number of bursts and saw strikes. The E/A eventually crashed in a field. This is the Squadron's 100th confirmed victory and everyone is quite excited. Captain Johnson of 122 Squadron also got one confirmed. The Squadron was next airborne at 1505 hrs to sweep the same area: Marauders this time bombing constructions at Calais. Nothing doing, the Squadron landed at 1635 hrs. The pilots attended a lecture at 1730 by Pilot Officer White of 485 Squadron who had just escaped from France. In the evening the Squadron Intelligence Officer, 'Spy' Dilks, came down to congratulate us on our 100th victory when we all adjourned to the local and drank the health of Flight Lieutenant Drinkwater.

Winston 'Spy' Dilks:

Unfortunately, at the beginning of the war, I was in a reserved occupation and so was unable to join up until late 1941. After training, in 1942, I was posted to 313 (Czech) Squadron, but on 20 June 1942, joined 19 Squadron at Perranporth. This was during their rest period but I can assure you that there was plenty of activity.

146. Flight Lieutenant Drinkwater DFC cuts the cake celebrating the Squadron's 100th kill. Holding it is the CO, Squadron Leader Vic Ekins DFC.

On most days there were sweeps over the French coast where many battles ensued, and many escorts around Brest where the enemy submarines were based. On one occasion the Squadron was jumped by Me 109s and we lost Flying Officer Jackie Henderson, a wonderful pilot and a clever artist. Pilot Officer René Roger, a Free Fighting Frenchman, was killed at the very end of the war while flying to meet his parents at a French aerodrome, where he crashed.

The Squadron was very good at spotting V2 ramps and as a result of the reports that I was able to submit to the Air Ministry the bombers had great success. When I arrived, the Squadron's total of victories was ninety-nine, and try as they could, as being engaged on a quiet sector of home defence German targets were few and far between, they could not get the 100th, although there were several probables. When Flight Lieutenant Drinkwater got the 100th kill there was a great party at a London hotel to celebrate. I attended with Squadron Leader Vic Ekins, our CO, and Air Vice-Marshal Dixon was also there.

Wing Commander Vic Ekins:

I knew Tommy Drinkwater very well and I had the greatest of respect for him. I always found him a quiet sort of man, respectful, and a very hard worker. He reported to me as 'B' Flight Commander in 1943 and carried out his duties as a fighter pilot with courage and enthusiasm. The 19 Squadron was proud of him. When

I was away on leave he would often lead the Squadron and did it very well. We had just changed over to Spitfire Mk IXs, a super aircraft with a four-bladed airscrew. A lot of Drinkwater's time with us was spent at 83 Group airfields in south-east England preparing for the invasion of Europe. I was so pleased that he got our 100th Hun. We certainly had a great party to celebrate!

The 99th victim, a Do 217, had been shot down in February 1942 over the east coast. According to a national newspaper, the Squadron had 'prepared the champagne bottles in preparation for the 100th, but they were to wait another 21 months for the 100th victory. Even the fierce air battle during the Dieppe raid failed to provide a victim for the squadron'. Apparently, the pilots and ground crew had since contributed sixpence each to a sweepstake before every sortie. The pot must have been substantial for the lucky winner!

The bomber-escort sorties went on. On 30 November 1943, 19 Squadron covered the withdrawal of 360 B-24 Liberators returning from the Rhineland. On 7 January 1944, twenty-four Spitfire Mk IXs of 15 Wing based at Gravesend, of which 19 Squadron was a part, took off at 1228 hrs on Ramrod 433. The Wing's objective was to provide cover for the withdrawal of American Liberator and Flying Fortress bombers. The rendezvous was made at Guise Villiers with the American 5th, 6th, 7th, and 8th Fighter Groups. The first box of bombers passed out at Cambrai and Arras, escorted by four Thunderbolts. When south-west of Arras, six Me 109s dived on a Liberator straggling on the port side. In the St-Pol/Douvellers area, eight FW 190s attacked the Fortresses but were chased away by 19 Squadron. Flight Lieutenant Drinkwater fired on an FW 190 and had a second in his sights when another Spitfire jostled in front of him and shot it down. The pilot baled out. The Wing crossed out with the last box over the Somme Estuary and left them only when twenty miles off the English coast. Flight Lieutenant Drinkwater reported:

> I was leading White Section when at 19,000 feet in the St-Pol area I saw eight FW 190s coming in out of the sun from the port quarter and at our height. The enemy aircraft broke immediately they saw us and dived away in disorder. I picked out one and started to fire from 400 yards, but I could not close the range. The enemy aircraft went into a vertical dive and was lost in cloud which was 10/10ths at 4,000 feet. I saw no strikes but base my claim of one FW 190 damaged on the assessment of my combat film, No. TAP184.

In January 1944, 19 Squadron began exchanging its Spitfires for Mustang IIIs, and over the next few weeks carried out numerous training and practice flights as the pilots familiarised themselves with their new mounts. The 19 Squadron had been the first in the air force to receive the Spitfire, in 1938, so this ended their association with Mitchell's fighter of over five years' standing. The Mustang was produced by North American Aviation Inc. and powered by an Allison engine. The first tested proved disappointing for high-altitude combat and were thus allotted to army co-operation roles. In late 1942, the flying trials took place of a Merlin-powered Mustang. The result was unquestionably superior in all respects. Within a year, Merlin–Mustangs were operational in England with the USAAC. Fitted with extra fuel tanks they acted as 'Little Friend' escorts for their 'Big Friend' bombers, and were able to operate deep within enemy territory. For many pilots the Mustang became the best single-seater fighter to see combat in the European Theatre, its attributes surpassing even the legendary Spitfire and FW 190.

On 5 February, 19 Squadron made its operational debut with the Mustang, flying two sweeps into Belgium and Holland, both of which were uneventful. That evening there was a party to celebrate the anniversary of 122 Airfield and at which the beer was free, no doubt a significant contributory factor to its success! The squadron diary also relates that 'there was screening of the airfield film, in which 19 Squadron figured prominently. Star of the show was undoubtedly 'Ace' Drinkwater (terror of the *Luftwaffe* and hero of the Squadron's century) who co-starred with 'Spy' Ellis saluting the airfield flag, which was the climax of the film'.

The Squadron's duties with the new Mustang became increasingly to provide an escort to American daylight bombers. An interesting sortie occurred on 6 March, when Flight Lieutenant Drinkwater's White Section shepherded a lone Flying Fortress which had to turn back but which they lost in cloud. On that day, the Squadron escorted 660 Fortresses withdrawing after bombing Berlin, the rendezvous with their charges being deep into the Reich, just ten miles east of the 'Big City'.

On 17 March, the 19 Squadron diary humorously recorded:

It is with great regret that we have to announce today that 'B' Flight Commander, Flight Lieutenant Drinkwater DFC, threw away his freedom and entered into holy matrimony. However, we really do wish both he and his wife very many years of happiness together. We were hoping to provide fighter cover for the happy event but as usual the weather washed out any likelihood of flying.

With the weather cleared a few days later, the escort missions continued. On 11 April, Flight Lieutenant Drinkwater's name comes to notice once more in the Squadron diary:

Announced this evening that Flight Lieutenant Drinkwater promoted to Squadron Leader and to take over 122 Squadron. While we are very thrilled to hear of his promotion, the squadron will miss one of its most capable and popular members whose efforts gained 19's 100th Hun. We all join in giving 'Drink' our congratulations and extend to him our very best wishes and good hunting with his new squadron.

147. Flight Lieutenant Peter Taylor listens to a 'line shoot'. He remembered the 'boys' being 'pretty shaken up' when Squadron Leader Drinkwater was killed.

The 122 'Bombay' Squadron was another of the disbanded former Great War fighter squadrons, and had reformed in May 1941, equipped with Spitfires from then until January 1944, when it also received the Mustang III. On 19 April, 'Drink' led his new Squadron up from Gravesend on a Ranger to attack an enemy airfield. Aircraft were damaged on the ground by Wing Commander Johnstone and Flying Officer Minchin. These were the Squadron's first successes flying Mustangs. Thereafter the unit flew an increasing number of Rangers and destroyed numerous enemy aircraft in similar circumstances.

On 2 May, six Mustangs of 122 Squadron each carried two 500 lb general-purpose bombs while another six acted as their escort. Railway marshalling yards between Nantes and Gassicourt were successfully attacked, but the Mustangs were the fleeting target for a heavy flak battery near Rouen. Six days later, Lille aerodrome was successfully dive-bombed. When the Mustangs left, both barracks and a hangar were ablaze.

On 14 May, the Squadron moved to Funtington in Sussex. On 18 May, Squadron Leader Drinkwater DFC, flying FZ164, led three other Mustangs off at 1800 hrs on a Ranger to the Tours–Nantes area. As the Mustangs bobbed along at low level, intense and accurate light and heavy flak were encountered from Chartres and Tours. 'Drink' drew more fire that the others. A gaping hole suddenly appeared in his starboard wing and the gallant, recently married, twenty-nine-year-old Cornishman crashed in flames east of Tours. Flying Officer Cush was badly hit, his starboard ammunition box exploding, and a bullet through the cockpit nicked his neck. Flight Lieutenant Pavey's external fuel tank was blown away, but Flight Sergeant Naish escaped without damage. The survivors returned to Funtington at 2030 hrs. Flight Lieutenant Peter Taylor, at that time flying Mustangs himself from Funtington with 65 Squadron, remembers the Mustangs returning, and that 'the boys were pretty shaken up'.

Squadron Leader Drinkwater DFC was buried at St-Symphorien cemetery at La Salle, as an 'unknown English soldier'. After the war, the RAF and other armed forces faced the massive task of identifying many servicemen so laid to rest, and collecting all such fallen warriors in communal war cemeteries. On 22 June 1946, Mrs Drinkwater received a letter from the Air Ministry:

> I am reluctant to distress you by referring after so long an interval to the loss of your husband, Squadron Leader T. H. D. Drinkwater DFC, but I am compelled to ask for your assistance. Some information has now been received which may enable us, with your help, to trace his burial place. We have received an exhumation report concerning a grave in St-Symphorien Cemetery. The cemetery records contain an entry: 'Unknown English soldier buried June 1st 1944'. The exhumation found that the body was that of a Squadron Leader with the DFC, wearing RAF battledress and a dark blue pullover. He had straight light brown hair. No means of identification could be found, but a cufflink was taken from the grave and has been forwarded here. The decorations and locality seem to indicate that this grave may be that of your husband, and if you could identify the cufflink, that would be conclusive. Unfortunately, it is in a very bad condition but it has marks of diagonal coloured stripes on a background of pale blue enamel. I am sorry to cause you distress, but I should be most grateful if you could say whether you recognise the link from this description. I hesitate to send it to you because of its condition, but should you wish to see it I will do so.

Mrs W. D. Drinkwater did indeed identify the cufflink. Squadron Leader 'Tommy' Drinkwater DFC was subsequently buried at the Nantes (Pont-du-Cens) Cemetery at Loire Sinfereure: Plot L, Row B, Grave 21.

Squadron Leader Drinkwater's career had truly been remarkable, considering his rise from lowly Aircraftman to Squadron Commander and distinguished fighter pilot decorated with the DFC. His period of operational flying, from just after the Battle of Britain until a few weeks before D-Day, saw great variety, spanning from the tentative offensive sorties of 1941, the escorting of massed American formations from 1943 onwards, and ground-attack in advance of the Allied landings in Normandy. This period of service also saw the appearance of the lethal FW 190, and indeed the P-51 Mustang – celebrated by many as the best

Above: 148. Drinkwater airborne in a 19 Squadron P-51 Mustang, called 'Wilf', which was his wife's nickname, in 1944. It was flying this type that he ultimately lost his life in action (Steve Brooking).

Right: 149. A section of 19 Squadron Mustangs, arguably the best fighter of the Second World War.

150. Squadron Leader Drinkwater's original grave marker at St-Symphorien, France.

fighter aircraft of the war. 'Drink's' flying career was almost entirely operational, and such strain must eventually have told. To conclude this chapter, reproduced below is the last letter that he ever wrote to his wife, and which requires no further comment.

Darling, let me tell you again, I love you, This past weekend has made me so pleased that you are my wife because I am so in love with you, and I will love you for the rest of my life. And Darling, thank you for loving me. My sweet, I am sure that you have something belonging to me, because I am always so happy when I am with you, but as soon as we are apart I'm just as flat as can be. I am like a man with no brain, but only a memory of you. Oh Darling, it is terrible. Please do not think me sloppy or stupid, though I may be, but I just can't get over it. Perhaps I am a bit tired tonight, and after a good night's rest will be better and able to write you a nice letter. Anyway, I'll see.

Darling, my operational flying days are nearly over. The Wing Commander has told me this evening that I can't go on so many shows, and he is very concerned about it. He said, 'out of fairness to you and your wife, I don't intend to let you stay on ops much longer, even if you want to'. You see, there was something in what I have said, but hell, I'm going to miss this life. I have had over three years of it and the trouble is that now I know nothing else. My sweet, I must off to bed now, I can hardly see what I am writing. I love you, my own precious darling, more than anything else in the world.

Yours forever, Tom.

20

SERGEANT JACK ALLEN

Over twenty years ago, I was contacted by an old Herefordian who told me the fascinating tale of the 'Sabatini Spitfire'. The pilot, he said, was the son of famous author Rafael Sabatini, whose books included *Scaramouche* and *Captain Blood,* both works becoming highly popular 1930s films starring the swashbuckling Errol Flynn. Apparently, Sabatini's son was killed in a Spitfire while performing low-level aerobatics over the family home at Winforton, and, according to my source, had an impressive effigy at Hay-on-Wye cemetery – sculpted by his mother and in his likeness. Now, this was exciting stuff indeed, but little did I know that the road would take me to two similarly tragic deaths in wartime Herefordshire – both having become one and the same tale in local legend as memories blurred over the years.

Back in the 1980s, of course, the internet had yet to change our lives and so we did not then enjoy the immeasurable benefit of information immediately available at our fingertips. It was therefore a case of good old-fashioned detective work, making enquiries in person. No record could be found, however, of a Spitfire having crashed at Winforton during the Second World War. At Hay-on-Wye cemetery we found the effigy concerned, discovering the pilot's name not to be Sabatini but Pilot Officer Lancelot Steele Dixon, killed on 9 April 1940. This was a mystery to be sure, as our source also insisted that the crash happened shortly after D-Day, in June 1944.

The MOD Air Historical Branch confirmed that Pilot Officer Dixon had been killed at Winforton, in Harvard P5864, while a student pilot at 5 OTU at Aston Down, near Stroud in Gloucestershire. We had some concrete facts but were disappointed that our D-Day Spitfire looked like being a red herring. Pilot Officer Dixon's story, however, is as fascinating as it is tragic, and is worth recounting here.

Lancelot Steele Dixon was the son of Hugh Wainwright Dixon and Christine Dixon, and born in London during 1917. Mr Dixon's sister Ruth was married to Rafael Sabatini, an Italian who had come to work in Liverpool in 1892. Writing

151. Sergeant V. J. T. 'Jack' Allen while training in Canada.

152. Pilot Officer Lancelot Steele-Dixon.

short stories as a hobby, Sabatini could never have imagined that today, fifty-nine years after his death in Switzerland, he would be remembered as one of the greatest historical adventure and romance storytellers of all time.

By 1909, the Sabatinis had a son, Rafael-Angelo, called 'Binkie', and had moved to London so Rafael would be closer to the publishing industry. During the Great War, Rafael became a British citizen and worked in British Intelligence as a translator. He continued writing, with modest success, but everything changed in 1921 with the astonishing success of *Scaramouche*, which sold in droves on both sides of the Atlantic. In 1922, followed *Captain Blood*, an even greater success, making Sabatini a rich man. By 1927, however, the prolific author was exhausted and, on the advice of his doctor, took time off and moved away from London. Renting Brockwier House in the picturesque Wye Valley, near Tintern Abbey, he was able to relax and indulge his passion for writing. Binkie, now aged eighteen, was a regular visitor in his new sports car. On 1 April 1927, however, the Sabatini's idyll was shattered. That day Rafael drove a friend to Gloucester while Binkie took his mother to nearby Monmouth. On the way home, Rafael encountered a wrecked car – Binkie's – alongside which the young driver lay dying. Ruth had been thrown clear and survived, but it transpired that only Binkie had kept the couple together during what had been an unhappy marriage and they divorced in 1931.

That year Rafael bought a new home, 'Clock Mill', on the banks of the River Wye, near Hay. Now completely withdrawn from London life, he remarried in 1935, his second wife being Christine Dixon, previously married to his brother-in-law, and the mother of Lancelot. Known as 'Lanty', the young Dixon had been named after the patriarch of the Dixon family, a wealthy Liverpool paper merchant. Lanty was not unlike Binkie, and Rafael became very fond of his stepson who also lived at Clock Mill. When war broke out, however, Lanty joined the RAF and was commissioned as a Pilot Officer in the RAFVR. By April 1940, Pilot Officer Dixon had completed both his elementary and service flying training, and was posted to 5 OTU for conversion to Spitfires. According to Mr Watkins, of Clifford, on several occasions during his training Lanty had flown over Clock Mill in figures of eight. On at least one occasion he apparently landed in the large field opposite the house before being rowed across the Wye by Mr Smiles, the local salmon ghillie, for tea with his parents.

Upon arrival at an operational training unit, student pilots would be checked out by an instructor in a Harvard aircraft, a dual-seat single-engined monoplane. After passing that test the pilot would go solo on type, then fly various exercises, such as aerobatics and map reading, before going solo on the Spitfire. On the morning of 9 April 1940, Pilot Officer Dixon was solo in P5864 and officially on a cross-country map-reading exercise.

At Winforton, the local populace was going about their business as usual: Mr Howells and Mr Preece were up on the imposing Merbach Hill, overlooking the Wye and Clock Mill; in nearby Winforton village, were Mr Morgan and Mr

Jones, who was in company with his young daughter Hazel. At about 10.10 a.m. all eyes were on an aircraft performing low-level aerobatics, the pilot climbing vertically before diving at high speed, pulling out only at the last minute, seconds before collision with the ground appeared unavoidable. Also watching Pilot Officer Dixon, from the garden of Clock Mill, were Rafael and Christine Sabatini and Mr Smiles.

Suddenly, the spectators' amusement turned to horror when the Harvard stalled while in a steep turn and started spinning, out of control. From Merbach Hill, Mr Howells saw that the aircraft 'had crashed into a very high hedge on the opposite side of the Wye to Clock Mill'. Mr Watkins was working about three miles away from the crash site: 'The aircraft flew over Merbach Hill and started the usual display of figures-of-eight. I heard the roar of the engine but then suddenly all was quiet. I arrived home later to find my worst fears confirmed. It would appear that when the aircraft nosedived there was insufficient height for the pilot to regain control.'

The child Hazel Jones (now Mrs Harris) saw everything: 'Suddenly there was an explosion and we realised that the aircraft had crashed. I cycled through the village, down Bakers Lane, and upon seeing the aircraft wreathed in smoke and flame knew that there was no hope for the pilot.' Mr Price, a gardener at Clock Mill, immediately fetched out the boat and rowed Rafael Sabatini and Mr Smiles across the Wye. The three men hurried to the blazing wreckage but, according to Mr Smiles, the pilot was dead and so badly burnt that he resembled a 'burnt pig'. Later, young Hazel Jones's father, Bill, helped remove the corpse and convey the remains to await the authorities in outbuildings at Winforton Court.

Unsurprisingly, Christine never fully recovered from the shock of seeing her son die in flames before her own eyes. Perhaps a part of the grieving process was creating the bronze effigy, in her twenty-three-year-old son's likeness, which adorns his grave at Hay-on-Wye. The piece is poignant, showing Icarus having fallen to earth, the wax, holding feathers on his arms, having melted. Rafael Sabatini died while on vacation at Adelboden, in Switzerland, in 1950, Christine also sculpting a moving tribute for his gravesite. This bronze shows a man who has fallen, face down, pen in hand. Christine herself died in a London nursing home during the early 1960s.

Having unravelled this story, I assumed that our original information was confused, and that there was no Spitfire but only Pilot Officer Dixon's Harvard. An RAF wartime veteran and Herefordian, Jim Thomas, however, assured me that there was a Spitfire down in similar circumstances. The pilot's name, he said, was Jack Allen, but he was not certain about where the crash had been. As research progressed, another story slowly unfolded.

Victor and May Allen lived at Buskwood Farm, Hope-under-Dinmore, near Leominster in Herefordshire. A daughter, Pearl, was followed in 1925 by a son, Victor Jack Trafford Allen. A popular boy in the village, a cousin, Eleanor, recalls Jack as 'super, very witty, with a great sense of humour'. Another cousin, Peggy,

153. Sergeant Allen poses in a Hurricane during operational training at Bagotville, Canada.

remembered him as 'quite a lad with a warm, loving nature; a daredevil with a great sense of fun'. Jack proved to be an excellent scholar who decided very early that he wanted to fly. A school friend, Mrs Apperley, recalls that when Jack was aged just thirteen he carved his name into the wooden bus shelter on Dinmore Hill: 'Jack Allen: Pilot'. Having attended the Larkhill Academy in Scotland and Herefordshire's Lucton School, Jack completed only one term at Trinity College, Cambridge, before joining the RAF on 6 October 1941, 'For the duration of the present emergency'. At the age of just seventeen, Leading Aircraftman V. J. T. Allen arrived in Canada to train as a pilot under the auspices of the Empire Air Training Scheme. In due course, Jack won his wings at the Elementary and Reserve Flying Training School at Caron, Saskatchewan, and then he converted to Hurricanes at 1 OTU, Bagotville. In the autumn of 1943, Sergeant Allen, as he now was, returned to England and learned to fly Spitfires with 53 OTU at Kirton.

Throughout this period, Jack's companion was Frank Day, a young Hertfordshire lad of similar wit, but at the end of their Kirton course the pair went different ways, never to meet again. Much to Frank's disgust he was sent to fly Hurricanes on the Scilly Isles, and later, more to his taste, Mustangs in India. Sergeants A. G. P. Jennings and V. J. T. Allen, however, went straight from Kirton to fly Spitfires with 616 Squadron at Exeter in 10 Group. The 616 Squadron was engaged on Home Defence duties, commanded by Squadron Leader L. W. Watts DFC, and equipped with the Spitfire Mk VII. This was a high-flying variant designed to

154. A Spitfire Mk VII, similar to the aircraft in which Sergeant Allen lost his life. Note the extended and pointed wingtips to increase manoeuvrability at high altitude.

combat high-altitude intruders. To reduce the drag of wing tip vortices induced when flying acute angles of attack at high altitude, the Spitfire's wings were given extended wing tips. The cockpit was pressurised and the aircraft boasted the most powerful Merlin yet produced: the 64.

In March 1944, Sergeant Allen flew several convoy-protection patrols as the CO's Red 2 and when the Squadron escorted Mosquitoes of 85 Squadron to attack targets in Northern France. He also flew No. 2 to Warrant Officer Des Kelly, an Australian, on a weather reconnaissance over Amiens and Lille. April continued in much the same vein, with patrols of Dover, Dungeness, and Portland. Towards the end of that month, the Squadron moved to Fairwood Common in South Wales, continuing to fly defensive patrols, although on 23 May, Sergeant Allen joined his Squadron escorting B-25s to Dinard airfield, where the Spitfire pilots witnessed some 'excellent bombing'.

By June 1944, 616 Squadron was based at RAF Culmhead, near Church Stanton, which is south of Taunton, in Somerset. This was, of course, during the intensive period immediately before the Allied landings in Normandy, and 616 Squadron found itself flying regular offensive patrols over France. On 1 June, Sergeant Allen flew YQ-F as Red 4 on a Rhubarb. A 'B' Flight commitment, the target was coastal railways, the Spitfire pilots destroying two locomotive engines, six wagons, lorries, and a gun position. Flight Lieutenant Barry returned safely to base after his aircraft was hit by 20 mm rounds, one of which was found embedded in the pilot's cockpit. On 2 June, Sergeant Alien flew on a cine-gun training flight, and at 3 p.m. the following day took off in YQ-E, in company with Flying Officer Mullenders, on 'low flying and cross country, landing at 4.40 p.m.'

The Allied landings in Normandy came at last on 6 June 1944: D-Day. Sergeant Allen, however, did not fly that historic day, but was up as Grey 2 on D-Day + 1, on a Squadron Rhubarb. Two locos and an army truck were damaged near Dinan. On 9 June, the Culmhead Wing Leader, Wing Commander Peter Brothers DSO DFC, led his Wing on a beachhead patrol. Jack Allen flew on that sortie and returned able to describe Allied warships shelling enemy positions inland, many of which were ablaze. The following day, Jack flew on 10 Group Rhubarb 275, to the area of Rennes-Lamballe. There was no opposition from either enemy aircraft or flak, and among targets attacked was a hutted camp by Sergeant Allen near Plougenast. During the return flight, Flight Lieutenant Graves DFC suffered engine failure and took to his parachute forty miles south of Start Point. Fortunately, the pilot was rescued by a Walrus, albeit with head and leg injuries.

By this time Hitler had unleashed a new menace against Britain, the V-l, or Fieseler 103 robot flying bomb, from launch sites in Northern France. Known

155. Buskwood Farm, Hope-under-Dinmore, near Leominster, Herefordshire. Occupied by the Allens during wartime, Sergeant Allen's Spitfire crashed into what was then an orchard in the foreground.

as 'No Ball' targets, the neutralisation of this threat was a priority and 616 Squadron found itself escorting heavy bombers on 'No Ball' raids several times in June 1944. That month also saw 616 Squadron's pilots start to attend Farnborough for week-long conversion to the new Gloster Meteor jet fighter. It was an incredibly exhilarating time, therefore: the long-awaited and spectacular invasion and the prospect of being the RAF's first jet fighter squadron. Heady days, especially for a daredevil nineteen-year-old like Jack Allen.

On 29 June, Sergeant Allen took off from Culmhead on 'a gunnery and aileron test flight to be carried out in the vicinity of the aerodrome'. In complete contravention of orders, however, the young pilot set course for his parents' home on Dinmore Hill, some ninety miles from the airfield. Dashing up to Herefordshire at speeds approaching 400 mph, Jack was soon racing very low down the valley towards Buskwood Farm. As the Merlin's roar shattered the silence, villagers came pouring out of their homes to watch the spectacle, including Jack's sister, Pearl, and her baby daughter. Although his parents were not at home, as both worked at the nearby Rotherwas munitions factory, Jack's grandfather was in a nearby field and also stopped work proudly to watch his grandson. On Jack's second low pass he intended to pull up sharply at the last minute and roar over Buskwood Farm. Somehow the young pilot misjudged the manoeuvre, his propeller clipping the ground in front of the pear tree orchard rising up to the house. The Spitfire tore through the trees, shedding panels and cowlings as it went. The engine broke free and bounded uphill, tearing through two hedges and coming to rest over 250 yards from the point of impact. Eventually the terrible sound of tortured metal subsided, a shocked silence descending over the remote Herefordshire countryside.

Eyewitness Tony Sampson:

At the time I was nine years old. It was a really hot day. I was playing with my friend Rex Evans and an evacuee called Ken Hardy. We were on a small hill north of the Bury Farm when a Spitfire came circling over the village. It circled over where we were and the Bury Farm and went into a dive north towards Queen's wood. I knew it was Jackie Allen because he used to fly similar stunts in a bi-plane. He circled back around again and we could see that the cockpit was open; he was close to us and waved. Then, as he was picking up revs, the engine gave a splutter and he dived again and then suddenly debris was flying everywhere. We ran as fast as we could to the house of his parents and as we came up over the brow of the hill toward his parents' cottage we could see grooves in the ground and pieces of propeller sticking out of it. A wing was propped against a pear tree on the left-hand side and there was debris everywhere. As we got to the front of the house we could see the cockpit which had detached itself but was still in an upright position. Jackie's sister was screaming and clawing at the cockpit to try and get him out. His granddad was on his knees crying nearby. Jackie's arm was resting on the side of the cockpit and we could see the Sergeant's stripes on his blue battledress. The Spitfire's engine had gone over a small lane at the side of the house. Our feet were soaked in high-octane fuel, as the ground was saturated with it. Soon a small crowd gathered and once the police arrived we were removed from the scene.

Aviation fuel, in fact, was spilling in all directions and the crowd nearly set upon a villager who produced a match with which to light his pipe! Bob Jaynes was also there, and remembers the wreckage being scattered over a large area, and black and white identification stripes on the wings. Soon PC 230 Dick Tanner of the Herefordshire Constabulary arrived and helped carry the body to a waiting RAF ambulance in the adjacent lane. The ambulance was from nearby RAF Shobdon, home of 5 Glider Training School, and the Station Operations Record Book states:

> 1535 hrs informed by Flying Control Officer of aircraft crash on Dinmore Hill, Herefordshire. Medical Officer and ambulance proceeded and found Spitfire MB762 wrecked. The pilot, 159427 Sgt J. Allen of 616 Squadron is dead, having suffered partial ablation of the skull and a fractured right clavicle.

Jack Allen was buried the following Monday at the village church, St Mary's. The service was taken by both Reverends Hughes and Charles. The latter had taught the young Jack at Lucton, and described having 'watched his career day by day until he had mounted to the height of his ambition. He was a brilliant scholar, intellectual and lovable'. Among the large congregation were two representatives from 616 Squadron: Flight Lieutenant Mike Graves DFC, the dead pilot's Flight Commander, and Pilot Officer Des Kelly DFC, who was recovering from an eye injury sustained in combat with FW 190s.

616 Squadron's Commanding Officer, Squadron Leader Watts, found himself in trouble with the Air Officer Commanding 10 Group as a result of the incident, and there is no doubt that a cover-up ensued. The Squadron's Forms 540 and 541 comprise the Operations Record Book, a mandatory diary of daily events which should record every flight and absolutely anything and everything of note. Although these now precious documents do differ in quality, depending upon the individual chronicler, there can be no other explanation for the fact that there is no record of Sergeant Allen even having flown on 29 June 1944, much less that he lost his life. Even the Form 78, or movement card, of the Spitfire concerned, MB762, makes no mention that the machine was written off on that summer's day, simply stating that the aircraft was 'presumed struck off charge on 21.6.47.' PC Tanner remembered being told at the time that 'Sergeant Allen was on a training flight and as he was many miles off course that fact must not become common knowledge'.

Squadron Leader Watts was later killed in a mid-air collision in a Meteor over Germany, and Flight Lieutenant Graves died when test-flying a Gloster Javelin in 1955. The Australian Des Kelly is believed to have survived the war, and is known to have visited the Allens at Buskwood before returning to Australia, but nothing more is known of him. The Culmhead Wing Leader, Air Commodore Peter Brothers, told me that he could recall nothing of either the particular pilot or incident, commenting only that 'it was a very busy time and we were taking casualties'.

After the accident a copy of the signal from 10 Group HQ to 78 MU, which cleared the crash site, appeared in the RAF training manual 'Tee-Emm' with the following warning to other headstrong pilots:

The sergeant pilot of a Spitfire was sent off to carry out a gunnery and aileron test, but half an hour later was flying low over his father's house. Only six weeks previously he had carried out the same stunts at a low altitude in order to show his father how well he could fly. This time on his second run across the village and up a valley on the far side he failed to allow sufficiently for the steepness of the hillside and crashed into it. On this occasion his father saw how badly he could fly for he killed himself instantly.

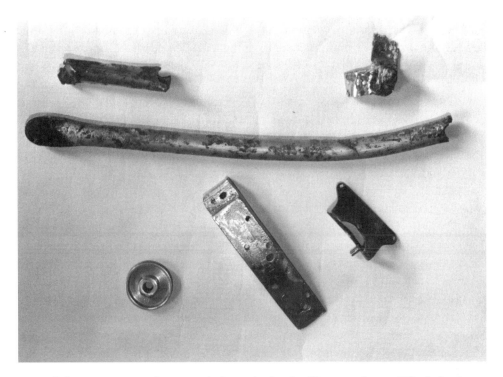

156. All that now remains: the canopy locking wheel and a fillet were given to Dilip Sarkar by an eyewitness in 1986, at which time the author found the other fragments of MB762 at the crash site. These are now displayed by the Worcestershire Air Museum, a mobile display unit.

Already the actual facts were becoming distorted. Jack had not 'beaten up' Buskwood six but three weeks before, probably on 3 June 1944, when he flew a low-level cross-country sortie of one hour forty minutes in company with Flying Officer Mullenders. It was not his father who witnessed the crash but his grandfather. In terms of conveying the necessary message, however, these were arguably unimportant details, but vital clues to the aero detectives of many years later.

Pilot Officer Lancelot Dixon and Sergeant Jack Allen were sadly not alone in the manner in which they met their premature ends. The 616 Squadron pilot Warrant Officer Bob George, who flew with Jack Allen in 1944, recorded in his logbook on 21 October 1943, that two other pilots 'pranged whilst shooting up girlfriend in Ringwood flying Tiger Moth. Both killed'. A 616 Squadron pilot also condemned Jack Allen: 'It is typical of him that his overconfidence and total disobedience to orders should cause the utmost pain and suffering to his family. His actions were not admirable but totally irresponsible.' Given the benefit of hindsight, Jack Allen himself would no doubt agree but, let us not forget, this extremely intelligent, fit, and confident young man was only nineteen years old and a part of what General Eisenhower called 'The Great Adventure'. The world was his oyster, and young Jack wanted everyone to know it. Countless other young pilots showed off their skill to family, friends, and peers, but lived to tell the tale. Air Vice-Marshal David Scott-Maiden, who flew Spitfires during the Battle of Britain, commented that

> When I was at Aston Down in June 1940 we used to fly beneath the Severn railway bridge. We used to do this right at the end of our course, when shortly to be posted to a fighter squadron and reasonably safe, therefore, from official retribution. None of these flights was ever recorded in the pilot's logbook, however – not if he were wise!

Like Christine Sabatini, May Allen never recovered from her son's tragic death. The Allen family remained at Buskwood for many years after the war but eventually returned to their native Scotland, where both Jack's parents later died.

Had Pilot Officer Dixon not been killed on 9 April 1940, he would undoubtedly have gone on to fly Spitfires during the Battle of Britain. Whether he would have survived that experience cannot be said, but at least if he had died in action his sacrifice would not seem such a terrible waste. Sergeant Allen was undoubtedly a young man of enormous ability and potential, so what someone with his drive, energy, and enthusiasm would have achieved in life is anyone's guess. At the going down of the sun, therefore, we must also remember them.

Right: 157. Eyewitness Tony Sampson saw things that fateful afternoon during the summer of 1944 that no nine-year-old should ever have to see.

Below right: 158. Sergeant Allen's original grave marker at Hope-under-Dinmore.

Below: 159. The CWGC headstone marking Sergeant Allen's grave today.

21

FLIGHT LIEUTENANT BRIAN HARRIS

I come from Droitwich, in Worcestershire, and attended the King's School in Worcester. My first flight was when I was a child; my father paid ten shillings for me to fly with Sir Alan Cobham's Flying Circus, which had visited Claines on the outskirts of Worcester. Although flying interested me, it was not a case of me being determined to be a pilot, or anything like that. After King's I went to Nottingham University and studied medicine, which was a reserved occupation, but as all of my friends were in the forces I decided to join up in 1941. I didn't much fancy the infantry, so volunteered for aircrew. Had I not passed the selection process, however, I would have been sent back to medical school. My objective, right from the outset when I joined the RAF, however, was to become a Spitfire pilot.

On the eve of my twenty-first birthday, we landed in Canada to start flying training, which we undertook in the United States, at various airfields in Alabama. There we flew Stearman PT17 bi-planes, which, having more power, were better than the British Tiger Moth, and then North American Texan monoplanes. Having won my 'wings', I returned to England and completed my advanced flying training at Ternhill in Shropshire. Then off to 55 OTU at Annan, flying Hurricanes. There we did various exercises, such as circuits and landings, altitude tests (each flight getting progressively higher), formation flying, low flying, aerobatics, dogfight practice, etc. We also practised forced landings, the landing strip being marked, and you had to come in with a throttled back engine and attempt to land between the two lines. We had already had a good basic training and the OTU prepared us very well for operational flying. After that, on 31 August 1942, I was posted to 74 Squadron, a famous fighter squadron with a proud tradition, so was well pleased, and travelled by troopship to the Middle East. The rest of the journey, from Lagos to Habbiniya, where I actually joined the Squadron, was completed as a passenger in a Hudson aircraft.

My first flight with 74 Squadron was on 9 December 1942, in a Hurricane IIB, BP708. I was impressed with the Squadron; I knew that I had joined a great outfit. There is an awful lot of teamwork involved both in the air and on the ground; I

160. Flight Lieutenant Brian Harris.

161. Brian Harris during flying training in Canada.

guessed that the existing members would all be pretty good, so if I behaved myself I hoped I would fit in. It really was all about teamwork, not individuals – you flew protecting each other. We started with the in line, line astern formation, and then began flying the new one, the 'Finger Four', in line abreast. That was better; you didn't have so much to look at as each pilot was responsible for a particular section of sky.

On 27 January 1943, I flew another Hurricane Mk IIB and practised air-to-ground firing with the 20 mm cannon. There was a mark in the desert, with lots of room round it, and we flew in and fired at it with coloured shells, so you could see where your rounds were hitting. The approach was quite steep, so the target was seen through the gunsight and the guns fired accordingly. When you fired the cannon you could really feel it – the recoil. Sometimes they jammed, and if only one jammed then you would get a real kick from the other one which skewed the aircraft. When you fired everything you obviously got a reaction, and it slowed the aircraft down a bit.

The flying became quite monotonous: lots of patrols protecting ships in the Med. We also had a lot of spare time, the reason being that we were waiting to fly our Hurricanes to the Russians, although in the event that never happened. I liked the Hurricane. It was easy to fly, very solid.

On 23 July, 74 Squadron flew a sweep over Crete. We were a part of the Sidi-Barrani Wing. One hundred fighters took part altogether, although I didn't see any apart from ours. There were a couple of lorries shot up, but that's all. It was costly: seventeen aircraft failed to return from that operation; some may have had problems with their auxiliary fuel tanks because it was a long flight: three hours and forty-five minutes.

In August 1943, I attended a Pilot Gunnery Instructor's Course at the Middle East CGS, although I can't remember now where that was based. There, on 27 August, I flew a Spitfire, a Mk VC, JG958, for the first time. It was the moment I had waited a long time for – a local familiarisation flight lasting forty minutes. I felt tremendous, very proud! I knew that it was something special, because she was – faster and more agile than the Hurricane, lighter on the controls. It was like going from a hunter to a racehorse! Both aircraft were good at their jobs, but the Spitfire was altogether more lively and definitely my favourite.

On 11 September, I re-joined 74 Squadron at Idku, by which time the Squadron had re-equipped with Spitfire Mk VCs. Everyone was absolutely delighted, especially the ground crews, because after a while in the desert everything becomes covered in sand – a fine dust that just gets everywhere. It had been quite a job to keep the old Hurricanes going. On 19 September, we flew to Cyprus, and from there, on the 28th, to the Dodecanese island of Kos, the position of which was crucial to our efforts to retake Greece. Then the fun started! That day we patrolled from Kos and I saw Me 109s above, which was the first time I had ever seen any, but there was no engagement. We were flying off the salt flats, because the Germans had bombed the real landing strip. And then on 2 October they invaded. First, we heard the thump of the landing crafts' heavy diesel engines, and paratroopers were also dropped. We had no armament, nothing to protect ourselves, no ack-ack, nothing. So all we could do was think about escaping, getting off the island. We were getting away, across open ground, when I dropped a packet of cigarettes. You could see tracer bullets flashing by. But would you believe it? I actually went back for those twenty fags! Three other pilots and myself made our way into Kos town, where there was a harbour, and commandeered a boat, in which we went over to Turkey, fifteen miles away. You could see it, but some of the lads were drowned trying to swim the distance. We then found an RAF launch and took that, crept along the coast and back to Cyprus where we joined the main body of 74 Squadron.

Back in Cyprus we were flying a mixture of Mk Vs and IXs by this time, although I can't say that I remember much difference in performance between the two. We moved around a bit, to Aboukir, back to Idku, and again the flying was all very routine. On 13 November, I was flying a Spitfire Mk IX, VS342 on a practice scramble when at 16,000 feet I suddenly realised that I was on fire! I told my leader that my engine had caught fire and that I had to go back, so I dropped out of formation, hoping to blow the fire out, which you could do sometimes. This one wasn't having any of that, so I slowed down a bit, and by the time I was coming in on the approach it was getting a bit warm! I decided to go in without wheels as I knew that I couldn't save the aircraft, slid along, and went over the side just as we stopped. My face was a bit scorched and my parents got a telegram from the Air Ministry, which frightened them to death, saying that I had been 'slightly injured'. I was off duty for a couple days and back in the air a week later.

In April 1944, we returned to England on a troop ship. We didn't have any leave, we were just posted to North Weald. Of course, things were hotting up for D-Day then, so it was very busy. My first flight back home was on 9 May, in a Spitfire Mk IX, MK681, and over the next few days we carried out quite a few Squadron Formation practice flights. On 17 May, we moved to Lympne, near Dungeness, where we joined the Spitfire Wing commanded by Ray Harries. After a Sector Recce we were flying sweeps over France straight away. It was very busy, the sky was full of aircraft and you could see the big formations of American bombers going out too. The *Luftwaffe* had been pretty well knocked about this time and wasn't much in evidence. Most of the casualties were not from aerial combat but from light ack-ack, because we had a lot of very low flying to do. It was a bit 'naughty' sometimes.

On 22 May, in Spitfire MK672, we were on a sweep around Ath in Belgium, strafing a German convoy. I was so low that I hit a poplar tree and knew immediately that the Spit wasn't going to fly any more. The prop was bent and it had ripped my off overload tank. I had to go down with a dead engine, so had no power. I spotted a couple of fields where I thought I could put down and I thought even if I went through a hedge it would be OK. The Spit was pretty good because you were sitting behind the weight, so if you could keep in straight then that would protect you. I then realised that I was heading for these big high-tension cables! As I had no power I couldn't climb over, so I had to go between the pylons and under the cables! I got through, hit the ground, and went through two or three hedges before coming to a stop. Again, the Spit started to burn, so I didn't have to worry about destroying the aircraft. I got over the side unhurt, got rid of my Mae West, hid it with my revolver at the bottom of a hedge, and took off towards the woods. I was very thirsty, possibly because of shock, and so I called at two or three cottages but the occupants would have nothing to do with me. They were very scared.

I was in the woods for a couple of days when I thought that I should try the local clergy because we had been told that the church was friendly. The Resistance then picked me up and carted me off, gave me food, water and coffee, which nearly took off the roof of my mouth it was so strong! Then they thoroughly interrogated me to ensure that I was British, being very wary in case I was a German stooge. Anyway, I was accepted and taken to a farmhouse in the village. There the local doctor examined me and said that I was OK before I was moved to a safe house. The Gestapo then found out where I was and soldiers surrounded the house. A German, whose English was excellent, shouted that if I didn't come out they would shoot me. So I surrendered and was carted off to Brussels with the family. They expected to be shot. The mother turned to me and said, 'Don't worry. We will all meet again in paradise,' such was her faith. She was quite convinced.

We were taken to an old-fashioned gaol where I was put into a cell with five Americans, with just a bucket for everything, which was emptied only when they felt like it; no other toilet arrangements, nothing. Two days before the Guards Armoured Division entered Brussels we were put on a train to be taken into Germany. Most of the guards were elderly, the younger people being in action. A young American and I decided that we were not going to Germany to be used as hostages, and if we got half a chance we would go over the side. The train slowed, a group stood around the

Right: 162. Brian Harris and
Spitfire Mk VC in the desert.

Below right: 163. All that
remained of Spitfire Mk IX VS342
of 74 Squadron.

Below left: 164. Living
accommodation, 74 Squadron
style.

165. Brian Harris (left) and an unknown 74 Squadron pilot in the desert.

166. 'There I was inverted, nothing on the clock but the maker's name!' Brian Harris shoots a line.

door while we rolled out and off we ran. Neither of us was hurt, so we shook hands and decided what to do. Do we go as a group or split up? We decided that our best chance was to separate and that was the last I saw of him, I don't even know whether he got away or was recaptured. I eventually found a friendly Belgian and stayed there until the Guards Armoured Division arrived the following day.

A couple of days later we were flown home. We were billeted in a very good hotel and treated like royalty by the Belgians. I had a steak and promptly shot the whole lot back up – the food while a prisoner had been awful: rotten fish, all sorts of rubbish. I got back home and into Ronkswood Hospital in Worcester. I weighed about six-and-a-half stone, was covered in scabies and had a lung infection. They even experimented with penicillin – stuck a harpoon in my leg and fed it in through that! Anyway, it was marvellous – worked like a dream.

I never flew again. The last flight was in the DC3 upon repatriation. After hospital I went back and had a couple of admin jobs before leaving in 1946. With hindsight I sometimes regret having left, but there you are. I thoroughly enjoyed my service career. It was fun, exciting, and an adrenalin rush. All these years later, some things stand out, other memories are vague. But, having flown Spitfires is something that I am very proud of and was the most exciting time of my life.

22

FLIGHT LIEUTENANT MAURICE MACEY

I was born in 1923 in Eastbourne. We lived at Langley, where there are only about half a dozen houses and the same number of bungalows, one of which was ours. We were surrounded then by fields and farms. And one day, when I was about eleven years old, a monoplane force-landed there in a field, just a couple of hundred yards away. A friend and I were most interested, went to see it, and were asked by the pilot to look after things while he went to fetch some petrol, would you believe? This was my first encounter with an aircraft and we both felt very privileged.

Some three years later, I was asked by a member of the flying club that used to be at Wilmington if I would like to have a trip in his Tiger Moth. You can imagine how I felt about the prospect of actually flying! We were airborne for an hour or so and after that I was absolutely hooked. When I was aged sixteen I joined the ATC and obtained a grounding in navigation and Morse code, theory of flight, etc. which enabled me to obtain my ATC Proficiency Certificate. This was a help towards acceptance for pilot training. Having also passed the written exam and medical I was accepted by the RAF at the age of eighteen. At that point the war had been going on for a couple of years.

A group of about eighty of us were sent out to Rhodesia where we had to cram the usual three-year pre-war university course into one year so, as you can imagine, we had to work very hard. We started training on Tiger Moths, this consisting of an instructor taking you up for the first six or seven hours and then immediately you become proficient enough you go solo. This went on: aerobatics, air-to-air, cross-countries, and eventually at the end of the course one goes up with the CFI who considers whether you are proficient enough to continue training. Afterwards we were sent to another aerodrome where we carried on our training in Harvards, which were a much more modern aircraft. Similar procedure: instructor until proficient at what you were supposed to be doing and then you just go up solo and practise all the time. This included night flying and when eventually we passed all our exams and flying tests we had a group presentation of our 'wings'. We were then given a couple of weeks' leave, which we spent at Victoria Falls and which

167. Flight Lieutenant Maurice Macey.

was a very enjoyable break, before being transferred to Egypt for our operational training.

It was in Egypt that we were first introduced to Spitfires. I shall never forget the first trip. With Spitfires there is no dual tuition, it being a single-seater. You learn the cockpit drill, get into it, and go! I remember that by then I had done several unremarkable first solos, but I will always remember *that one*. One lines up on the runway, opens the throttle, and all you hear is the beautiful sound of the Merlin engine as you take off. This I carried off with no problem at all. I climbed to about 5,000 feet and threw the thing about for about an hour, delighted to be flying a Spitfire at last, and then one suddenly realised, of course, that one has to get down again! Landing a Spitfire is unlike landing almost any other aircraft because there is such a long nose in front, with this enormous engine. In a landing attitude there was no forward vision, so one has to turn in on the end of the runway and straighten up to do a three-point landing. It was advisable to do three-point landings because if you did a two-point the propeller was only a few feet away from the ground, which is a bit dicey. However, it all went off very well and left a great feeling of elation at what was the first of hundreds of safe Spitfire landings.

I was then posted to Fighter Command HQ in Cairo, and from there to 127 Squadron which was based in Hyfa, near Tel-Aviv. Half the Squadron was there, the other on Cyprus. Upon arrival, we had to do a 'Tail Chase', which meant taking off with the Flight Commander and doing everything that he did: climbs and turns and everything else you might need in combat. It seemed that I satisfied the powers that be, and was posted to Nicosia in Cyprus. There we had about a dozen pilots, most of whom had been there quite some time. They were very cosmopolitan: some English, some Australians, some Canadians, and one South African. We all got on very well together and were a good team.

My first operational flight was rather memorable. There were two of us on an offensive sweep over the Mediterranean and we carried enough fuel for a round trip of about 500 miles. The actual capacity of a Spitfire was 90 gallons and we worked on a gallon per minute. But mostly we carried a drop tank underneath, an overload tank, which allowed us to stay up for approximately three hours. On this particular trip there was no sighting of any enemy aircraft or shipping, so it was rather a dead loss from an action perspective. After we had been airborne for about three hours, I called up my companion and asked what he thought our estimated time of arrival back at base was. He reckoned about thirty minutes. But my fuel gauge indicated that I only had enough fuel for about fifteen minutes, so a certain amount of panic ensued and we contacted the Air Sea Rescue Service in case I had to ditch in the Mediterranean. Normally when we took off we used the fuel in the overload tank first, so that if there was any action we could jettison it, and then work from our main tanks. Because there was always a possibility of an air lock when doing this one always left a little bit of fuel in the overload tank, and on this instance I switched back to that to drain it, to get a few more minutes flying. Fortunately, when I switched back to the main tanks the engine picked up without cutting out and I got another quarter of an hour's flying out of it. When we arrived back at base I could see the runway dead ahead of me, so instead of doing the normal circuit and landing I went straight ahead and landed. Halfway down the runway my engine cut out. I was completely out of fuel! It was a very close call.

In those days we used to do early morning dawn patrols, flying along the coast looking for enemy aircraft and shipping, and that sort of thing, and then return for breakfast. After March 1944 there wasn't much happening in the Middle East: Tripoli, Benghazi, Tobruk, and El Alamein had all fallen to us, so our squadron returned to the United Kingdom in preparation for the liberation of enemy-occupied Europe. We came home by troopship and landed at Port Glasgow, then travelled by train to North Weald, near Epping Forest. We went on ten days' leave, during which time I received a telegram to report to Lympne in Kent on 30 April, my twenty-first birthday. I never did get round to celebrating that!

Back in Cyprus we had handed over our Spitfire Mk Vs to a French squadron,

168. Flight Lieutenant Macey prepares for a sortie in a 41 Squadron Spitfire. Note the five propeller blades of this powerful Griffon-engined variant.

but at Lympne we were given the much better Mk IX. The IX was more powerful and more heavily armed, with two 20 mm cannons and four 0.5 inch machine-guns, which were pretty effective. We also carried either a ninety-gallon overload tank or a 500 lb bomb, so we were pretty versatile. We did quite a lot of dive-bombing, our main target in those days being launch sites for the V1 'Buzz Bombs'. Of course, these sites were fairly mobile and sometimes difficult to find. If we couldn't find them for that reason or due to bad weather, meaning that we were unable to attack the intended target, we would bomb the railway marshalling yards at Douai. I remember a particular hazardous offensive sweep when a mass of flak erupted from a forested area. An Australian colleague of mine was shot down. I was absolutely certain that he had been killed but was very relieved to hear, over fifty-four years later, that he was actually still alive and well in Australia! We all got separated on that occasion and I found myself flying at low level along a valley. A couple of miles ahead of me there was a heavily armed troop train crossing my line of sight. I switched on my camera-gun before firing my guns, so as to get a good view of the result, and the train blew up in a most spectacular fashion!

It was a busy time and usually we would have one, maybe two, cross-Channel trips a day, except when weather didn't permit, which was not often. We had a variety of tasks: escorting bombers, dive-bombing, air-to-air interception, strafing ground targets (transport mostly) – trains, lorries, barges, airfields, troops – in fact anything that moved and could be identified as enemy. The *Luftwaffe* was not very much in evidence before, during, and after the invasion, and we had so devastated their fighters that most of them seemed to be in and around Germany defending the Reich against American and British bombers.

On the way back from one bombing trip one of our pilots, 'Chalky' White, had to ditch. He was about five miles out when he was hit by anti-aircraft fire and was extremely lucky. He ditched in the Channel and got away with it. He was picked up by a Walrus seaplane and undamaged except being covered with the yellow dye that spreads out on the sea when the dinghy opens to make the airman's position more obvious. It is well known that the odds of surviving after ditching were very slim indeed; there was a far better chance of survival if there was sufficient altitude to allow the pilot to bale out.

It was about this time that D-Day happened, the Allied landings in Normandy on 6 June 1944. We did three trips over the beaches on that day, a very interesting, hectic, and exciting one, all these masses of gliders being towed by bombers, and over on the invasion beaches all these masses of different-coloured parachutes where the troops had either landed or dropped supplies. We patrolled the beaches, day after day, making ourselves as useful as possible, and by about day three the beachhead was being organised with the prefabricated Mulberry Harbour, which was a brilliant idea and which enabled supplies to be unloaded. The Navy was very much in evidence but they were rather touchy, and not very good at aircraft recognition, as they often shot at us!

One day we patrolled the eastern beaches in the morning, then in the evening met a formation of bombers over Littlehampton, our job being to escort them and provide top cover. Their job was to bomb the E-boat bases at Le Havre. By the time we arrived over the target it was dark and, not having been on a nocturnal bombing operation before, the anti-aircraft fire struck me as spectacular – a constant stream of molten metal, rising to about 5,000 feet. We were able to stay on the periphery, but the Lancasters just flew through it, dropped their bombs, and turned away. We certainly took our hats off to those chaps. However, we were not equipped for night flying and our base at Lympne was just a field, so we were diverted to West Mailing, near Maidstone, where they had a very large runway and switched the lights on briefly so we were able to land quickly. One of the squadrons there, a Norwegian one, was celebrating its anniversary, and so they invited us to a very good party with a liberal supply of gin; I don't recall going to bed but I must have done! I woke up at 0830 hrs and went down for breakfast. The waitress asked if I was the 'Spitfire chap'. I confirmed that to be the case and was told that there had been a tannoy call about two hours before because there was a bit of a panic on at Lympne and we were needed back there at 0730! We went straight back to base where fortunately the weather had clamped down and the operation had been cancelled. It must have been at least thirty years before I drank gin again! The following day was also rather interesting as King George VI and Winston Churchill visited the Normandy beaches and we provided their escort.

Around that time we started operating from temporary airfields in Normandy. Engineers had laid sheets of tracking which created a primitive landing strip, enabling us to spend more time over hostile territory. We would land there after our first morning trip, make several sorties during the day, and return to Lympne at night. This made us a bit more cost-effective, as it were, and went on day after day – bombing and strafing, etc. Pilots were lost, new ones arrived. We tried not to make friendships too meaningful as it was very possible that they wouldn't last all that long. So far, all that had happened to me were a few holes in my aircraft, in places that were not too vulnerable, and I started to think I was invincible, and that it wouldn't happen to me.

I have good reason to remember one particular trip made around that time. We were escorting about half a dozen American Mitchell bombers, their task being to destroy a bridge over the River Seine – just an ordinary road bridge way out in the country. There should not have been any sort of problem, but all their bombs dropped into the countryside, quite a way from the target. We had to return that afternoon and dive-bomb it. We completely destroyed it and I was to have positive proof of this some weeks later (of which more in due course).

I also have very good reason to recall 14 August 1944. We had escorted a group of Boston bombers to a target south-east of Paris, which was quite a long trip for us. Upon return to base we were told that we were on stand-down. We had just finished lunch when we were ordered back to fly and told that there was no time for a proper briefing but just to patrol the bomb line near Argentan. 'Johnnie' Johnson's Wing had problems and we were to relieve them. Having been rather busy for a while strafing tanks and troops, etc., there came an enormous bang under my feet, my right knee hit me on the chin, and my cockpit burst into flames. My engine was still working, so I pulled up to about 3,000 feet, which takes very little time at 350 mph, with a view to doing the only sensible thing when one is flying a blazing Spitfire and that is to get out quickly! The drill for this is to pull a little black ball on the right-hand side of the canopy, the canopy is then supposed to fly off, which it didn't. However, I managed pull the hood back instead, but was getting rather scorched, and started to wonder at the state of my parachute, upon which I was sitting. The next procedure is to release the harness holding me into the aircraft, then turn the aircraft on its back, and push the control column forward so that you dropped out. This all worked perfectly and there I was tumbling over and over near the plane, which blew up shortly after I left it. After about ten seconds I pulled the ripcord; there was quite a big jerk and I looked up to see that beautiful dome of silk above me, which made me a member of the exclusive Caterpillar Club – members of which are those whose lives have been saved by an Irvin parachute. I recall a great silence, broken only by the sound of a skylark. I then heard much-less pleasant sounds – of bullets whizzing past, all of which fortunately missed me. I drifted towards a farm and quite a large orchard and lots of people. I missed the trees, landed in a field, and was immediately rounded on by a troop of the German army.

Surprisingly, in view of the problems they were having at that time, I found the German soldiers pretty reasonable. After searching me – and being very surprised at the quality of the tobacco in my pocket – and after a cigarette, a motorcycle and sidecar arrived, an officer on the pillion. There were a lot of 'Heil Hitlers' and much clicking of heels, etc. and I just couldn't believe that this sort of thing really happened! I couldn't avoid a bit of a laugh, which sounds silly but is true. I just burst out laughing! Anyway, I was ordered into the sidecar, the officer on the pillion holding a Luger a couple of inches from my head, and I was taken to a farmhouse a few kilometres away where I was left in the living room with an armed guard. I remember there was a grand piano, and on it were several loaves of German rye bread, all mouldy on the outside, with a couple of pounds of local Normandy butter. After a while a guard picked up a loaf, cut off the mould, plastered it with butter and started eating it. He saw me staring him but misconstrued why – he thought I wanted some! He offered it but seemed quite surprised when I refused. Ironically, few months later, when food was in even shorter supply, I would have jumped at the chance! Of course, on that day I had enjoyed a good meal back at base only a couple of hours earlier.

About an hour later an unpleasant SS officer arrived to interrogate me. Suffice to say that since that time I have not been very keen on black leather clothing! According to the Geneva Convention, the procedure is that a POW does not have to give any information other than number, rank, and name. I feel that my interrogator was not only an arrogant bully but also rather stupid; he kept asking me to tell him where was the rest of my crew! I certainly wasn't about to tell him that a Spitfire is a single-seater that doesn't have a crew. He seemed convinced that I was a bomber pilot and started brandishing his Luger and getting quite excited when I kept repeating my number, rank, and name. We were only about a mile from where I had landed, so the German troops must have seen me bale out. The anti-aircraft gunners who shot me down must have seen me too. Also, I had been in a certain amount of pain, since having my rather abrupt drop out of the sky I had a piece of shrapnel in my instep and some nasty burns on my neck, face, and legs. As the SS officer was the first person I had met who spoke English, I asked him for medical attention; he wasn't interested. In fact, the change of subject seemed to upset him. He stalked out of the room, thankfully never to be seen again.

So far as my foot was concerned, I thought that I had better do a DIY job. The flying boots we wore in those days were known as 'Escape Boots' because if the leather upper was removed they looked like ordinary shoes. There was a penknife tucked into the lining of the boot for that purpose, so I used that penknife to remove the shrapnel and eventually felt very much more comfortable. I had to put up with the burns, and my eyebrows never did fully recover!

Late that night a lorry pulled up at the farmhouse and I was ordered to get in the back. I found quite a few other chaps in there already, but when I tried to start a conversation I was ignored, which I thought was rather strange because I had heard what I thought were American or Canadian voices. Anyway, I insisted and eventually they started talking, asking questions, and it seemed they were under the impression that I could have been a German stooge. They turned out to be a dozen Canadian Tank Corps chaps who had been captured during the Battle of Falaise, and proved very good companions. We were together several weeks as we were taken through France on our way to Germany.

That first day we were together, we were going through a Normandy village and stopped for a break in what I can best describe as a low-walled compound off the main street. Within minutes, dozens of the local inhabitants started arriving with food and drink. In fact, we soon had quite a pile of it! The guard had obviously been bribed by some of them with a couple of bottles. We really felt for these local people, who couldn't have had all that much themselves, but they were really doing their best to help. A middle-aged man approached and said that he was with the Resistance, and that they would try and rescue me during the night. He gave me a bottle of Calvados and some lump sugar to drink it through. Then a very irate SS man drove up in a jeep, flourishing his pistol, shouting at the guards. I thought he might shoot them for allowing it he was so furious. The civilians were herded out, he got into his vehicle and drove back and forth over our sustenance and completely ruined it. He shot out into the road, knocked over an elderly Frenchman who looked to be in a very bad way, and we were moved out. I still had my bottle of Calvados, which later went down well, but it didn't go very far between thirteen of us. I have driven around that area many times since the war to identify the village concerned, to give my thanks for what the villagers did, and to ask about the old gentleman who was run over. But I have never found it.

While on that journey we came across a lot of German troops, and it was noticeable that they were becoming aware that all was not going their way. They seemed to treat the Canadians with a certain amount of respect, but so far as I was concerned they considered me a *terrorflieger* and sometimes got rather rough and nasty. After this had occurred a couple of times the Canadians made a point of surrounding me so that I was not too visible, and life became a little easier. We did quite a lot of walking, mostly at night; our captors were not too happy walking in broad daylight due to too much strafing by the likes of me. By then I had managed to obtain a bandage for my foot, but too much walking did not amuse me. One day we were on a road leading to the River Seine, but upon arrival we found that there was no bridge. I had first-hand confirmation that we had made a very good job of destroying it! We were then rowed across the Seine by German soldiers. So how is that for coincidence?

After a few more days another Spitfire pilot joined us who had his arm in a sling. He had got a bit caught up in his parachute harness and wrenched his shoulder, but he was otherwise OK. The day after he arrived we were put into a large open trailer towed by a lorry. After about an hour we parked a few hundred yards away from what looked like an isolated factory. As we sat watching, we noticed that a succession of corpses were being carried out, placed in a series on those French one-horse carts, and taken away. We were all a bit bothered, to say the least, as to what this place was. The thought was there: are we going to end up in body bags like them? We were then herded into the building, given some water and chunks of bread. It turned out to be a field hospital and most of the dead we had seen were German soldiers. We were told that the Allies were only about twenty to thirty miles away and that they were evacuating the hospital of walking wounded and leaving a couple of German nurses with those too ill to be moved.

We were soon joined by a Tempest pilot. We were being walked along a country lane when we heard the sound of very low and fast aircraft. The guards dived into the hedges at the roadside and trained their guns on us, so that we stayed on the road. We were just about to take our chances with the guards and dive for cover when the Tempest turned away without firing. The leader must have realised what was going on and our new member said that it was his Squadron in 'Bee' Beaumont's Wing. A few weeks later, in a transit camp in Frankfurt, I met 'Bee' Beaumont! He had recently been shot down by flak at low altitude and crash-landed.

Soon after that episode we were taken to what in peacetime had been a French artillery barracks at Amiens, where we stayed for several days. On several occasions we saw lorries painted with red crosses loading up with mortar shells, guns, and ammunition – very much against the Geneva Convention, to which Germany was a signatory. Storing arms and ammunition in a POW camp and transporting them under protection of the red cross was just not on. We had been told by the powers that be that if we saw vehicles with red crosses to ignore them and strafe them anyway, so they must have known a thing or two about what was going on. On several occasions I had had the opportunity to strafe vehicles with red crosses but I refused to do so; perhaps, however, I had been wrong? From there we were taken to Douai, to, would you believe, a cattle truck in the marshalling yards? Again, I had the best of all possible views of the damage we had caused with our many raids. There was just a single track leading out of the rubble. It was with some trepidation that I kept looking out of the three-feet-square and barbed- wired window for signs of the lads coming to bomb the marshalling yards! Fortunately, it was a nice day, so visibility was good enough for them to find their No. 1 target. After an hour or so we started a very long and uncomfortable trip to Germany. The truck was one of these carriages built for two horses and six men, or something like that. There were fifteen of us but only two buckets: one for water, the other for all other human requirements. The next morning we arrived at Limberg where we were separated from our army chums. There were quite a few air force chaps there and we were then taken to Frankfurt, from where some of us went to Sagan, near the Polish border – the notorious 'Great Escape' camp where fifty Allied officers were shot when recaptured after escaping.

It was now the end of September 1944, and by the second week of October about a dozen of us were transferred to an especially built escape-proof camp for RAF aircrew. When we arrived it was incomplete, so what we were housed in were really chicken sheds with no bunks – in fact, no anything. Fortunately, after a few days, representatives of the International Red Cross from Switzerland arrived and raised quite a stink about our conditions. Apart from anything else, the temperature was well below zero. In a few days we were housed in our new quarters where we had a wood-burning stove.

The major problem was food, or the lack of it. Our daily ration consisted of a loaf of bread between four, so we would cut cards to see who should have which piece in case there were a few crumbs more in one piece than another. Very sad, really, to be in that state. We also had several potatoes, cooked in their skins, a pint of soup – mostly one we called 'Whispering Grass' made mainly from turnip tops and other rubbish they could find. It looked and tasted like rusty water. Sometimes we had a special treat: soup made of dried peas. But there were so many weevils in it that we used to call it 'Meat Soup'. About twice a week we had about an ounce of *ersatz* margarine, a blob of a sort of jam made from beetroot, coffee made from roasted acorns, and a supply of herb tea. We were supposed to be given a Red Cross food parcel each week, but this never happened. Occasionally we were given one between two or six, but mostly one between four. This was about every other week. The American parcels were our favourite because they contained a tin of Spam, a tin of margarine, a tin of concentrated orange juice, Klim milk powder, soluble coffee, a packet of raisins, processed cheese, and some cigarettes. I am quite sure that without food parcels a very great many of the POWs would not have survived, and I am talking about POWs who were down for three or four years. The cigarettes were very useful as currency, as some of the guards would sell bread in exchange for cigarettes. At one time during a particularly hungry spell I acquired two loaves for my watch. I have often since regretted that as it was a rather nice watch!

One of our fellow POWs was a physiotherapist in civvy street and he started a course which several of us joined. I found it very interesting and learned quite a bit about giving a practical massage which enabled me to give some help to quite a few of the lads, particularly some with bad burns. I remember one chap in particular, a New Zealander, with a hand so badly burned it was like a claw. After many hours of massage using some oil I managed to scrounge from a guard, he was able to use it again. We also spent many hours a day playing bridge, and I became quite an addict, although strangely enough I have never played since.

We also had a very good tunnel, supported by slats from our bunks. The main problem was disposing of the sandy soil. Someone had an idea to build an ice rink between the two barrack blocks, permission for which was granted. Soil from the tunnel was then surreptitiously disposed of around the legally disturbed soil of the ice rink. Meanwhile, Christmas was approaching and rumour had it that there was a consignment of Red Cross parcels arriving at the local railway station, about two miles down the road, to be distributed for Christmas 1944. Of course, it didn't happen. The only Christmas highlight was that some of us had made a brew of potato and raisin wine, and so we were able to toast our absent friends and loved ones at home.

Early in January 1945, the *Kommandant* told us to prepare to evacuate the camp as the Russians were approaching. We said 'To hell with that, we'll wait for the Russians!' The *Kommandant*, who was quite a nice chap actually, then read out the order he'd received from Hitler's headquarters, which virtually amounted to an order to kill all the prisoners and return to Berlin. So, in the light of that, we decided to co-operate.

Having already taken part in a forced march through France, it was logical to make use of the experience I had gained, so I had a chat with my friends Peter and Dennis and stressed that the most important thing was to keep as near to the front as possible (there were about 1,600 of us), and we would then have the best chance of scrounging food and somewhere to sleep at any stop. I also suggested that we wore every article of clothing we had, took a blanket each and any food we could find, together with a tin or dish in which to cook or warm up snow and a container for water. Everything else was abandoned.

We started what became called the 'Death March', because so many didn't make it in a howling blizzard, having been told that transport to a new camp would be available in two or three days. It took several hours to cross a bridge over the River Oder, which the Germans destroyed immediately we had reached the other side. We spent the first night in a deserted warehouse, a perk, really, for being at the front. It was actually several weeks until we were taken the last sixty miles or so to a camp at Euchenwald. Although we had originally been promised to be at a new camp within several days, the march actually took weeks to complete. Along the way we managed to scrounge things like sugar beet and frozen carrots and potatoes, which were supposed to be fed to the pigs. Most of us survived, however, although we had been virtually starved. Upon arrival at the new camp we were given a feed of barley soup and rye bread, a meal to remember! The following day they shared out some Red Cross parcels.

We had no beds or bunks, but lay in rows on the floor, several hundred bodies at least keeping the temperature reasonable. Being in such close proximity, however, lice rapidly became prevalent. This worried us somewhat, and we killed off as many as we could because next to us were Russian prisoners who were dying of typhus. We felt really sorry for them as they were completely despised by the Germans, and as Russia had not signed the Geneva Convention their troops were not protected by it. They had no more rations than we did and I very much doubt that they ever saw any food parcels. They were put to work as well.

While we were on the march we had seen many hundreds of civilians, mostly women and children and the elderly, fleeing west from the Russians, of whom they were terrified. They dragged along their possessions on makeshift sleighs and handcarts, so very sad and desperate with nowhere to go and no help. What an evil, useless thing war is.

At the end of April 1945, the Russians we had all been fleeing from caught up with us. We awoke one morning to find all the Germans gone. We took over the camp and the following day Cossack troops on horseback, led by a female major, arrived. Then a couple of American lend-lease lorries, a lot of foot soldiers, and many horse-drawn carts with a couple of pigs inside and a cow tied behind; they obviously lived off the land. I remember that my first thought was for the Russian POWs, thinking that they would now be looked after. But how wrong can you get? They were taken out of their compound, given guns, told to get on with it and that they should never have become prisoners in the first place! They tried to get us to do the same, but we told them what they could do. Apart from the fact that we were in no fit state, the war by then was virtually over and in fact on 8 May it was. We expected to be repatriated quickly, but it didn't happen like that. There were rumours that we were being kept as pawns in the political game of splitting up Europe, but whatever the reason we were kept for at least a month after the war ended.

There was one rather memorable incident at this time. A fellow POW who I had seen around asked me to accompany him to the local town to see what we could barter and scrounge at the local village. We broke through the wire and the first person we met was a rather inebriated Russian officer who had a couple of Nazi dress swords tucked under his belt and greeted us like long lost friends. We indicated our intent, he went into the farmyard, lashed out with a sword, and handed me a headless chicken! He then insisted that we accompany him into the farmhouse, where, to our surprise, there was a man sat at the table having a meal wearing jodhpurs, an American tunic, and an Australian bush hat. He was a New Zealander, had been there since the Germans ran off and had been entertained extremely well by the farmer, his wife, and daughter. We joined him for an exceptional meal and he remarked that it was a shame we had not joined him before as his Russian friend had got him a horse and he was about to leave for the west, to find the Americans. Anyway, we had a good time and said cheerio, and off he went.

On our way back to camp we had to pass by some woods and found ourselves surrounded by six or seven armed Germans. I immediately thought, 'After all we've been through, the end of the war now seems to be the end of us'. But these Germans had had enough and gave themselves up. They asked if we would take then to the British or Americans, but had no choice and had to hand them over to the Russians. There was one very nasty incident when one of our chaps had his watch taken by a Russian, and when he complained was asked to identify the culprit. After a while he saw him and pointed him out; the supervising officer just withdrew his pistol and shot the thief! You can imagine how our chap felt at such a drastic measure just over a watch. Life was, indeed, very cheap.

By 18 May 1945, the total strength of the camp was between 16,000 and 17,000 including both men and women of twenty-five nationalities. The total number of female refugees in the camp was 450. You can imagine the problems faced by the *Kommandant* in housing and feeding them all! About a week later we felt hopeful of repatriation when a convoy of Americans arrived to take over the RAF contingent, but a senior officer told them that if they took any of us they would be interned too. The Americans had to return without us, but the political scene must have changed, because two weeks later the Russians took us on the most hair-raising journey I have ever experienced – long roads that were frequently impassable so that we were diverted through pine forests and past the corpses of people and animals. The stench was appalling. Ultimately we did reach the River Elbe and were handed over to the Americans. What bliss! We had hot showers, the first clean underwear for nearly a year, the first real lavatory paper for the same period. In fact, we nearly gorged ourselves to death. Those Yanks were certainly well looked after!

The following day, after a blissful sleep on a bed with sheets, we were flown to Brussels. Civilians there were absolutely wonderful to us and we must have been among the last to be repatriated. Yet they still enthused. After being dusted off with delousing powder we were given vouchers to take to a bank to withdraw the equivalent of £10 and go out on the town. Peter and I joined up and as we came out we were accosted by two beautiful and well-spoken English WAAFs who asked if we would take them out for the evening. We didn't say no! They took us to what must have been the city's premier hotel, with a superb dance floor, where we drank and danced the night away. I regret, however, that I didn't do the floor much good as I was wearing my flying boots, which had been repaired by the Germans with wooden slats and hobnails. However, we had a really wonderful time and arranged to meet the girls the following day.

To our dismay, Peter, half a dozen others, and I were then crammed into a Lancaster bomber and flown to Duxford in Cambridgeshire, so we were unable to see the girls a second time. We were met by a squadron leader (desk type) who said, 'Jolly good show, chaps!', and by a WI lady who gave us a packet of Woodbines, a bar of chocolate, and a shaving kit, and then by a lady from the Salvation Army, who gave us the same! We were ushered into an office and given a travel warrant to Cosford. At the railway station it was very noticeable that civilians kept well away from us. I suppose we did look rather scruffy! But the comparison between the civilians in Brussels and those in England was quite amazing. At Cosford we were given new uniforms, back pay, and another travel warrant to our home stations.

It was really wonderful to be back home with my parents and sister, although I was a much thinner version than they had previously known. I may have mentioned that in those days my parents owned one of the six bungalows in the hamlet that was then Langley; the following day when I came out of the front door with my family to go into Eastbourne for a meal, who should come out of the house opposite but the New Zealand chap I had seen off on his horse a month previously!

I was on a sort of indefinite leave, a pay check arriving every fortnight. I had a sailing boat in storage throughout the war so had it transferred to the beach that had been the Eastbourne Sailing Club before the war, where I had started sailing. There I met up with Brigadier-General Davey, also on ex-POW leave, he having been caught up in the Arnhem business. The old clubhouse was in ruins, so a group of us got together to refurbish and rebuild it, and got the club going again. It needed a lot of work on it so it kept us very busy. After six weeks I received a telegram ordering that I report to West Malling aerodrome for rehabilitation, as did my very old friend Tony Clark, with whom I had been reunited in the delousing showers at Brussels. We drove to West Malling together, where the programme was as follows: day one, a visit to a coal mine; day two, a visit to a brewery; day three, tickets to the Paris Theatre in London to see a BBC show. And that was it! We stayed the night in the RAF Club and went to Lyon's Corner House in Oxford Street for breakfast. We were the only people there when in came a very smartly dressed man who asked if he could join us, which seemed a bit odd. He gave us his card. He was a film director and asked if we would be interested in being film extras for a few days at Elstree where they were making Cleopatra – the pay was £3 a day! We contacted West Malling to ask if we could sort out our own rehabilitation and the outcome was a very interesting few days.

169. Flight Lieutenant Macey with another 41 Squadron Spitfire in 1945.

I sometimes wonder about the youth of today, even those in the armed forces; if something not very nice happens they invent the word 'trauma' and expect to be compensated with large amounts of cash. On my return to the United Kingdom, however, I signed on for another year, because the Far Eastern conflict was still going on. Just after West Mailing I went on a flying refresher course but by the time this had finished the atom bomb had been dropped and the war was over. It was very nice to be airborne again, though, especially without being shot at! We had Spitfire Mk XVIs – very nice aircraft. I then had fourteen days' leave before being posted to an army co-operation squadron, 577, flying both Spitfires and twin-engined Oxfords.

Upon arrival I was shown the cockpit drill in an Oxford, taken up by the flight commander for familiarisation, and after the fourth circuit and landing, to my surprise, he said, 'You will do. Take the plane up, do about eight or ten circuits and landings, then come in for lunch.' I did this and quite enjoyed myself. Never having flown twin-engined aircraft before it was quite an experience. In the Mess afterwards I had the best ego boost I can remember: I was approached by the Aerodrome Control Officer who asked if I had been doing the circuits and landings. I thought, 'What have I done wrong?' But he said, 'I have been here a few years and I was watching you. That was the best series of landings ever!' So I thanked him and bought him a beer!

We were based either at Castle Bromwich, near Birmingham, or Hawarden near Chester, and liaised with an army artillery training outfit at Oswestry. We would fly more or less on a straight course, at various altitudes, to enable them to train their guns on a moving target. If in a Spitfire, we would come in low and fast, as if we were strafing them, so that they could get some idea of what to expect, and again to learn to train their weapons on a fast-moving target. It was a fun posting, not only getting to fly the Airspeed Oxford, but low flying was always a bonus. In fact, the army officers invited us over one evening for a spot of hospitality and they certainly knew how to give a great evening!

I had one charming episode one evening while walking from the airfield down to town, quite happily enjoying the walk, when a car drew up alongside and the driver asked if I wanted a lift. I was about to thank him but decline when he said, 'Well, hard luck mate. The war is over!' and drove off! It takes all sorts, I suppose.

Early in June 1945, my squadron was disbanded and I was posted to 41 Squadron at Wittering. There we were upgraded to Spitfire Mk XXIs, with their more-powerful engine capable of 450 mph on a straight and level flight – which is quite something, and obviously a great deal more in a dive. A week after I joined them, the Squadron moved to Lübeck in northern Germany and I was sent to fly ahead of the others to ensure that the living accommodation was suitable for the ground staff. As I taxied off the runway to park my aircraft, a jeep drove up to meet me. It was my Wing Commander from Lympne, Ray Harries! It was great to see him. He had survived the war. He was a really great pilot and leader – DSO and bar, DFC and bar – flying constantly from the Battle of Britain onwards, amazingly without a scratch. He led from the front, but was extremely fortunate not to get hit. The only problem I knew he had was that he was dating a blonde from the Met Office at Lympne and I was dating a brunette. My friend and I went around on bicycles but Ray Harries had a sports car. One evening while returning from a party he overturned and broke his collar bone! Sadly, a couple of years after our chance meeting at Lübeck I heard that he had been killed in a flying accident flying a Meteor jet.

Unlike my previous time, this sojourn in Germany was extremely pleasant. The all-round facilities were good: good food, a really good gliding club, and a marvellous selection of horses. We were looked after by many women in the age-group eighteen to forty of Latvian and Estonian origin, displaced by the Russians taking over their country. I spoke to one of them, who kept our room tidy and did the washing and ironing. She spoke good English, was a university graduate and was married with a child. She had not seen her husband or child for over two years, and had no idea where they were or whether they were dead or alive. All of these women were in a similar situation. They were just grateful to have work.

When I joined 41 Squadron I met up with Peter Clarke. We had been in the same POW camp, knew each other by sight, but hadn't collided, as it were. We had also been on the refresher course together and now we were sharing a room and getting on together very well. If the weather prevented flying we all used to gather in a lecture room where we would have input on various aspects of aviation. One day, Ray Harries said, 'Today, Macey will be telling you about the trials and tribulations of being a POW.' I was not amused, as I prefer to be forewarned about this kind of thing. But I flannelled away for half an hour, not helped by Peter sitting in the front row, chuckling away. When I had finished, he called everyone together and presented me with what he called the 'Stein Hager Cross', which was the local gut-rot gin. He had made a German Iron Cross out of tin, with a piece of ribbon, and attached this to me with a dirty great safety pin, which was all good for a laugh.

We were there for about two months. I did a lot of interesting flying, gliding, and even horse racing across the aerodrome. I won quite a lot of races. I had a little mare that the other horses seemed to prefer to follow rather than overtake! Anyway, we returned to Wittering via Windhaven, Calais, and Manston on 30 April, my twenty-third birthday. On 9 September, we went to Duxford. This was my second time there. The first time was in a Lancaster from Brussels, coming home from POW camp, and this time we were there to take part in the first Battle of Britain fly-past, led by Douglas Bader. It was memorable. I have never seen so many aircraft formatting at one time. It must have looked quite spectacular from the ground.

A new chap joined the Squadron at this time and was sent up in one of our more powerful Mk XXIs for a familiarisation flight, but he did a very quick circuit and landing, saying that his engine was running rough. When we looked he had retracted his wheels too early and knocked about six inches off each of his five propeller blades! Not surprising, then, that the engine was running rough! It was a good job that the propellers were made of laminated wood and not metal; it took him a long time to live that one down!

We were now overdue to be demobbed, but I wasn't bothered as I was content doing what I was doing. Peter, however, wanted to get out and get married. He told the adjutant, who said that if he was overdue then so was Macey, so we were both demobbed in January 1947. On my demob leave I married my dear wife, who has now had to put up with me for over fifty years!

Two years after my demob, I joined the RAFVR, and used to fly from Redhill at weekends, first of all in Tiger Moths, then Chipmunks. In June 1951, I was called up for three months' training for conversion to jet aircraft when the Korean War was on. With regard to Spitfires, it occurred to me that I had enjoyed the privilege of flying every mark from I to XXII, but I was then switched to de Havilland Vampire jets, a very interesting experience. As it happened, we were not required in Korea, so it was back to flying at Redhill. I thoroughly enjoyed these last five years in the RAFVR. But then the Air Ministry decided that the VR was too expensive and had served its purpose, and they closed it down.

Finally, there is something that occurs to me, that has always occurred to me: so many novelists and people consider being a fighter pilot to be glamorous. I can assure you that there is nothing glamorous in killing and being killed. Exciting – very exciting – sometimes too exciting. But definitely not glamorous.

SELECT BIBLIOGRAPHY

PUBLISHED SOURCES

Foreman, J., *Fighter Command Victory Claims: A Listing of Combat Claims Submitted by RAF Fighter Pilots 1939 to 1940* (Red Kite, 2003).

Franks, N. L. R., *Royal Air Force Fighter Command Losses of the Second World War*, i–iii (Midland Publishing, 1992–2008).

Mitchell, R. J., *Schooldays to Spitfire* (Tempus Publishing, 2002).

Morgan, E. B., and E. Shacklady, *Spitfire: The History* (Key Books, 1987).

Price, A., *The Spitfire Story* (Jane's, 1982).

Ramsey, W. G. (ed.), *Battle of Britain Then and Now, Mk V* (ATB Books, 1989).

Sarkar, D., *Bader's Tangmere Spitfires: The Untold Story, 1941* (Patrick Stephens Limited, 1996).

—— *The Few: The Story of the Battle of Britain in the Words of the Pilots* (Amberley Publishing, 2009).

—— *The Spitfire Manual 1940* (Amberley Publishing, 2010).

Shores, C., and C. Williams, *Aces High* (Grub Street, 1994).

Wynn, K., *The Men of the Battle of Britain* (Gliddon Books, 1989).

WEB RESOURCES

Dilip Sarkar <www.dilipsarkarmbe.co.uk>
Commonwealth War Graves Commission <www.cwgc.org.uk>
Imperial War Museum <www.iwm.org.uk>
The National Archives <www.nationalarchives.gov.uk>
RAF Museum <www.rafmuseum.org.uk>
Spitfire Society <www.spitfiresociety.co.uk>

ACKNOWLEDGEMENTS

First, I must thank all the former Spitfire pilots, the relatives of casualties, and eyewitnesses to the dramatic and often tragic events involved who have so kindly supported and contributed to my research over the past thirty years. Secondly, there are certain organisations without the help of which it would be impossible to reconstruct the past: The National Archive, Imperial War Museum, RAF Museum, MOD Air Historical Branch, RAF Personnel Management Centre, and the Commonwealth War Graves Commission are all essential sources of information. John Foreman was always extremely helpful and knowledgeable regarding losses and claims, and Don Caldwell likewise concerning JG 26. Thirdly, Jonathan Reeve and the team at Amberley Publishing are always a pleasure to work with. Finally, my wife, Karen, whose support is immense and without whom my 'resurrection' would not have happened.

Available from September 2010 from Amberley Publishing

Dad's Army by the men who were there —
profusely illustrated with cartoons

In May 1945, as the Home Guard stood down, an enterprising small publisher in Birmingham produced
Home Guard Humour — a lighthearted look at the five-year history of the Home Guard. Within the
pages of the booklet are contained all of the standard 'Dad's Army'-style jokes and one wonders if it was
this booklet which encouraged the writing of one of Britain's most loved sit-coms.

£4.99 Paperback
30 illustrations
32 pages
978-1-4456-0186-1

Available from September 2010 from all good bookshops or to order direct
Please call **01285–760–030**
www.amberleybooks.com

Also available from Amberley Publishing

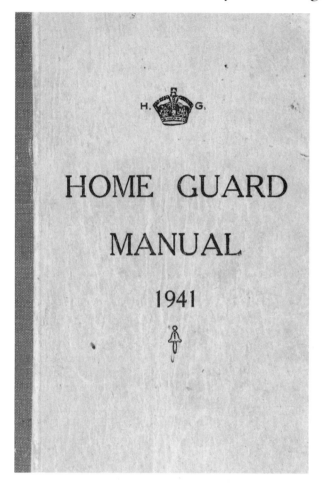

*Find out about the real Dad's Army, from the manual
used to train them*

Over a period of a few months, this rag-tag group was armed, uniformed and trained, using the *Home Guard Manual*. Learning how to construct booby traps, destroy tanks, ambush the enemy, survive in the open, basic camouflage, read maps and send signals, the fledgling volunteer was turned into a veritable fighting machine, leaving the Army to retrain, re-equip and fight elsewhere.

£7.99 Paperback
50 illustrations
240 pages
978-1-4456-0047-5

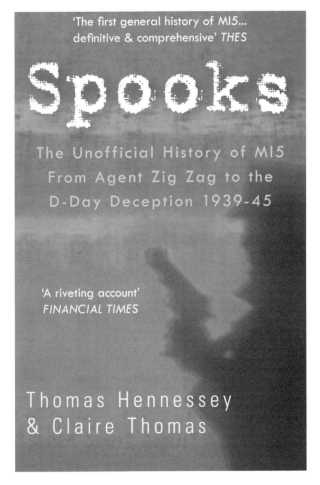

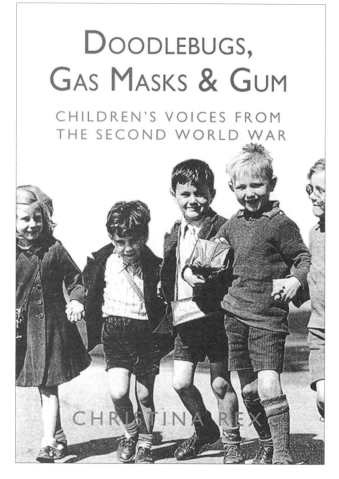

Also available from Amberley Publishing

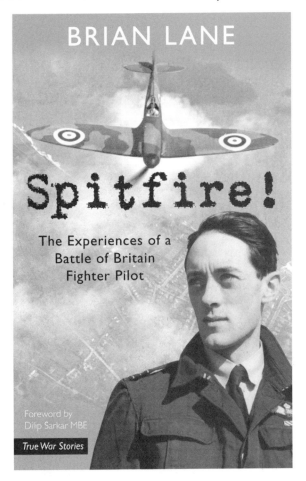

The remarkable Battle of Britain experiences of Spitfire pilot
Brian Lane, DFC

'A very fine and vivid account' MAX ARTHUR

Brian Lane was only 23 when he when he wrote his dramatic account of life as a Spitfire pilot during the Battle of Britain in the summer of 1940. Lane was an 'ace' with six enemy 'kills' to his credit and was awarded the DFC for bravery in combat. The text is honest and vibrant, and has the immediacy of a book written close the event, untouched, therefore, by the doubts and debates of later years.

£9.99 Paperback
44 illustrations
192 pages
978-1-84868-354-9

Available from all good bookshops or to order direct
Please call **01285-760-030**
www.amberleybooks.com

Available from November 2010 from Amberley Publishing

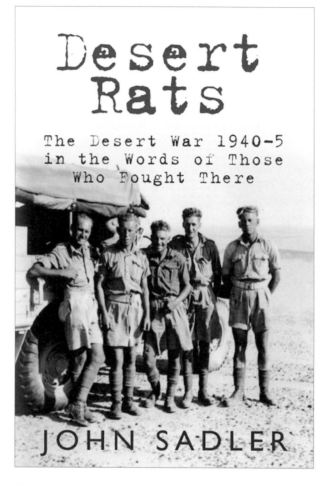

The story of the last surviving 'Desert Rats' in their own words and their experience of war in North Africa

From 1940-3 Britain was engaged in a life and death struggle with the Axis powers in North Africa, a titanic, swaying conflict that surged back and forth across the barren wastes of Egypt, Libya and Tunisia. Those British servicemen who were to form the legendary 'Desert Rats' were, for the most part, not professional soldiers; they were drawn from all walks of civilian life. They were ordinary men who did extraordinary things in most extraordinary circumstances.

£20 Hardback
80 illustrations
320 pages
978-1-84868-337-2

Available from November 2010 from all good bookshops or to order direct
Please call **01285-760-030**
www.amberleybooks.com

Also available from Amberley Publishing

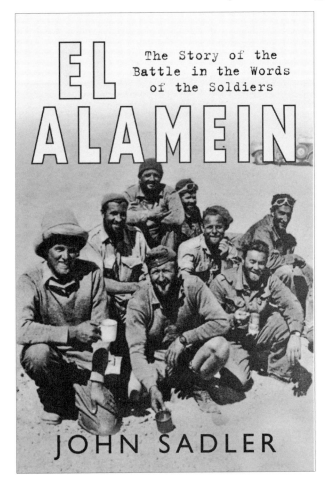

This is the story of El Alamein and the British soldiers who fought in it

'There was for me no excitement in the charge. I'd seen it all before, and after a certain time you look round the faces of your mates and you realize with a shock how few of the original mob are left. Then you know it's only a matter of time before you get yours. All I wanted to do was to get across that bloody ground and through the guns.' *BRITISH INFANTRYMAN*

The epic battle in Egypt between the Axis forces led by Rommel 'the Desert Fox' and Britain's 'Desert Rats' in the words of the soldiers themselves.

£20 Hardback
50 illustrations (15 colour)
336 pages
978-1-84868-101-9

Available from all good bookshops or to order direct
Please call **01285-760-030**
www.amberleybooks.com

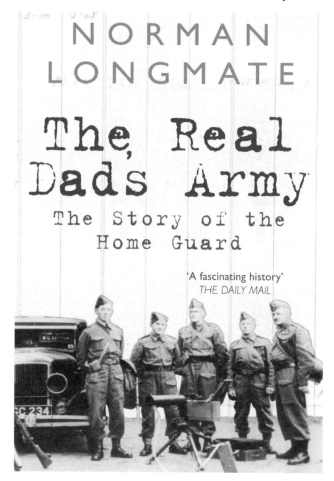

NORMAN
LONGMATE

The Real
Dads Army

The Story of the
Home Guard

'A fascinating history'
THE DAILY MAIL

*A narrative history of the Home Guard from its creation in May 1940
to the end of the Second World War*

'A fascinating history' *THE DAILY MAIL*
'Wonderful stories… a well-written account of the last line of defence' *THE DAILY MIRROR*

The enduring popularity of the BBC tv series *Dad's Army* has focused attention on one of the strangest and least military armies ever formed — The British Home Guard. Norman Longmate, an ex-member of the Home Guard and an authority on wartime Britain, has collected together a wealth of hilarious anecdote as well as all the unlikely facts to produce the first popular history of the Home Guard to be written since the war.

£18.99 Hardback
50 illustrations
160 pages
978-1-84868-914-5

Also available from Amberley Publishing

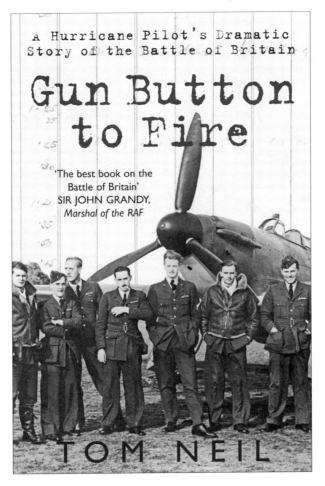

The amazing story of one of the 'Few', fighter ace Tom Neil who shot down 13 enemy aircraft during the Battle of Britain

'A thrilling new book...Tom Neil is one of the last surviving heroes who fought the Luftwaffe'
THE DAILY EXPRESS

'The best book on the Battle of Britain' SIR JOHN GRANDY, Marshal of the RAF

This is a fighter pilot's story of eight memorable months from May to December 1940. By the end of the year he had shot down 13 enemy aircraft, seen many of his friends killed, injured or burned, and was himself a wary and accomplished fighter pilot.

£20 Hardback
120 Photographs (20 colour)
320 pages
978-1-84868-848-3

Available from all good bookshops or to order direct
Please call **01285–760–030**
www.amberleybooks.com

Also available from Amberley Publishing

A fabulous slice of wartime nostalgia, a facsimile edition of the propaganda booklet issued following victory in the Battle of Britain

First published in 1941, *The Battle of Britain* was a propaganda booklet issued by the Ministry of Information to capitalise on the success of the RAF in defeating the Luftwaffe. An amazing period piece, hundreds of thousands of copies were printed and sold for 6d and it became one of the year's best selling books. It is the first book to embed in the public imagination the heroics of 'The Few'.

£4.99 Paperback
25 illustrations
36 pages
978-1-4456-0048-2

Available from all good bookshops or to order direct
Please call **01285-760-030**
www.amberleybooks.com

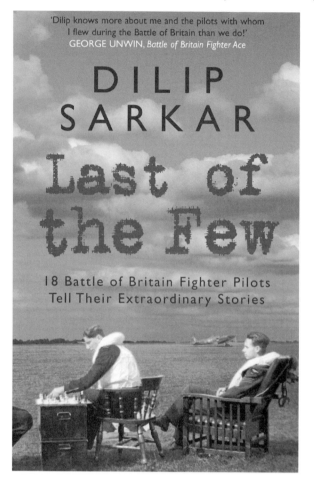